Venice in History

The Remarkable Story of the Serene Republic for Travelers

John D. Irany

Clipper Ship Publishing

Table of Contents

Venice in History

Chapter 1: The Serene Republic

In 1581, Francesco Sansovino a Venetian who greatly admired his city wrote that the name Venice derived from the Latin phrase *Veni etiam* which he said meant "come back again, and again, for however many times you come you will always see new and beautiful things."

Nice story.

Probably untrue as to the origin of Venice's name.

Yet it conveys the sense that Venice is unique. It is different from any other city. It is a special place. Each year hundreds of thousands of tourists visit Venice. All admire the city's beauty and vitality. The observer cannot fail to be seduced by the elegance and charm of the canals, the opulent palaces, and the numerous large and small churches glistening by the waters edge. The Basilica, the Doge's Palace, the Piazza San Marco invite the traveler to enter and to explore. All agree. Venice is different from any other city in the world.

Most of us, however, know little of Venice's history and past importance. This is unfortunate, for to fully appreciate the presence of Venice, one must understand the richness of its past.

Visitors who walk across the Piazza San Marco, or who ride a gondola on the Grand Canal, or who look in awe at the magnificent buildings and art, must take one more step and reach back to examine the history of the people who created this wondrous place.

This book is the story of the Republic of Venice from its settlement on a few remote islands in the Adriatic through its rise to become the most powerful state in Europe. The history of Venice is about simple things: the price of cloth, the design of ships, the transportation of spices and other goods. And it is about how such simple things affect the power and prosperity of nations. Like the Venetians themselves we must approach their history from a worldview.

For hundreds of years, Venice was rich when the nations of the rest of Europe were poor. While London, Paris and Rome were mired in the Dark Ages of Medievalism, the Republic of Venice – the Serene Republic – expanded in commerce, art, learning and power. As such, Venice played a crucial role in the dynamic development of Europe.

In time the changing fortunes of world events would allow other nations to successfully challenge the pre-eminent status of Venice.

But five hundred years ago, and for a thousand years before Columbus set sail to find a westward route to Asia, the Republic of Venice was the most exciting place to be. The citizens of the European nations that would later become great powers – England, France, Spain, and the Netherlands – could look only wistfully at the prosperity and wealth of the Venetians.

The Venetians readily expended their wealth in artistic and scientific achievement. Bellini, Tintoretto, Giorgione and Titian were great masters of painting.

The architects Andrea Palladio, Baldassare Longhena and Jacopo Sansovino created churches, palaces, and even administrative offices of unsurpassed beauty. Galileo made his first astronomical discoveries while a professor at the Republic's university, and later referred to his time in Venice as "the happiest years of his life."

With seemingly inexhaustible economic resources, and with unabated confidence in a bountiful future, Venetians built the glorious city that captivates all who see it, even today. In art, architecture, and scientific accomplishment, Venice in its time was the center of the world.

Venice, of course, is a masterpiece. It is a work of art in itself. No photograph or set of photographs can fully capture the beauty of the city. Venice must be experienced. We must walk the narrow *calli* in the shadows of surrounding buildings and suddenly stumble out into a sun-filled plaza dominated by a Renaissance church. We must wend our way down a winding pedestrian-filled street and be surprised by the changing view around each corner. Only a traveler who has been to Venice can appreciate a boat ride up the Grand Canal. Only a visitor who has entered a church and looked upon an altarpiece or painting by Titian, Bellini, Carpaccio, Giorgione, Tintoretto or Veronese can truly admire the greatness of Venetian art. To see the most beautiful city in the world one must go to Venice.

Chapter 2: The Rise to Supremacy

In the first centuries of the Christian era, Venice was an unimportant fishing village. As the Roman Empire disintegrated, people seeking refuge from the invading barbarians of the north founded Venice as a haven from terror and violence. Standing on the beaches of the northern Adriatic Sea, the first settlers looked out at the uninhabited islands in the lagoon and saw places of safety beyond the grasp of the land based, civilization destroying marauders. Soon, they established isolated hamlets on the islands. In 537 in the first historical record mentioning Venice, Senator Praetorian Praefect Cassiodorus reported to the Tribunes of the Maritime in Rome that the Venetians live as fishermen and harvesters of salt and that they have built houses on islands in the lagoon "after the manner of water-fowl."

As the population grew, however, the people recognized that their common interests were best served by forming one government on the most centrally located and best protected islands. Thus, Venice came into being. Since the islands chosen were low and muddy, wooden pilings were pounded into the sand and ooze to provide a base for buildings. The first structures were made of wood timbers that were laboriously hauled from the abundant forests on the mainland. In time, though, the ever present danger of fire made clear the necessity of building in stone and brick.

In this manner, Venice existed in quiet obscurity for hundreds of years. As the Dark Ages descended upon

Europe, Venice was a mere town in the shadows of Rome, Constantinople, and Jerusalem.

Yet despite its isolation, Venice was claimed by Byzantium to be part of its empire which stretched to the east with its capital at Constantinople. This connection with the east was important for reasons of culture and trade. Much of Venice's early architecture derives from Byzantium. The Basilica of San Marco, for example, was modeled after the sixth century church of the Holy Apostles in Constantinople. In trade also Venice benefited from the Byzantine connection as spices, silk, and other products of Asia were brought west. In time, of course, these articles of commerce would become the mainstay of Venice's wealth.

In the early Middle Ages, some of the fishermen of Venice seeing the potential of commercial ventures turned to trade and shipping as a means of earning a living. They transported goods up and down the Italian rivers that flowed into the Adriatic Sea. The Po, with its headwaters in the Italian Alps in the region of Lombardy, is the largest of these rivers. It flows across northern Italy to find its outlet on the Adriatic, a few miles south of Venice. The Po River valley, from the earliest times, was a rich source of timber and agricultural goods that could be traded for the products of nearby regions and far off countries.

As the commerce thrived, the Venetians became the merchants who handled the trade. In time, they were buying and selling products throughout the Mediterranean and as far north as England and southern Russia. With each successive outreach, their prosperity increased.

As the wealth of the Venetians multiplied, the people of the rest of Europe were in awe, for, as the amazed Europeans said, the Venetian "Non arat, non seminat, non vendemiat" – he plows not the land, sows not the seed, and reaps not the grain. In the Middle Ages, Venice was a state thriving on commerce and trade, while the rest of Europe, adhering stubbornly to the feudal past, drew its wealth, almost entirely, from farming the land. The Venetians became the merchants of Europe.

Naturally, Venice had competition for this lucrative business. In the early Middle Ages, Ravenna and Comacchio, both closer to the Po than Venice, were well placed to become the leading trading centers of the northern Adriatic. In a series of military engagements, however, Venice emerged victorious, and the other cities of the northern Adriatic never again threatened the Venetian dominance of the region.

A more serious challenger to Venice's position came from Constantinople, the powerful Byzantine city that controlled the principal land and sea routes between Europe and Asia. In the twelfth century, Constantinople was the richest city in the world. If Venice was to dominate European commerce Constantinople had to be defeated. But Constantinople was too strong to be militarily taken on by Venice alone. To defeat Constantinople, which was then a Christian city, Venice needed help. Mainly, Venice needed a large army. Venice simply did not have sufficient population to provide the enormous number of foot soldiers needed to successfully attack the Byzantine city.

As the thirteenth century began, though, an army was formed in western Europe that precisely met the needs of the Venetians. The army's stated purpose was to seize Jerusalem from the Muslims. By the grace of God, the army was the Fourth Crusade. What Venice needed to do was to hijack this army and use it for the national interests of the Serene Republic – that is, to attack Christian Constantinople rather than Islamic Jerusalem.

The Fourth Crusade, which set out for the Holy Land in 1202, was passing through Venice on its way to the East at a most advantageous time. In contrast to the army-deficient Venetians, the Fourth Crusade had foot soldiers in abundance. The Venetians looked upon the unexpected availability of the military apparatus of the Fourth Crusade as an opportunity not to be missed, and the leaders of the Serene Republic immediately began to scheme to find a means to use this fighting force for Venice's own needs. The Venetian conscience was not troubled one wit at the prospect of using these Crusaders to attack Christian Constantinople. The only problem was to convince the Crusaders of the righteousness of such an act.

Some cynical historians believe the Venetian role in the Fourth Crusade was entirely self-serving and an example of opportunism carried to an extreme. These historians may be right. The Venetian plan was at least an example of the strategy that the Venetians used to make the Serene Republic the most powerful state in Europe. History does not provide many other examples of such inspired arrogance.

The Fourth Crusade was conceived when Pope Innocent III challenged the Christian world to retake

Jerusalem from the Muslims. The knowledge that the land of Christ's crucifixion was a possession of the followers of Islam gnawed at the Christian soul. Three earlier crusades had failed to capture and permanently hold the city. Despite some successes against the Arabs, the Crusaders' hold on the most sacred city of Christianity was always tenuous, and Jerusalem always returned, in time, to Muslim control.

The Pope's call, however, went unanswered until November 28, 1199. On that day at a tournament at a castle in the Ardennes region of France, powerful nobles rose to the command of Pope Innocent III. In the Middle Ages, the tournament was the social event of the day. Knights and their ladies got together for several days of merriment, banqueting, and social engagement. At a time when the landed nobility lived in castles and manor houses somewhat isolated from one another, a tournament was a joyous occasion for the renewal of friendships and the enjoyment of good food, good wine, and good entertainment. Included in the festivities were the jousts in which the knights could prove their prowess with horse and lance before the crowd of their elegantly dressed fellow nobles and their ladies. All in all, tournaments provided welcome diversions for people who lived rather dull lives.

The tournament at the castle in the Ardennes on November 28, 1199 was no different from the ordinary such event until Count Thibaut of Champagne rose to make a spectacular announcement. Although he was only in his early twenties, Count Thibaut was one of the most powerful and distinguished nobles of France. To the assembled aristocrats, he proclaimed that the time had come to accept the challenge of Pope Innocent. They must commit themselves, he said, to a crusade to regain Jerusalem for Christianity's faithful. Immediately, the barons, like missionaries in pursuit of unrepentant sinners, swept forward with unrestrained enthusiasm. Religious fervor ran through the crowd. Those not imbued with the hysteria of the prospect of the audacious venture were nevertheless carried away by the passions of their fellow men, and by the sheer enjoyment of the anticipation of going forward and doing battle with the enemy.

In the months that followed the tournament at the castle in the Ardennes, other nobles in France and in Flanders joined the commitment to the Crusade. Soon they pledged an army of over 30,000 men to complete the divine task of making Jerusalem a Christian city. The nobles were possessed of a religious zeal that promised to move all before them.

When the barons met again, they resolved questions of strategy. They would move their soldiers, horses, and supplies to the Holy Land by sea. They realized, of course, they could not move 30,000 soldiers across the Mediterranean without ships. Given the small size of the ships of the Middle Ages, many ships would be needed. These ships would have to be acquired from a foreign source. No French port had sufficient shipbuilding facilities. Nor did the Italian maritime states of Pisa or Genoa. England, in 1200, was an economic backwater. Only Venice, as Europe's supreme maritime power, had the shipbuilding resources to build the number of vessels required. If the ships were to be built, the Venetians had to be approached. Accordingly, the French nobles chose six envoys led by, Geoffrey de Villehardouin, to negotiate with the Doge, Enrico Dandolo.

Enrico Dandolo was as sharp a trader as Venice ever produced. He was at least eighty years old, and he was blind. But his age and lack of sight had not diminished his sharpness of mind, his strength of character, or his understanding of what policies were in the long term best interests of Venice.

He entered into an agreement with the French representatives. Venice would build 200 ships, enough to transport the 4,500 knights, 9,000 squires, and 20,000 foot soldiers whom the French confidently expected would join the Crusade. The Venetians also agreed to feed this horde for a year. In addition, the Venetians would support the expedition with fifty armed galleys and with the thousands of sailors needed to man the ships. In return, the Venetians were to be paid 85,000 marks of silver, and to receive one half of the booty and conquests.

After the agreement was reached, however, the French realized that they had one very large problem. They were financially over-extended. The 85,000 marks of silver that they promised to pay far exceeded their resources. Indeed, 85,000 marks of silver exceeded the annual revenue of the kings of France and England combined. It was impossible for a few French nobles to amass such a sum. In the end, they could raise only 51,000 marks, which they gave to the Venetians. Nevertheless, the Venetians went ahead with the full shipbuilding program.

It is likely that Doge Dandolo knew from the beginning that the French had promised more than they could possibly deliver. The terms of the agreement were basically outrageous. Now, the Crusaders were short of funds. They were also short of men. As the hour of departure arrived, only 10,000 Crusaders showed up, less than one-third the number expected by Villehardouin and the other French barons. Somehow, when faced with the actual decision to leave their castles, their farms, their vineyards and towns, most of the advocates of the Crusade found pressing reasons to remain at home.

Nonetheless, ten thousand men did make it to Venice, and for the Venetians, a fighting force of 10,000 men was too valuable an asset to waste fighting infidels. A much more important use for this armed rabble was at hand, namely the destruction of Venice's chief economic competitor – Constantinople. At the time, the population of Venice was only about 100,000, so a force the size of the Crusader army was a significant resource that would not likely ever be available again. If God had seen fit to make available to the Venetians this army, they reasoned, God must have meant for them to use it.

In the spring of 1202, the Crusaders who did decide to honor their pledge left their homes in France and Flanders, and began the journey to Venice, from whence they were sure, they would be sailed to the Holy Land. Upon arriving in Venice, they were transported by the Venetians to the Lido, then called San Nicolò, to pitch their tents and to wait. Today, the Lido is a fashionable summer resort community. In 1202, it was a hot, sandy, and barren island, cut off by the lagoons from the inhabited islands of Venice. The choice by Doge Dandolo of this isolated piece of scrubland for the Crusaders' bivouac area was made with much thought. For one thing, an army separated from Venice proper could not get into mischief. On an individual basis, this mischief could include rape, theft and murder. It could also include, on a collective basis, an insurrection to overthrow the Venetian government.

Dandolo well knew that there were many times in the historical past, when a city invited an army in as a savior, only to see the army stay as a predator.

Another reason for placing the Crusaders on an isolated island was that the Crusaders, being without boats, were totally dependent upon the Venetians for food and fresh water. If the Crusaders proved to be unruly guests, the Venetians could always forget to send the lunchwagon. The Crusaders would quickly get the point.

But Doge Dandolo had another point he wanted to make: the Crusaders still owed him 34,000 marks of silver. He declared that Venice had fulfilled its part of the bargain. The ships were built and ready to sail. The Crusaders acknowledged that the Venetians had done even more than they had agreed to do. Upon first seeing the fleet that the Venetians had built, the Crusaders were amazed at its size and readiness. The fleet consisted of galleys, warships, merchantmen and special transports to carry the horses. The Venetians had employed all the resources of their shipyards for over a year to accomplish the feat. The Crusaders conceded that they owed the Venetians the money. The only problem they had was that they were broke. They could not pay.

Thereupon, Doge Dandolo, rapacious businessman that he was, declared that Venice would keep the money the Crusaders had already paid. Furthermore, he announced to the Crusaders, isolated on the dry and barren Lido: "You shall not move a foot from the island until we have been paid. Quite apart from which, you will not find anyone who will bring you anything to eat or drink."

So the situation in the summer of 1202 was thus. Ten thousand Crusaders, who had set off from their homes in France and Flanders in the religious exaltation of returning Jerusalem to the Christian people, were now being held captive by a Christian state on a forlorn island because they were broke and could not pay their bills. Moreover, the Christian captors, lacking any semblance of Christian charity, intended to keep the money they had already received and to let the Crusaders starve until they received the rest.

The barons, of course, were very upset. Was there no way out of this dilemma, they asked. At this point, Doge Dandolo, not surprisingly, presented a solution to the problem. Down the Adriatic coast was a city named Zara. (Zara is the present city of Zadar in Croatia.) Zara was a thorn in Venice's side. It was a Dalmation city that challenged Venice's control of the Adriatic. By its geographical location, and by its vigor as an economic competitor, Zara was a threat to the prosperity and security of Venice. . In addition, pirates from Zara occasionally preyed upon Venetian shipping.

By themselves, the Doge acknowledged, the Venetians were not strong enough to overcome the military superiority of Zara. In the previous dozen years, Zara had twice defeated Venetian armies sent to conquer the city. Enrico Dandolo himself was doge when the second unsuccessful attempt was made.

Therefore, to counter the threat posed by Zara, and to provide a way for the Crusaders to pay their bills, Dandolo proposed that a new agreement be drawn up.

To compensate the Venetians for the failure to provide the entire payment of 85,000 marks of silver, the French would have to agree to a new contract: the Crusaders would have to help the Venetians conquer Zara. Some Crusaders balked at this agreement. After all, Zara was a Christian city. The original purpose of the Crusade was to fight Muslims, not to aid one Christian state in a war of aggrandizement against another Christian state.

The papal legate, Peter Capuano, moreover, was outspoken in his objection to the use of the Crusaders to attack a Christian city. Such an attack had been expressly forbidden by the Pope. Doge Dandolo responded by not allowing Capuano to sail with the Crusaders as the papal legate. Capuano could join the expedition as a simple priest, but nothing more. No meddlesome envoy from the Holy See would be allowed to disrupt this venture. Faced with the intransigent doge, Peter Capuano decided to forgo the Crusade and returned to Rome.

The money issue too was an argument without merit. Although not receiving the total amount due, the Venetians were being well compensated for their efforts. They only had to feed one-third the number of Crusaders originally contracted for, resulting in considerable cost savings. And because so few

Crusaders had made their way to Venice only about one-half of the galleys and merchantmen, and two-thirds of the horse transports were needed. The rest were to be left tied to their docks in Venice. In addition, the ships built to transport the Crusaders to Jerusalem including those not needed remained the property of Venice, and could be put to other uses.

Under the circumstances, the demand by the Venetians for full payment was an act that today can only be appreciated by American lawyers specializing in the arcane reaches of contract law. Any reasonable Crusader must have easily formed the impression that it was a situation of simple French folk, accustomed to the courtly and honorable ways of agrarian life in Burgundy, Bordeaux, and the Ardennes, being taken for a ride by the wily and sophisticated businessmen of Venice.

In retrospect, historians have even speculated that Dandolo never intended to transport the Crusaders to the Holy Land. It has been argued by some historians that while Dandolo was promising the Crusaders to lead the fight against the Muslims, he was also cutting a deal with the Muslims to receive trade concessions in return for not allowing the Crusaders to reach Muslim territory.

The Muslims had much to fear from the Crusaders. The plan of the Crusaders was first to attack Egypt, then to turn against Jerusalem. By seizing Egypt, the Crusaders would prevent the Muslims of northern Africa from coming to the aid of their brethren in Jerusalem. With Egypt captured, the Muslim world would be physically divided, and the Crusaders could take the Holy Land without worrying about a counter-attack from the south.

The Sultan of Egypt, al-Adil, realizing that his country was in peril, resolved to do whatever had to be done to spare his people a war that could bring them no benefit. Secret negotiations with the Venetians may have ensued.

As a result, in the spring of 1202, several months after concluding the agreement with the French noblemen to sail the Crusaders to Egypt, the Venetians may have made a separate undisclosed agreement with the Egyptian Sultan.

The existence of a treaty with the Egyptians is questioned however. A diligent, careful and highly regarded nineteenth century historian, Carl Hopf, claimed to have seen evidence that the treaty existed. Modern historians though have not been able to substantiate his claim.

In the treaty according to Hopf, the Venetians promised to prevent the Crusaders from reaching Egypt. In return, the Venetians were granted advantageous trading rights in Egypt. Since many of the Asian luxuries and spices coveted by wealthy European aristocrats were transported up the Red Sea and through Egypt, the Egyptian grant of trading rights was a prize of enormous economic value. To seal the agreement, the Egyptian Sultan paid the Venetians a considerable sum of money.

Of all this, nothing, of course, was told to the Crusaders, who were at that very moment making their way through France and over the Alps into northern

Italy. The Venetians in effect may have double crossed the Crusaders, played one side against the other, and pocketed the substantial payments made by each.

Aside from Doge Dandolo's double dealing, his demand that the Crusaders assist in the attack on the Christian city of Zara raised significant ethical issues for the idealistic young soldiers and squires from France and Flanders. They had come this far to do God's work. Making war on a Christian city went against their most holy tenets.

But even the French opponents of the agreement to attack Zara conceded that only the Venetians had sufficient ships to transport all the Crusaders to the Holy Land. That, and the fact that the Venetians had all their money convinced nearly all the Crusaders to accept the new arrangement. Some of the Crusaders could not in good conscience go forward with the plan. They returned home, poorer but morally pure.

Most, however, decided to continue with the venture, perhaps motivated by greed, for Dandolo, in a gesture of benevolence, proposed to apply the value of the booty taken at Zara toward the debts owed by the Crusaders. In addition, winter was approaching. To the Crusaders bivouacking in tents, the capture of Zara offered a warm, sheltered place to stay, and a chance to get off the bleak, inhospitable island, where they were held in virtual captivity by the Venetians. Enrico Dandolo, the shrewd doge, blind and in his eighties, held all the cards.

The fact that the Crusaders had been kept stranded on San Nicolò for the entire summer of 1202 rather than sailing for Jerusalem in August when they were ready is further evidence that Doge Dandolo never intended to use this force against the Muslims. The Crusaders had left their homes in France and Flanders after Easter and began arriving in Venice by mid-May. By the end of July they were ready for the armada to get under way. But Doge Dandolo kept them imprisoned through early October by which time it was too late to sail for Jerusalem. Dandolo blamed the Crusaders for the delay.

Whatever his intent, Dandolo did have a sense of the dramatic. After the French agreed to attack Zara, Dandolo addressed his countrymen in the Basilica San Marco. He said that he was an old man, in need of rest, and in failing health. Then to the crowd's amazement, he announced that, despite his infirmities, he would personally lead the Venetians in the battles to come. Thereupon, he knelt at the altar and wept. It was pure theater, but it was an act that no opponent to the plan could surpass.

A few weeks later, in the first days of October, 1202, the Fourth Crusade was under way – with the Christian city of Zara as its first target. At the head of the armada was Doge Dandolo. He led the fleet of warships down the Grand Canal and out to sea in a vermilion colored war galley, with a silken vermilion awning unfurled above. Music added to the martial aura of the occasion with cymbals clashing, drums beating and trumpets sounding from the ships. Overhead, the crimson and gold flag of Saint Mark flew defiantly, perhaps arrogantly. Never before, had such a large fleet been assembled in the Adriatic. The Venetians cheered. Everyone wept with joy and pride. Never had there been such rejoicing. Two hundred and fifty warships carrying 10,000 soldiers, thousands of cavalry horses, equipment and supplies were an awesome sight indeed.

On November 10, the flotilla was at Zara. The attackers found the city fortified with encircling walls and towers. Across the entrance to its harbor, the defenders had stretched a heavy chain as a barrier. The Venetians and Crusaders attacked from both land and sea. Ladders were thrown up against the walls, while stone throwing machines were used to batter the towers. Soldiers on the galleys meanwhile broke the chain blocking the harbor entrance. After two weeks, it was over. Zara surrendered. The city was pillaged. The lucky leaders of the city were exiled. The unlucky ones were beheaded.

But in the end, the Venetians found, perhaps to no one's surprise, that the booty collected at Zara was not sufficient to pay off the debt owed by the Crusaders. Money, said Doge Dandolo, was still owed.

Pope Innocent, however, was not concerned with money or debts. The Pontiff was furious at this attack on a Christian city. He was so angry, in fact, that he on the advice of Peter Capuano, the papal legate, excommunicated both the Venetians and the Crusaders. Upon review of the actual events, he realized that the Crusaders were not at fault, and he granted them absolution. But he left intact the edict excommunicating the Venetians.

The Venetians ignored the excommunication, and settled into Zara along with the Crusaders for the winter. Before leaving Zara in the spring, the Venetians leveled the city. They destroyed the fortifications, the protective walls, the shops, the palaces, the modest homes. They left only the churches and the bell towers to stand and mock those who had opposed Venetian power.

It was while wintering at Zara that Doge Dandolo finalized the even more audacious move: the attack on Constantinople.

Constantinople was the largest city in the Byzantine Empire. It was built along a deep bay which formed a natural harbor on the vital waterway that flowed between the Black Sea and the Mediterranean. Past the city's gates traveled much of the trade of Russia and Asia with the countries of the Mediterranean. It is a natural place for a great city, which is today called Istanbul. Whoever controlled the city, controlled the straits of the Dardanelles, as the waterway is known, and thereby controlled the sea-borne trade between the major eastern and western nations. Due to this location, the city became a great center of commerce, and grew in wealth and power.

And with wealth and power came conflict with the Venetians. The confrontations between Venice and Constantinople in their efforts to dominate the trade of the eastern Mediterranean became contentious. Decades before the Fourth Crusade the Byzantine Emperor without reason arrested thousands of Venetians living in the lands he controlled and threw them into prisons where some languished for over ten years. Trade would resume. But the shared animosities remained.

At the dawn of the Christian era, the city was called Byzantium. As the Roman Empire disintegrated in the centuries after the birth of Christ, Byzantium acquired new importance.

The word 'Byzantine' in the English language is often used today in a pejorative sense. When we describe something as being Byzantine, we usually mean that it is unnecessarily complex and involved. Our use of the word deprecates the grandeur of the Byzantine Empire, and ignores the vitality and magnificence of its arts. During the centuries immediately following the collapse of the Roman Empire, Byzantium was a thriving civilization. During this same period, civilization in western Europe sunk into the depths of the Dark Ages, from which it would not fully emerge for a thousand years. There were no dark ages in Byzantium.

In the early years of the fourth century, the Roman Empire was divided from within by competing rulers. One of these leaders was named Constantine. He was a fearless warrior, who adhered to traditional pagan religious beliefs. But he was to have an experience that caused him to convert to Christianity. On the day before a crucial battle, it is said, Constantine looked into the sky and saw there a flaming cross, emblazoned with the Greek words "en toutoi nika" – "in this sign thou shalt conquer." That night he had a dream, in which he heard a voice commanding him to fight under the sign of Jesus Christ. The next day he followed the dictates of the apparition of the night before, and his army routed the enemy. Other victories followed until Constantine was the most powerful of the emperors. Thereupon, Constantine embraced Christianity.

In becoming a Christian, the Emperor Constantine felt that Rome, which still followed the pre-Christian, pagan ritual, could no longer serve as the capital of the Empire. A new city would have to be chosen as the capital. He looked east and saw Byzantium. It was a city with many attractions. It was strategically located, it was easily defended, and it would offer a new beginning for an old and crumbling empire.

Under the direction of Constantine, Byzantium became the center of the Catholic faith. In time the city came to be called Constantinople, and the set of Christian beliefs that its people followed came to be called Greek Orthodox.

Thus, it was a Christian city of ancient heritage that the Venetians and the Crusaders planned to attack in 1203.

The reasons for the Crusaders attacking Christian Constantinople were no better than the ones for the attacking Christian Zara. The professed purpose of the attack was to place on the Byzantine throne a young man named Alexius, who, claimed the Venetians, had been wrongfully deprived of the crown by his uncle, the current emperor. No one believed that either the Venetians or the Crusaders had such reverence for legitimacy in the Byzantine state that they would go to war for such an issue.

A more plausible reason for the Crusaders was the need for money. The plunder from Zara had failed to produce enough loot to pay off the Venetians. Moreover, Alexius, the young claimant to the throne, promised to pay the Crusaders 200,000 silver marks after the city was seized. The money would come from Constantinople's treasury. Thus, the Crusaders would be able to pay off the Venetians and have enough silver marks left over to return to France richer than they ever thought possible. Greed was overwhelming their Christian souls.

The Venetians' reasons for attacking the city were just as obvious. Constantinople in 1203 was the richest and most powerful state in the Mediterranean, possibly even in the entire world, and presented an imposing obstacle to Venetian ambitions.

Doge Dandolo also had personal reasons for wanting Constantinople to be destroyed. Over thirty years earlier, he had been sent to Constantinople as the head of a Venetian diplomatic mission. It may have been while he was in Constantinople that he lost his eyesight. Some said the cause of the blindness was a wound suffered in a fight. Others maintained that he had been deliberately blinded by the Byzantines. There is convincing evidence, however, that he did not even begin to lose his sight until several years after he returned from his diplomatic mission. Whatever the true cause of his blindness, Dandolo in his soul had a deep-rooted hatred of Byzantium.

Yet attacking Byzantium entailed risks. Many Venetians resided in Constantinople. They were the merchants and traders who bought the spices and other luxury goods transported from central Asia. These Venetians in Constantinople then shipped these goods to Venice for resale throughout Europe. It was a very profitable venture that would be severely undermined by a failed attack. Failure would mean that the Byzantines would likely direct the spice and luxury trade towards merchants from Pisa and Genoa. Venice's prosperity would suffer a devastating blow.

Nevertheless, Doge Dandolo perhaps driven by personal animus considered the potential gains of a Constantinople much reduced in power to be worth the risk. The attack proceeded.

When the fleet appeared before Constantinople on June 23, 1203, the Venetians and the Crusaders could scarcely believe their eyes. Never had they seen such a large metropolis. In the year 1203, Paris and Venice were hardly more than large towns compared to Constantinople. The European cities seen by most Crusaders were mere villages compared to the size and grandeur of the city that now lay in front of them.

A few years earlier, a Jewish merchant from Spain named Benjamin of Tudela had described the wealth of the city and of its Greek citizens. "Warehouses," wrote the merchant, "are filled with garments of silk, purple and gold. There is nothing in the whole world to be found to equal these storehouses and this wealth. The Greek inhabitants are very rich in gold and precious stones, and they go clothed in garments of silk with gold embroidery, and they ride horses, and look like princes. Indeed, the land is very rich in all cloth stuffs, and in bread, meat and wine. Wealth like that of Constantinople is not to be found in the whole world."

High walls with imposing towers completely encircled Constantinople. The main walls were forty feet high and fifteen feet thick. They had been built eight centuries earlier. During those centuries, armies of the Persians, the Avars, the Bulgars and the Arabs had attacked these walls, but so strong were the fortifications that no army had ever succeeded in entering the city.

The Byzantine leaders of Constantinople were so confident of the invulnerability of the walls, however, that they had neglected to maintain a trained army. Behind the walls, the Byzantine army had declined to the point where it barely constituted a fighting force. The navy was in a similarly unprepared state. The Byzantines at Constantinople relied upon the strength and height of the walls to deter all aggressors. Their main fighting forces consisted of mercenaries, hired to defend the city and protect the emperor. Ironically, the mercenaries for the most part were Englishmen and Italians. The Byzantine army, itself, was riddled with corruption. The navy was no better.

In contrast to the deplorable state of the Byzantine defenders, the knights of the Crusade were equipped with a recent military invention for the protection of the fighting man. This invention, which promised to revolutionize warfare in the thirteenth century, was the suit of armor. The suit of armor was made up of small metal ringlets, interlaced with one another to form a fabric-like metal garment that was impenetrable by the weapons of the day. The knight's head, chest and legs were protected by solid pieces of metal. The suit of armor had been developed as a defense against swords, lances and other weapons of the era prior to the European discovery of gunpowder. It was heavy, and it was hot. But it was effective.

At the very first encounter between the Byzantines and the Crusaders, the inadequacy of Constantinople's defenders was quickly demonstrated. This encounter occurred on July 1, when a reconnaissance party of eighty Crusaders blundered into the camp of 500

Byzantine troops. The greatly outnumbered Crusaders prepared to defend themselves to the death. They need not have bothered. The Byzantines broke ranks and fled, running away, said one observer, "like frightened deer."

Much fighting and political wrangling occurred between the two opposing armies during the summer and fall of 1203. But the results were inconclusive. As the year 1204 began, the Venetians and Crusaders were still pitched in tents outside the walls of Constantinople, which looked as formidable as ever. For good reason the walls had never been breached in the eight centuries since they were built. Within the walls, the citizens of the city had ample food and water to endure a lengthy siege.

The Venetians knew that breaching the walls would be a formidable hurdle. New tactics were required. To accomplish the task, the Venetians decided to use new and ingenious devices: assault gangways that would rise from the galleys to the top of the walls facing the sea. When hoisted into place, the gangways would provide a ramp for the knights to run up to the top of the wall. The gangways were covered with sailcloth to protect the knights from stones, lances and other missiles thrown by the defenders. With luck the assault gangways might protect the Crusaders long enough for the attackers to seize a portion of the walls. If they were able to do so, the city might be taken.

The decisive battle commenced on April 9, 1204. The lower ends of the assault ramps were attached to the galleys while the upper ends were hoisted to the tops of the walls. The attack began. And quickly failed. From the tops of the walls, huge rocks, boulders, and buckets of burning pitch rained down on the attackers. The defenders were determined not to let the Crusaders get a foothold in the city. The Crusaders and Venetians retreated.

Three days later, they tried again. This time the Venetians massed their ships into a smaller attack zone, putting two ships against a section of wall, where earlier they had put only one. The new tactics decided the issue. The knights in their chain mail armor gained control of the contested part of the wall. The axes, swords and lances of the defenders were unable to pierce the knights' chain mail suits. Simultaneously with the success at the top of the wall, a group of knights hacked through a heavy wooden door at the base of the wall. Once the wall was breached, the effects of the Byzantine failure to maintain a large, trained army became apparent. The Crusaders simply streamed into the city overwhelming the little opposition that did appear. On April 12, 1204, Constantinople, for the first time since its founding nearly a thousand years before, was in enemy hands.

The looting of the great city now began. With the exception of the imperial treasury and arsenal, which were placed under guard, no structure was spared. The looting by the Crusaders and Venetians was indiscriminate, shameless, and barbaric. "Never since the world was created," wrote Villehardouin, after he observed the plundering, "was there so much booty gained in one city. Each man took the house that pleased him, and there were enough for all. Those who were poor found themselves suddenly rich. There was captured an immense supply of gold and silver, of plate and of precious stones, of satins and of silk, of furs, and of every kind of wealth ever found upon earth."

Included in the booty taken from Constantinople were statues of four large, gilded, cast in copper horses. These four horses were sent to Venice, where they were placed triumphantly above the main entrance to the Basilica San Marco. From this perch, the horses gazed down upon the multitude in the Piazza, and served to remind all that Venice was now the dominant state and master of the Mediterranean. The statues had been cast in the last days of the Roman Empire, and had stood defiantly in Constantinople since that time. (The original horses were recently moved indoors to protect them from environmental pollution. The statues in their place are copies.)

Constantinople's churches were also targets to be plundered. The fact that they were Christian churches and that the plunderers were Crusaders who had originally set out to liberate the Holy Land changed nothing. Precious stones were ripped from chalices and other religious artifacts. Beautiful embroidered altar cloths, into which were woven jewels and threads of silver and gold, were torn apart for the value of their materials. Into the Hagia Sophia, the largest church in Constantinople and one of the most magnificent churches in Christendom, the Crusaders and Venetians brought horses and mules to better carry off everything of value, no matter how beautiful or sacred. Before the fall of Constantinople, one observer had described the beauty of the Hagia Sophia as "a glimpse of heaven itself." Now it was a mere shell of a building.

Any bronze sculpture or ornament that was not carted away was melted down for the value of its metal. Many of these works of art, which had endured unscathed for centuries, were destroyed in this manner in a centrally located crucible. For this metallurgical furnace, no object was sacred enough, or beautiful enough, or of sufficient historical value to be spared. The plundering of Constantinople continued until nothing worth taking remained.

Nor was theft the only thing on the minds of the soldiers and sailors. In satisfaction of their sexual desires, they spared no attractive woman who was so unlucky as to fall within their grasp. Young, unmarried women were raped, as were nuns who had committed their lives to the Church. These Christian marauders were worse than the Arabs, noted one observer, for the Arabs "at least respected women."

The terror, of course, affected all citizens of Constantinople. A prosperous Byzantine named Nicetas later recounted the frightening experience endured by himself, his family and friends in fleeing the city. They had taken refuge in a small house near the Hagia Sophia. The house was inhabited by a Venetian merchant, who had resided in the city for many years. This Venetian merchant was a good friend of Nicetas and was willing to risk his life to aid Nicetas and other threatened Byzantines. He pretended that he was a Crusader, put on the uniform of a soldier, and by speaking in his native Italian was able to prevent those engaged in pillage from entering the house.

As the situation became increasingly dangerous, though, Nicetas feared for the safety and honor of his daughters, and decided to attempt to flee with his family to the countryside. The others, including other fathers with their daughters, agreed to join him. They dressed as paupers wearing the shabbiest garments. They smeared dirt on their faces to make themselves less conspicuous. Finally, they stole into the street, leaving the sanctuary of the house, and headed for the city gate.

Once outside the city walls, they met many other refugees, including the Patriarch of the Eastern Church. He was, wrote Nicetas, "without bag or money or stick or shoes." But like a true follower of Jesus Christ, Nicetas observed, the Patriarch "was seated on an ass, with the difference that instead of entering the New Zion in triumph, he was leaving it."

Like all conflicts, the Fourth Crusade inflicted grievous harm on innocent non-combatants. People died, people were injured, people lost their worldly belongings. For most citizens of Constantinople life was never the same after April 12, 1204.

From a larger perspective, however, the sacking of Constantinople had a profound and beneficial result. Unexpectedly, it set in motion a chain of events of major significance. Besides increasing the fortunes of the Crusaders and Venetians, the looting of Constantinople had an entirely unintended effect upon European cultural development. As the art treasures of Constantinople were carted off by their new owners to adorn castles and manor houses in France, Italy, Germany, and Flanders, the makers of cultural opinion in those countries looked for the first time at artistic masterpieces far more advanced than their own crude endeavors in the arts.

Some historians believe that the European Renaissance, which was to burst forth in the coming centuries, had its inception with this dispersal of Byzantine masterpieces throughout the countries of western Europe. These treasures of Byzantium, acting as seeds thrown upon a fertile land, served to stimulate the European mind, and, in time, to touch the souls of Giotto, Michelangelo, Leonardo da Vinci and countless other masters of the Renaissance. In Venice, itself, now awash with Byzantine art, the captured works of art were used to embellish buildings and public places. The Byzantine style of Venice, with its abundant use of gold and gemstones in decoration and building, and with its love of ornamentation dates from this period.

The total value of the plunder, of course, far exceeded the amount owed the Venetians for building years earlier those galleys that were supposed to take the Crusaders to the Holy Land. Once the Venetians were paid the debt due for their shipbuilding efforts, the remaining loot was divided among the Crusaders and the Venetian soldiers. Although estimates of the value of the plunder have been made, the true value remains unknown because many soldiers stole many valuable objects for themselves, rather than pooling them for common distribution.

The Venetians and the Crusaders had previously agreed to collect the booty at three churches, where it would then be equitably divided. Although most of the soldiers, under threat of excommunication, brought what they found to the churches, some, perhaps many, did not turn in everything. Villehardouin reports somewhat piously that "the covetous began to keep

back, and our Lord began to love them less" –
apparently the Lord loved less those who stole
individually than those who stole collectively. But
continued Villehardouin, "stern justice was meted out to
such as were found guilty, and not a few were hanged."
Villehardouin cites one case where the Count of St. Paul
hanged one of his knights "with his shield to his neck,"
for keeping back certain spoils.

So ended the Fourth Crusade. It never did get to
Jerusalem. The Crusaders simply collected their booty
and returned to their homes in Europe. They returned
though many times richer than when they had left. But
Doge Dandolo, the blind Venetian leader who had so
skillfully manipulated the Crusaders, did not return to
his homeland. He died in Constantinople the year
following the fall of the city. In 1453, two and a half
centuries after the Fourth Crusade, the city fell again,
this time to the Turks, who made it an Islamic
stronghold. The city was subsequently renamed
Istanbul.

The capture of Constantinople, despite its enrichment
of the Crusaders, nevertheless, did not please Pope
Innocent. He remembered that Byzantium was a
Christian state. He also remembered that the original,
and only blessed, purpose of the Crusade was to retake
Jerusalem from the infidels. The Holy Father was not
reticent in making known his anger. He wrote one of
the French barons responsible for the original plan:

"You took upon yourselves the duty of delivering the
Holy Land from the Infidel. You were forbidden under
pain of excommunication from attacking any Christian
lands, unless they refused you passage or would not

help you (even then you were to do nothing contrary to the wishes of my legate). You had no claims or pretensions to the lands of Greece. You were under the most solemn vows of Our Lord – and yet you have totally disregarded these vows.

"It was not against the Infidel but against Christians that you drew your sword. It was not Jerusalem that you captured but Constantinople. It was not heavenly riches upon which your minds were set, but earthly ones. But far and above all of this, nothing has been sacred to you – neither age nor sex.

… "In the eyes of the whole world you have abandoned yourselves to debauchery, adultery and prostitution. You have not only violated married women and widows, but even women and virgins whose lives were dedicated to Christ.

"You have looted not only the treasures of the Emperor and of citizens both rich and poor, but have despoiled the very sanctuaries of God's Church.

"You have broken into holy places, stolen the sacred objects of altars – even including crucifixes – and you have pillaged innumerable images and relics of the Saints. It is hardly surprising that the Greek Church, beaten down though it is, rejects any obedience to the Apostolic See. It is hardly surprising that it sees in all Latins no more than treachery and the works of the Devil, and regards all of them as curs."

The Venetians were unimpressed by Pope Innocent's understandable outrage. Regardless of what the Pope thought, for the Venetians, the Fourth Crusade had achieved its aims. By the thirteenth century Venice was one of the world's great powers.

Chapter 3: A Glorious and Heavenly City

For the traveler of the Middle Ages and Early Renaissance, the first sight of Venice was a spectacle of unprecedented magnitude. No other city of that time rivaled Venice in its stupendous glory. The city's wealth was displayed for all to see in the sumptuous palaces that lined the canals, and in the broad piazzas and public buildings that invited citizens from all nations to celebrate the achievements of the Venetians in art and enterprise. Recording his first impressions a visiting awe struck Englishman named Thomas Coryate wrote in 1608, "I saw Venice ... which yieldeth the most glorious and heavenly shew upon the water that ever any mortal eye beheld, such a shew as did ever ravish me both with delight and admiration." Dreary London with its persistent rain, crampted Medieval streets, and dour Puritans could not compare. England though in 1608 did have William Shakespeare.

Venice is located in the north of Italy, at the northern end of the Adriatic Sea. It is east of most of the rest of Italy, and just south of Germany. On the other side of the Italian peninsula is Genoa. South of Venice, are the Italian cities of Florence, Pisa, Rome, and Naples.

From the Adriatic, the Venetians had access to all the ports of the Mediterranean. The Mediterranean Sea is made up of several lesser seas, including the Adriatic. The Tyrrhenian Sea lies to the west of Italy. The Ionian is between Italy and Greece. The Aegean is surrounded by Greece and Turkey, and is adorned with the most beautiful islands in the world. The Adriatic is bounded on the west by Italian peninsula and on the east by Croatia, which in the sixteenth century were known as Dalmatia. On the Adriatic, Venice is one of the European ports closest to the riches of Asia.

From the Republic's very beginning, the sea brought it protection and wealth. The city is built around shallow lagoons on pilings driven into the sand and clay beneath the water. A traveler best approaches Venice from the sea.

The sea was the lifeblood of Venice. It was the source of Venice's prosperity. By controlling the sea, the Republic of Venice grew rich and powerful, and became a place of academic achievement and artistic expression. The importance of the sea to the Republic's well-being was underscored by a simple ceremony performed each year on Ascension Day by the Doge of Venice. The ceremony was called the Wedding of the Sea – *lo Sposalizio*. In the ceremony, the doge, as the supreme ruler of the Venetian state was known, took his place on a specially gilded galley called the Bucentaur. He was then rowed out to sea by three hundred appropriately attired oarsmen to the sounds of trumpets and horns. A parade of vessels decorated for the occasion followed. At a select point while the highest dignitaries of Venice and other states looked on, the doge cast a gold wedding ring into the water, and announced that he was taking dominion over the sea in the same manner as a husband takes dominion over a wife.

If the ceremony had been continued into the twenty-first century, the part about a husband taking dominion over a wife undoubtedly would have been modified to reflect modern values and to preserve domestic tranquility. Nevertheless, the ceremony with its underlying meaning was performed for several hundred years. In a sense, it displayed the characteristics that Venetians employed to achieve commercial supremacy in Europe. The Venetians take dominion of the sea, they do not humbly ask for the sea's bounty. The Venetians arrogantly reduce the sea to the role of a wife, which at the time that the ceremony was performed was a very low role indeed. In time, of course, Venice ceased to have dominion over the sea, but the avenging agents were men of other nations, sailing better ships and using more ruthless tactics.

The gold ring cast into the sea, by the way, was retrieved.

The doge was the Venetian head of state. He was chosen from one of the influential families of the city by a committee of the aristocracy. Like the pope, the doge was elected for life. By the late Middle Ages, however, he ruled with the advice of counselors, who in turn were chosen by a general assembly consisting of the nobles and wealthiest merchants of Venice. The doge and the top counselors constituted a body called the Signoria, which was the chief policy making organization of the state. A governmental body with separate responsibilities was the Senate. The members of the Signoria and Senate drew their authority, directly or indirectly from the Great Council – the *Maggior Consiglio* – a body of over a thousand nobles and merchants.

The most feared government agency, though, was the Council of Ten – the *Consiglio dei Dieci* – which was responsible for state security. The suppression of treason, rebellion, and menacing foreign activity was the duty of the Ten. Murder and torture were its tools. To aid in enforcement, the Ten conveniently placed denunciation boxes around the city where citizens could secretly report on the suspicious activities of their neighbors. The denunciation boxes were in the shape of a lion's head. Accusers inserted the letters of accusation into the lion's mouth, from which the boxes drew their name – the *Bocca di Leone*.

Even the activities of the doge were subject to review by the Ten, which as a matter of course opened and read the doge's private correspondence.

Members of the Council of Ten served for only twelve months before returning to private life. In a body invested with such authority, Venice wanted no person or group of persons to hold office long enough to develop troublesome ideas.

The Ten had the power to act swiftly. If an accused was found guilty of treason and sentenced to death, the sentence – frequently carried out by strangulation – was performed the same night, and the following morning the citizens of Venice would find the body of the convicted hanging by one leg from a gibbet in the Piazzetta. No explanations were offered. None were expected.

When deemed necessary, though, the Ten would combine brutality with humiliation. In one such case, in 1509, Bertuccio Bagarotto was convicted for treason and then was publicly hanged from gallows erected between the columns in the Piazzetta while his wife and children were forced to look on.

Signor Bagarotto was convicted, some think unjustifiably, for siding with Venice's enemies in a war against a coalition of anti-Venetian states known as the League of Cambrai.

In 1539, the Ten added three *Inquisitori di Stato* to assist in the suppression of activities considered harmful to the Republic.

The Republic of Venice was not a democracy. It was ruled by a tightly defined nobility of about one hundred forty families. Their names reoccur throughout Venice's history—the Contarini, the Loredan, the Giustinian, the Grimani, the Priuli. In 1297 the *Maggior Consiglio* in a measure called the *Serrata* conferred upon these noble families the hereditary right to govern the Republic. The english meaning of *serrata* is lock which accurately suggests the hold the nobility held upon the governance of Venice. In 1506 lest there be some ambiguity the hierarchy of the elite was further spelled out with the institution of the *Libri d'Oro* – the Book of Gold – in which the names of all noble male births were to be registered. Later it was required that the mothers of the noble male children also be of noble lineage.

Only a member of the nobility could serve in the *Maggior Consiglio*, or be a doge, or be a member of the Senate or of the Council of Ten. With this concentration of power in the hands of the few, the potential for abuse was ever present as every Venetian knew. But abuse rarely occurred. The Venetian government was self-regulating with an effective system of checks and balances.

Although Venice did not have a written constitution, by common consent, the doge would not act against the advice of his counselors, the Senate, and the Council of Ten. It was perhaps the most successful system of government conceived by man for his control, protection, and general welfare. It provided the citizens of Venice with freedom, prosperity, and security for more than a thousand years. The United States has eight hundred years to go. By the fourteenth century Venice had a well-established, republican, orderly form of government at a time when in England Plantagenet claimants to the throne were hacking each other to pieces in the War of the Roses while ignoring the weak and powerless Parliament.

The Venetians affectionately called their state the *Serenissima Repubblica*, the Serene Republic. The name was a misnomer, though, since Venice, to protect its interests, was frequently at war.

"Venice can only be compared to itself." So wrote Goethe, the eighteenth century German observer of the European scene. By the Late Renaissance of the sixteenth century, the physical appearance of the city was close to what one sees today. As Goethe said, Venice can only be compared to itself.

The most renowned building in Venice, now and in the time of the Republic's greatest glory, is the Basilica of San Marco. Facing the great open plaza called the Piazza San Marco, the Basilica is a structure that finds its architectural heritage in the east. In an effusion of Victorian prose John Ruskin, the nineteenth century English architectural critic, described the Basilica of San Marco as "a multitude of pillars and white domes, ... a treasure heap, it seems, partly of gold, and partly of opal and mother of pearl, ... beset with sculpture of alabaster, clear as amber and delicate as ivory." Where the roof meets the sky, continued Ruskin, "the crests of the arches ... as if in ecstasy ... break into a marble foam, and toss themselves far into the blue sky in flashes and wreaths of sculptured spray."

Inside the Basilica, mosaics of multi-colored stones adorn the walls and ceilings with a medieval display of pageantry and self-glorification. The mosaics, which date from the twelfth and thirteenth century, depict the early history of Venice. Of course, the history portrayed is history as the Venetians had wished it to have been. Like people of all centuries, the builders of San Marco's Basilica enshrined myth as well as fact.

The domes of the Basilica, the mosaics, the polished marble surfaces, the lavish use of ostentatious decoration, all reflect the influence of the Byzantine civilization to the east. This love of lavish ornamentation, though, was perfectly in tune with the Venetian character.

On the loggia above the central portico of the Basilica of San Marco stand statues of four horses. These statues are copies of ancient statues that were taken as booty from Constantinople in 1204 after the destruction of that city by the misdirected Fourth Crusade. The original statues have been moved into the Basilica to prevent deterioration from modern day pollutants, and can be viewed close-up by the public.

The horses have fascinated visitors to Venice from the beginning. Even in 1204 the statues were over a thousand years old. They are made of copper and were cast in the second century.

The horses have a jaunty appearance. With their sidelong glances each relates to the others giving them the sense of a coherent team. Their manes are short and cropped. Yet their tails are full and free flowing. Each has a foreleg raised as if ready to gallop forward. Their well-developed shoulder, neck and hindquarter muscles indicate that these horses were bred to pull chariots. Work horses they were not.

Scholars believe the statues were commissioned by the Roman Emperor Septimius who conquered Byzantium in 195. The horses would have been mounted upon a triumphal arch. And there they stayed for a thousand years until 1204 when the Venetians carted them off to stand vigil over the Piazza San Marco.

The horses were meant to be elevated so as to be seen from below. Physically they do not represent a true horse. Their legs are too long, their necks and backs too short. But the effect when viewed from below is of a horse of grace and beauty.

During the period that Venice was an independent republic, that is up until 1797, the seat of the patriarch – Venice's highest religious leader – was not the Basilica of San Marco. Thus for the period of the Republic, San Marco should properly be referred to as a church, not as a basilica. (However, since guidebooks usually refer to San Marco as a basilica, that usage is often utilized in this book to avoid confusion.) During the period of the Republic, San Marco served as the private chapel of the doge. The seat of the patriarch was the church of San Pietro in the sestiere of Castello.

The second great building in Venice, the Doge's Palace, is adjacent to the Basilica. As the seat of the government, the Doge's Palace faces the Canal di San Marco near the entrance to the Grand Canal. It is one of the world's most ornate buildings. Within, were the chambers of the governing councils and the residential quarters of the Doge. Paintings of Titian, Tintoretto, Veronese, and other artistic masters of the Renaissance cover the walls of its rooms. Even the ceilings are decorated. No space was too unimportant to be left untouched by the work of an artist.

The staircases, themselves, are artistic marvels. One of these, the Scala d'Oro, the staircase of gold, is adorned with gilded reliefs and painted panels, and remains perhaps unrivaled as Christendom's most opulent, even most arrogant, staircase. The Doge and the procurators, as the members of the ruling council were known, climbed the Scala d'Oro to reach the chambers where they held the governing sessions of the council.

The exterior walls of the Doge's Palace are of masonry, colored rose and white. The walls sit delicately over two series of arcades. The arches on the lower arcade are traditional Gothic, heavy and substantial. But the arches in the upper arcade are so lacy and intricate that they give the entire palace an ethereal sense of well-being and harmony.

Overall, the building, which was completed in the fifteenth century, is a balanced design incorporating elements from Gothic, Classical, and Islamic architecture. As such, the Doge's Palace was perfectly designed to be the center of government for a city that drew its vitality from both eastern and western cultures. Its Classical and Gothic influences can be seen in its columns and arches. The Eastern heritage is visible in the diamond pattern of the inlaid tiles on the upper facade, which is reminiscent of the decorative tradition of Persia and Turkey. This decorative pattern over the wide expanse of wall amuses the eye and comforts the soul.

The Doge's Palace was also accessible to the people. Architecturally at least it was open to the Piazza where the merchants and tradesmen went about their daily business. The governing authorities in other Italian Renaissance cities, in contrast, hid in fortress-like structures that were designed to intimidate the populous, and to impart a sense of power and control. In Florence, the Palazzo Medici and the Palazzo della Signoria with their heavy solemnity sent a very different message than did Venice's Doge's Palace. In Ferrara, only a day's journey from Venice, the center of government was a stronghold, surrounded by a moat, and entered by way of a drawbridge. The leaders of Venice, confident in their ability to govern, needed no such artifices.

Across from the Basilica and the Doge's Palace, the bell tower called the Campanile rises higher than all other structures. Compared to the ostentatious display of the buildings surrounding it, the Campanile is of simple and restrained design.

Beside the Campanile is the Library, which has been described as one of the richest and most ornate buildings ever erected. The Library – the *Libreria* – was completed in the late sixteenth century. It was designed by Jacopo Sansovino and is considered a masterpiece of Late Renaissance architecture with its ornateness complementing its overall sense of harmony and beauty.

Unfortunately for Signor Sansovino, though, a vault supporting part of the roof collapsed during its construction. As a result, he was jailed and held to be financially responsible for the mishap. He was only released from prison after leading citizens convinced the authorities that jailing a noted architect was not an appropriate response for construction problems in a building he designed. Moreover, it was agreed, such jailings would discourage artistic development, an endeavor prized by all nations in Renaissance Europe.

Adjacent to the Libreria, Sansovino designed another building – the Zecca, the mint and treasury. In this fortress-like structure that reflects its original use, Sansovino introduced to Venice many attributes of Renaissance architecture that had earlier been developed in Rome and Florence.

From the Zecca, the traveler can see vessels entering the nearby Grand Canal and passing before the Santa Maria della Salute, which might be the most photographed church in all of Christendom. The Salute was designed by Baldassare Longhena and was built in the decades following 1630. Longhena was one of the great architects of the Baroque. In the Salute with its scrolls and statues and dynamic composition, he captured the whimsical spirit of seventeenth century architecture. With the Dogana da Mar, the customs house, the Salute provides the perfect entrance to the Grand Canal.

From this entrance near San Marco, the Grand Canal starts its meandering course through the city. Along the canal, the palaces of the patrician class compete for the observer's attention. At the uppermost point that can be reached by a sea-going ship, the Grand Canal is crossed by the Rialto Bridge. Until the seventeenth century, this was the only bridge across the canal. For hundreds of years, the Rialto Bridge was made of wood. The present stone structure replacing the wooden bridge was only completed towards the end of the sixteenth century. Anyone not wishing to use the bridge to cross the canal could take one of the traghetti or ferryboats that operated from many points.

The area at the eastern end of the Rialto Bridge was the financial district of Venice. In the fifteenth and sixteenth centuries, it was the Wall Street of its day. The government offices were at the Doge's Palace on the Piazza San Marco. The road connecting the Rialto and the Piazza San Marco was called the Merceria, and though it was narrow, crooked, congested, and unpaved until 1675, it was the most frequently used street in Venice, and a most desirable location for shops of every sort.

The other streets of Venice retained their medieval character. Like the Merceria, they were narrow and crooked, and ran simply from the edge of one canal to the edge on another, following the paths laid out centuries earlier. Since goods were transported on the canals by gondola, and the streets were used only by pedestrians, there was never a necessity to widen and straighten the streets of Venice to accommodate wagons, carriages, and other vehicles.

On the Rialto also were the fish, meat and vegetable markets. Fish, caught in the Adriatic, were always fresh and available in wonderful variety. Vegetables and olive oil were brought in from the countryside, as were lamb, veal and kid goat. One Venetian wrote in 1493 that "in this city nothing grows, yet whatever you want can be found in abundance."

Along the Grand Canal, the Venetian patricians and merchants built magnificent palaces with the profits garnered as the masters of European commerce. During the fifteenth century, the money from the spice trade flowed in torrential quantities, and it was during this time, not surprisingly, that many of the Venetian palaces we see today were built. They were delightfully ostentatious, glittery, and innovative. During the fifteenth century, the two Giustiniani palaces were built, as were the Ca' Foscari, the Palazzo Contarini-Fasan, the Palazzo Pisani-Moretta, the Palazzo Dario, and many more.

The mansion that reached the height of unrestrained exuberance, though, was the Ca' d'Oro, which literally means the "House of Gold." The Ca' d'Oro is a jewel. Its facade, facing the Grand Canal, is an abundant display of columns, arches, and intricately carved windows. It is as if the architectural traditions of Western Gothic and Eastern Byzantine collided at this spot. Ostentatious as the Ca' d'Oro appears today, it was even more so in the fifteenth century, when nearly its entire facade was gilded with real gold leaf. To add color to the prospect, ornamental details were painted ultramarine blue and red.

The Venetians who built the Ca' d'Oro and the other palaces could foresee no end to the prosperity of the fifteenth century. They were the strongest power in the world. They could conceive of no challenger to that role. Certainly, they thought, no other European state, with their backward, illiterate people, posed a threat to the supremacy of Venice.

Passing the Ca' d'Oro and following the Grand Canal as it unwinds past the other great marble palaces, the traveler comes upon a less prosperous district on the north side of the city. This was the Jewish quarter.

When in need of money, the workman or even perhaps the aristocrat or merchant was likely to seek a loan from a Jew. The seeker of a loan would travel by gondola up the Grand Canal to the Ghetto, as the Jewish district was called. This district was on an island that once contained an iron foundry for casting cannon. The island was still called "the Ghetto" from the Italian word for foundry. It was from this place that the word "ghetto" went forth into the languages of the world, taking on different meanings to reflect different times and different conditions.

The ghetto of sixteenth century Venice was a walled community, cut off from the rest of Venice by canals and drawbridges. At the gateways in the high walls, guards prevented unauthorized entrance or exit. The Jews were allowed to leave the district during the day, but were required to return by dusk. To further contain the Jews in the Ghetto, patrol boats watched the community, and windows facing towards the city were bricked up. The government ever frugal billed the Jews for the cost of the patrol boats.

Conditions within the Ghetto were crowded and unhealthy. Nevertheless, the district was of necessity the center of Jewish social life. Within were five synagogues, many shops and bakeries, and a kosher butcher. The wooden multi-storied apartment buildings fronted on alleys and courtyards. None of the buildings within the Ghetto, however, was owned by a Jew, since they were forbidden to own real estate.

As a further stigma, the Jews were required to wear hats of bright crimson when venturing outside the Ghetto. For a Jew to wear a black hat such as worn by Christian Venetians was a criminal offense, and the Jewish community had regularly to pay the fines of persons imprisoned "by reason of the black hat." This practice continued into the eighteenth century. It was thus a common sight to see these red-hatted people going about their business. If there on a Friday evening, the beginning of the Jewish Sabbath, one could see the entire multitude of red-hatted men moving toward the Ghetto to be home before sundown, when, according to Jewish custom, all work must cease.

Jews throughout Europe were required to wear red hats. In Rome, though, the requirement that Jews wear red hats was replaced by a rule that they wear yellow hats. The cause of the change was a near-sighted cardinal who mistook a red-hatted Jew for a fellow member of the College of Cardinals, who also wore red hats. As the Englishman, John Evelyn explained in 1645: "The Jews in Rome wore red hatts til the Card: of Lyons lately saluted one of them, thinking one of them a Cardinal, as he passed by his Coach, being it seemes short sighted, upon which an order was made that they should use only the yellow colour."

Far more serious for the Jews than the color of their hats, was the continuous threat of expulsion. The fears of the Jews were justified. In 1571, the Venetian Senate decreed that within two years all Jews were to leave the city and were never to return. The decree came only months after the great naval victory of the Venetians over the Turks in the Gulf of Lepanto. The order expelling the Jews was justified as a means of thanking the Almighty for the victory of battle.

For a year and a half, efforts to rescind the 1571 decree were unsuccessful. The Jews packed and prepared to leave. However, a few months before the deadline, the Venetian Senate in a reversal repealed its order of expulsion. Precise reasons for the repeal are lost in time, but a significant factor appears to be the realization that in expelling the Jews, Venice would be losing many of its most industrious and best educated people. Moreover, Turkey was resurgent. Despite their defeat at Lepanto, the Turks again presented a threat to the autonomy of Venice. The Almighty, it appeared, might not be on the side of the Venetians after all. Venice needed all the resources it could muster, and the Jews were allowed to remain. Thereafter, the Jews lived peacefully until modern times.

The Ghetto had been the Jewish quarter since the year 1516, when the Signoria, concerned with the number of Jews living among Christians mandated that all Jews live in a separate district. Hundreds of years earlier, Jews had begun settling in Venice as a natural development of the commercial trade between Venice and the Holy Land.

As their numbers grew, they were forbidden by the Christian authorities to practice all but a few occupations.

One occupation left open to the Jews was that of money lender, a source of wealth that the Catholic Church deemed to be unholy, tainted, and against the commands of the Bible. If non-Christians wished to engage in this sin of usury, so much the better. The souls of non-Christians were lost anyhow. The Jews, thereby, to earn a living, opened loan banks, which were in effect pawnshops where Venetians in need of cash could get a loan by leaving some article as collateral. A second occupation left open to the Jews was that of strazzaria—the trade of secondhand articles, usually clothing, but occasionally of jewels and other articles. The Jews were also allowed to sell various household items, such as pots and pans.

In Venice, Christian working people, as did the Jews, lived in conditions much different from that of the aristocrats in their palaces on the Grand Canal. From the paintings of Giovanni Antonio Canaletto, an eighteenth century painter who was fascinated by the dynamic and picturesque character of all of Venice, we get a glimpse of everyday life in the less prosperous sections of the city. His paintings, such as those titled *Rio dei Mendicanti* and *The Stonemason's Yard*, portray in wonderful detail sections of the city few foreign travelers ever saw. The buildings are tenements, three or four stories tall. Laundry hangs from clotheslines strung between convenient windows. Workmen, often shabbily dressed, perform their tasks as stonecutters and shipbuilders. Well used wooden sheds provide places to store materials and tools. Old people sit complaisantly in the sun. And nearby always is the gray-green water of a canal.

We can also see the Piazza San Marco as it was. Most notably, the Piazza was less tidy than it is today. In Canaletto's paintings we see blue and white canvas awnings hanging over the Romanesque windows of the Procuratie Vecchie on the north side of the Piazza. Goats wander about on the Piazza itself. Before the Basilica, vendors of sundry goods sell their wares under multi-colored tents. The whole area thrives with commercial activity.

Much of Venice's food was brought in from farms on the mainland, where Venice possessed rich agricultural territories. The people on the mainland naturally engaged in pursuits quite different from the commercial enterprises of Venice itself. They were farmers and herdsmen, and were far removed from the transactions of international trade taking place on the Rialto. In the midst of this rural countryside was the town of Padua, where the Venetian Republic maintained a university that from the fourteenth to the seventeenth centuries was one of the foremost institutions of higher learning in the Western world. During this period, the University of Padua surpassed in fame and standing the universities at Oxford, Cambridge and Paris.

As the Renaissance expanded interest in the learned subjects, students from many countries came to Padua to study. In the early years of the sixteenth century, a brilliant young Polish cleric named Nicolas Koppernigk came to study canon law. Years later, after having changed his name to Copernicus, the cleric would theorize that the sun, not the earth, was the center of the universe. Others, also, came.

In the autumn of 1592, as a favor to an influential aristocrat, the University hired an instructor of modest accomplishments to teach mathematics. The twenty-eight year old man was out of work and needed a job to support his widowed mother and younger brother and sisters. Despite little in the way of credentials, the aristocrat thought the man showed great promise. Thus, Galileo Galilei became a junior faculty member at the University of Padua.

Galileo had been born in Pisa, but grew up in Florence, where his father scratched out a living as a music teacher. As a young man he returned to Pisa to study and to teach at the University of Pisa.

In those early years of his professional life, Galileo was interested mainly in the physical laws governing the speed of falling bodies. In contrast to the established belief of the time that a heavy body falls faster than a lighter body, Galileo believed that all bodies fall at the same rate of speed, regardless of weight. There has grown up the story that Galileo, to prove his theory, went to the top of the Leaning Tower of Pisa and simultaneously dropped a light and a heavy object. Both objects, it is said, struck the ground at the same time, proving his own theory and disproving the establishment view. Appealing as this story is, it appears to have no factual basis. In his voluminous writings, Galileo makes no mention of such an experiment, and the story of the Leaning Tower itself makes its first appearance only after Galileo's death.

There are abundant facts, however, to indicate that Galileo, a feisty and combative character, did not get along with his fellow faculty members at the university. His personality may have been a factor in his contract not being renewed at Pisa after three years of teaching. He was out of work when he was asked to teach at Venice's university at Padua.

The invitation to join the faculty at the University of Padua was a crucial event in Galileo's life. He quickly made friends with high-ranking people who would influence his future career. Through these friends, he frequently met with the most powerful men in church and state. His easy access to and association with these men of power may have led Galileo to assume that he could publicly articulate positions considered heretical by the Church. He was to learn that he could not.

For most of his years at Padua, Galileo continued to study the motion and the speed of falling objects. Important, but not exciting stuff. If he had done no more than continue his experiments in this field, he would today be referred to only in obscure academic journals. He would be regarded as an early pre-Newtonian scientist of minor importance.

In 1609, though, he received news that would radically change his area of study. While visiting friends in Venice, he was told that a Flemish maker of eyeglass spectacles had invented an instrument that greatly magnified distant objects. By looking through the instrument, it was said, objects that were so far away as to be barely visible could be seen as if nearby. Galileo spoke with many in Venice who refused to believe that such an instrument could be made. Within days, however, the initial report was confirmed in a letter to Galileo from a French nobleman, who had been one of Galileo's students.

Upon receiving the letter from France, Galileo began to think how such an instrument might be constructed. Although he had not seen a "telescope" and the description was sketchy, Galileo with his knowledge of optics quickly built a superior model.

At one end of a lead tube, he placed a convex lens, at the other end, a concave lens. When he looked through the end with the concave lens, he saw that objects appeared nine times larger than they did to the unaided eye. Galileo had constructed his first telescope. He did not call it a telescope, though. He called it an *occhiale*, the Italian word for eyeglass. Only later was the device named a telescope, from the Greek words meaning "to see at a distance."

The news of Galileo's telescope soon reached the ears of Venice's highest authorities. The leaders of Venice immediately realized the significance of this instrument. The future of Venice depended upon the control of the sea, and for any maritime power, the telescope was of obvious military importance. With it a naval vessel or commercial ship would be able to see hostile forces long before they became visible to the unaided eye.

Galileo was called to the Doge's Palace to show his device to the full Senate.

On August 24, 1609, the appointed day of the demonstration, Galileo arrived at the Doge's Palace and ascended the Scala d'Oro—the stair-case of gold—to meet the highest ranking members of the Venetian

government. As he walked to meet Doge Leonardo
Donà in the Sala del Collegio—the cabinet meeting
room—Galileo passed paintings and frescoes by Titian,
Tintoretto, and Veronese. He then followed the Doge
into the large Sala del Senato—the Senate chamber.

Those present in the large, ornate Senate chamber wore,
in conformity with the custom, special robes indicating
their status. The procurators, who were the members of
the highest governing council, wore red silk robes with
cut velvet stoles. The senators, a little below the
procurators in rank, wore red silk robes without a stole.
The heads of the various ministries, if they were
present, would have worn robes of dark blue. The
Admiral of the Fleet, if he was present, would have
been adorned with a robe of red and gold brocade, a
glittery outfit that perfectly symbolized the importance
of the naval forces to the survival and prosperity of
Venice. The Doge, of course, was the most resplendent
of all. Galileo, as a mere university professor, probably
wore a robe that was plain and black.

Galileo demonstrated his telescope to the assembled
patricians and senators. The telescope was about two
feet long and less than two inches in diameter. Knowing
how to put on a good show, Galileo had dressed up the
appearance of his instrument by covering the outside of
the tube with crimson satin.

Since the senate chamber was not an appropriate place
to display the magnifying power of the telescope, it was
decided to adjourn and reassemble at the top of the bell
tower, the Campanile of San Marco, where ships could

be seen entering the harbor many miles away. Located on the Piazza San Marco, across from the Doge's Palace, the Campanile is the highest structure in Venice.

The group trooped outside, climbed the tower's many stairs, and reassembled at the top of the Campanile. From there, with a view of the seaward approaches to Venice, the astonished senators saw ships that were fifty miles away. Incoming ships that would not be visible to the naked eye for at least two more hours could now be clearly seen through the telescope.

When these highest ranking leaders of Venice turned the telescope toward Padua, the dome of the church of Santa Giustina, which was twenty miles away, could be seen. Turning the telescope south, the Doge and senators clearly saw Chioggia, fifteen miles distant.

The value of the telescope was apparent to all. The highly pleased senators soon rewarded Galileo with lifetime tenure and a large salary increase.

Galileo, however, was not interested in using the telescope to see distant ships. Galileo's main interest was to use the telescope to observe the heavens. A few months after the triumph at the Campanile, he pointed his best model of this optical device towards the moon and the planets. He soon discovered that much of what was believed about astronomy was simply wrong.

He quickly wrote a small book, titled *The Starry Messenger*, to describe his discoveries. The moon, he reported, had tall mountains and deep valleys, and was not perfectly smooth as had been believed. Moreover, the planet Jupiter had its own moons – something no one had expected. Later he would discover that the planets Mercury and Venus showed evidence of orbiting the sun, and that the sun contained sunspots. With these revelations, Galileo headed into dangerous territory.

The discoveries reported in *The Starry Messenger* along with his later discoveries clearly gave credence to the theory of Nicholas Copernicus that the sun, not the earth, was the center of the universe. The Church regarded the Copernican theory as contrary to Holy Scripture, and therefore judged belief in the theory to be heresy.

Yet Galileo was a man who felt compelled to speak his mind. Inevitably he would come into conflict with the Church and the Inquisition. If he had remained in Venice, he may have been able to avoid much personal hardship. But shortly before publishing *The Starry Messenger*, he decided to return to his native Florence.

His friends were distressed. Francesco Sagredo, perhaps Galileo's closest friend, asked him pointedly, "Where will you find the same liberty as in the Venetian territory?" For all its faults, Venice was still the European state most tolerant of diversity in opinion, and most willing to protect oddball professors with crazy ideas about the shape of the universe. Nevertheless, Galileo left the University of Padua for the Florentine court of Cosimo de' Medici.

When Francesco Sagredo asked Galileo, "Where will you find the same liberty as in the Venetian territory?" he knew that Venice was unique amongst the nations of the world in protecting individual freedoms. This toleration of dissident ideas led to a thriving publishing industry.

Although movable type and the printing press were developed by Johannes Gutenberg in Germany in the mid-fifteenth century, Venice, probably because of its light regulatory touch, became the center of Europe's publishing industry.

It is not surprising, therefore, that the world's first newspaper was published in Venice sometime around 1630. It was a four page weekly called the *Gazzetta*. The paper took its name from a Venetian coin of little value called the *gazzetta*.

This openness to free inquiry led to a robust academic environment. The university at Padua, where Galileo did much of his most important work, continued to be unsurpassed in academic excellence. Of particular significance, the University was home to the leading medical school in Europe. At the time that Galileo was conducting experiments in physics, other professors were doing research that greatly expanded knowledge of how the human body works.

The main effort of the medical research at Padua was to scientifically study the human anatomy. For the first time in man's history, physicians made a systematic effort to understand the function of each organ. At the University of Padua during the sixteenth and seventeenth centuries, the mysteries of medical science began to unravel as knowledge of physiology increased exponentially.

The professor most involved in medical research was Girolamo Fabrici. His principal method was to dissect and scientifically examine the cadavers of executed criminals. At Padua, Fabrici benefited from the enlightened environment indigenous to the Republic of Venice. In other European states at this time, there remained a political and religious bias against the dissection of the human body. For example, the city of Paris, which maintained a university that rivaled Padua in excellence, allowed only two autopsies a year. The worldly Venetians, though, placed no such restrictions on the academicians at Padua.

The biggest problem the researchers had was to get good corpses. Andrea Vesalius, a predecessor of Fabrici at Padua, and one of history's great scientists, had to overcome much opposition to convince the local authorities not to draw and quarter criminals, a process that satisfied the citizenry's appetite for blood and gore, but which at the same time ruined the body's usability for medical research.

Fortunately, the authorities found less destructive means of executing criminals, and the flow of cadavers to the examination table at the University of Padua began in earnest.

The bodies were dissected in a special room designated for that purpose. The anatomy theater, as it was called, consisted of the dissection table in the center with six tiers of circular balconies rising above the examination floor. From the balconies, students and other observers could look straight down at the autopsy being performed. It provided the most advanced facility in the world for the medical study of the human body.

Not surprisingly, the medical school at Padua attracted the best students from all of Europe. In 1600, at the same time that Galileo was teaching mathematics at the university, William Harvey, a twenty-two year old Englishman, arrived to study for a doctorate in medicine. Harvey studied under Fabrici. Expanding on Fabrici's work, Harvey, after returning to England, discovered the circulation of blood. Fabrici had determined that valves in the veins allowed blood flowing in the veins to flow only towards the heart. From this and other evidence, Harvey deduced that blood is pumped by the heart through the arteries, capillaries, and veins, and is thus forced through a closed loop back to the heart.

Although both Galileo and William Harvey left Padua to continue their research in Florence and London, respectively, their experiences at the university maintained by the Republic of Venice were crucial in opening their minds to the possibilities of uninhibited inquiry into the world of science. At Venice's University of Padua, the scientific revolution of the seventeenth century took root.

Chapter 4: Ships at Sea

Constantinople was vanquished. No Eastern state now challenged the Serene Republic. The power of Venice was not absolute, however. The Venetians still had to be ruthless in defending their sovereign rights.

With the fall of Constantinople the Italian city of Genoa became Venice's principal adversary. Throughout the Middle Ages and early Renaissance, these two great Italian cities engaged in a commercial rivalry that frequently erupted into recurring warfare.

In the last half of the thirteenth century and first half of the fourteenth century, Venice and Genoa fought three wars and engaged in countless naval battles of more modest proportion. The issue was always the same – which of these city-states would control the trade of the Mediterranean and Black Seas. The result was also always the same—a stalemate in which neither power could decisively defeat the other. In 1379 the intermittent warfare that had been going on for over a century and a quarter resumed. But this time the result was conclusive. The Genoese were annihilated at the Battle of Chioggia. Divided by civil war, and decimated by the plague, Genoa never again mounted a serious challenge to Venice. Venice was triumphant.

As the final act in this period of struggle for supremacy, the Venetians turned their military forces against nearby Padua, an independent region controlled by the Carrara family. In the wars, the Carraras had made the mistake of supporting Genoa. For the Venetians, this was an unforgivable offense. Accordingly, when three members of the Carrara family had the misfortune to be captured, they were summarily strangled by order of the Council of Ten, the agency of the Venetian government responsible for security. No one in Venice protested the killings, even though the cover story that the Carraras had died of pneumonia was not believed. The Venetians after all had a saying "uomo morto non fa guerra," "dead men wage no wars." Of course, it was a violent age, with poisoning and beheading of rival political leaders a regular occurrence.

Moreover, besides the politically inept move of joining the unfortunate Genoese, the Carraras had lost the sympathy of the Venetian people years earlier when they inflated the prices of hens, geese, eggs, vegetables, fruit and other agricultural products sent to Venice from the Carrara controlled countryside. The Carrara family was eliminated and the town of Padua and its adjoining region were incorporated into the Venetian state.

With the defeat of Genoa, the Mediterranean Sea became a Venetian domain.

To the Venetians' great fortune, their control was aided by significant developments in maritime technology. In the hundred year period between 1250 and 1350, changes in the size and design of ships, and in the methods and technology of navigation were so dramatic that maritime historians refer to the changes in the period as the nautical revolution.

One of the most important technological advances was the invention of the compass. For a simple device – it is only a magnetized needle allowed to swing freely – the compass allowed major changes in sea-borne commerce.

The compass was invented in China, and then apparently re-invented independently in Italy centuries later. The first compass consisted simply of a magnetized needle inserted into a straw that was allowed to float in a bowl of water. The straw with its magnetized needle always swung into a north-south orientation.

Between 1295 and 1302 a tradesman or seaman in the southern Italian town of Amalfi created the modern compass by placing a freely rotating needle balanced on a pin in a box that contained a card imprinted with the compass points. This greatly improved and more useful device was called a *bussola nautica*—a nautical box.

Prior to the invention of the compass, mariners navigated by the sun and stars, or by dead reckoning – the practice of navigating by estimating the distance and direction traveled from a known point. The problem with determining one's position by the sun and stars is that the sun and stars are often obscured by clouds and fog. In the Mediterranean, overcast weather with long periods of limited visibility is especially a problem during winter. Navigating over long distances by dead reckoning also presented problems in determining one's position accurately, since a seaman's estimate of distance and direction traveled would most likely be rendered unreliable due to the unseen effects of ocean currents.

Before the invention of the compass, ships rarely ventured out of port between October and March.

Staying close to land was not a solution for the mariner, because ships were in great danger of crashing into hidden reefs on dark and foggy nights, or of being hurled upon rocky shores in stormy weather. Indeed, the experienced mariner, caught at sea by bad weather, knew that he was safer riding out the storm on the water than attempting to reach port.

The compass, of course, was a revolutionary development. Within a few years it changed the methods of navigation that had been in place from the time man first sailed a boat beyond the sight of land. With the compass the experienced mariner could now find his way around the Mediterranean despite persistent overcast skies. His sailing season was extended by many months into late fall and winter. Due to the length of the typical voyage, moreover, the addition of only a few months to the sailing season greatly expanded the amount of commerce that could be carried in a single year. Whereas, before there was time for only one voyage between Venice and certain other ports, now there was time for two.

The extended sailing season resulting from the invention of the compass also enabled seamen to take advantage of the shifting pattern of prevailing winds late in the year to shorten the time and distance of a voyage. During the summer and early fall, for example, prevailing northerly winds make the sail from Egypt to Italy an arduous task. In late fall, however, the prevailing winds turn easterly, making the Egypt to Italy journey a delightful run, with the wind on the seamen's backs.

Along with the compass, other changes came in the size and design of ships. Foremost among these changes was the development of a new ship, the merchant galley.

A galley, by definition, was a ship using both sails and oarsmen for power. The Venetians had used small versions of the galley for centuries. The ship was ideally suited for the Venetians' needs. The sails provided the means to move the galley long distances under the power of the wind, and the oarsmen furnished the muscular energy to maneuver the ship into port when the wind was calm or when it blew from the wrong direction. The oarsmen also provided the vessel with a necessary fighting force for protection against pirates, who lurked in many remote coves and inlets, waiting to spring upon any ship that appeared to be a tempting target.

In the early years of the fourteenth century, a much larger version of the traditional galley came into use. This new design, called the merchant or great galley, carried more sail, engaged more oarsmen, and provided more capacity for cargo.

The principal purpose of the great galley was trade with the countries of northern and western Europe. In the spring of nearly every year, a fleet of Venetian ships known as the "Galleys of Flanders," assembled on the Grand Canal, sailed down the Adriatic, continued west across the Mediterranean through the Straits of Gibraltar into the Atlantic, and up along the coasts of Portugal, Spain, and France to the Flemish city of Bruges.

Bruges in what is today's Belgium was a major commercial center in pre-Renaissance Europe. At Bruges merchants from Flanders, the Netherlands, England, Germany, France, Spain and Italy met and traded the specialized goods of each region. Flemish cloth and English wool were especially in great demand.

The merchants from Venice as the purveyors of the highly desired products of Asia – silk and spices – were in an advantageous position for profitable trade. Another important product carried to Bruges by the Venetians was the sweet wine of Greece, for which the most fashionable Northerners had developed a taste.

In the thirteenth century, Bruges which was then twice as large as London built Cloth Hall to facilitate trade. In this emporium, Venetian merchants sold Asian spices, Asian silk and other products of the East at premium prices.

Not all the merchants of Venice preferred to send their goods by sea. The voyage was dangerous, and in case of peril, the Venetians lacked a friendly port in which to regroup and refit. The merchants, who did not wish to send their goods north by sea, sent them overland in wagons and on the backs of horses and donkeys on primitive roads cut through the Alpine passes into Germany.

In addition to the "Galley to Flanders," other ship convoys set sail nearly every year to every corner of the Mediterranean. The Galley of Beirut sailed to Palestine and Syria; the Galley of Northeast Africa to Tunis and Tripoli; the Galley of Barbary to northern Africa and Spain; the Galley of Alexandria to Egypt; the Galley of

Romania to Constantinople, the Black Sea and Russia; the Galley of Aigues-Mortes to Messina, Naples, Pisa, and France. These fleets transported the products of one nation to another – with the Venetians always making a profit.

The fleets were organized by the Venetian government so as to provide protection against pirates who roamed the Mediterranean beyond the reach of any naval force.

Although the great galleys were the brightest stars of the Venetian merchant fleet, most goods were transported on more mundane vessels called round ships or cogs. The round ships carried no oarsmen, and thus were more vulnerable to attack by pirates. They were, however, cheaper to operate than the galleys, due to their lack of oarsmen, and also due to their being able to use more efficient sails and rigging. As a result of their economy of operation, although at the cost of less protection against armed attack, the round ships were mainly used for carrying bulk commodities, such as grain and salt. The round ships also sailed in the annual voyages to Flanders and other foreign destinations.

A less desirable use of the round ships was to convey slaves to Venice. By the end of the fourteenth century most of the slaves were Russians or Tartars from Central Asia. Able bodied men were transported to Crete and Cyprus to be used as farm workers. Young women were sent to Venice and other Italian cities to be used as concubines. Children were used as domestic servants. The slaves were purchased by the Venetians at the Sea of Azov port of Tana, at the mouth of the Don River, which flows south through the Russian heartland. As the years went by, the Venetian conscience became less willing to accept the slave trade. Enslavement of Christians was condemned, and in 1366, slave auctions were forbidden in Venice, although private sales were still allowed.

Most of the galleys and round ships were manufactured in the Arsenale, a government run shipyard that was built in the early years of the twelfth century. The word *arsenale* is derived from an Arabic word meaning "place of industry," and had a broader interpretation than the modern use of the word. The Arsenale in Venice was the forerunner of the modern shipyard. Wood was aged and then shaped into ship hulls, masts and booms. Sails were cut. Rope was spun. The place thrived with activity. For centuries it was the largest manufacturing operation in the world.

Thus as Europe emerged from the darkness of the Middle Ages, the Republic of Venice held an unassailable grip on the trade of Europe's most valued products. It controlled the trade routes. It had superior technology and manufacturing capability. And it had the government leadership and the entrepreneurial class to vigorously defend its position. No nation could defy the economic superiority of Venice. No challenger was in sight.

Chapter 5: Venice and the Spice Trade

By the fourteenth century, the Republic of Venice was
the most powerful state in Europe. While the rest of
Europe slumbered in the remnants of its medieval
experience, Venice vigorously established supremacy
over the trade routes traversing the Mediterranean Sea.
With a vise-like hold on the trade of the most profitable
products sold in Europe, Venice in the fourteenth and
fifteenth centuries faced no serious challengers to its
pre-eminence as the most wealthy and politically
powerful state in the western world. All other
contenders for power, such as Spain, England, France,
the Netherlands, Turkey, and the Italian city-states of
Florence and Genoa, had been beaten in battle, or were
lying in the shadows, awaiting their own day in the sun,
when fortune and the changing course of events would
allow them to surpass those states which had faltered.

The nations that would dominate future centuries –
Spain, England, France, and the Netherlands – were
each consumed with civil strife. Kings sat warily on
their thrones as warring fiefdoms within each country
battled for supremacy. Power would not be unified into
national monarchies for many generations. Meanwhile
internal warfare between contending factions destroyed
commerce and suppressed the vitality of the people.
Against this turmoil, the Republic of Venice was an
exception. The Serene Republic looked at the rest of
Europe with benevolent arrogance. While other
Europeans sought only to survive the ravages of

marauding armies, the Venetians expanded their trade
and accumulated legendary wealth.

At the heart of the Venetian prosperity was the spice trade. Europeans craved Eastern spices – pepper, cloves, ginger, nutmeg, mace, turmeric, tamarind, and cinnamon. Until the sixteenth century, Muslim traders brought these spices from Asia to eastern Mediterranean trading centers where they were exchanged for Western woolen and cotton textiles, and metals such as copper and silver. With a near monopoly on the Mediterranean portion of the trade, Venetian merchants grew rich.

The spices were of many varieties. Ginger alone was classified on one ship's manifest as: *zenzeri buli,* coated ginger; *belledi,* ginger native to the west coast of India; *sorati,* ginger from Surat; *mordassi,* ginger with a biting taste; *mechini,* ginger from near Mecca; and *zenzeri verdi,* green ginger. Each variety had its unique flavor, and no doubt many an argument raged over the relative merits of each. Prior to the Middle Ages, these spices were virtually unknown in Europe, where food was prepared entirely with indigenous ingredients.

Many a Frenchman's culinary delight had to wait until a Venetian merchant found that Asian spices were salable products in the west. Disparate civilizations had to interact before a French chef could produce his first chicken dinner requiring peppercorns or turmeric. With these new ingredients, however, pepper, cinnamon, and nutmeg became as vital to the success of the cuisine of France as butter, cream, and truffles. The same was true in other countries. The European culinary experience would be bland indeed without the scintillating addition of nutmeg, ginger, and cayenne. By the fourteenth century, the spices were the rage in France, England,

Germany, Spain, and Holland. The upper classes were especially taken with these imports from Asia. The spices were so expensive, in fact, that they became a status symbol. To serve spicy food meant one was doing very well. The spicier the better.

In 1260, not many years after the conclusion of the Fourth Crusade, two Venetian brothers, Niccolò and Maffeo Polo, set out on a voyage of discovery to the east. Niccolò and Maffeo Polo were merchants of obvious wealth. They wanted to find out more about the lands from whence these spices came. Asian spices had only recently reached Venice by way of Arabia – the first known reference to pepper occurs in 1214.

The Polos reached the Forbidden City in what is now Beijing and were cordially received by Kubilai Khan, who was as interested in their description of Europe as they were in their quest for knowledge of Asia. They returned to Venice nine years after leaving for the east.

They did not remain home long though. In 1271, they set out again for the land of the Kubilai Khan. But this time they were joined by Niccolò's seventeen year old son, Marco. They would be gone for twenty-three years. When he returned as a middle-aged man, Marco Polo published an account of his travels. Most Europeans believed the story he told was an extreme exaggeration. No land could be as rich as Marco Polo said.

The spices grown in Asia were transported by Muslim traders across the Arabian Sea to ports on the Red Sea, and thence overland by desert camel caravan to Cairo, Alexandria, Beirut, and Damascus, where the spices were sold to the Venetians. By the fifteenth century, the quantity of spices shipped was so voluminous that the caravans leaving Mecca, a popular assembly point, often took two days and nights just to pass through the city gates.

The chief advantage of the Red Sea route was the protection offered by the ruler of Arabia, the Mamluk soldan. Outside the area of the soldan's control, bandits would attack even the largest caravans. Alternative routes, through Central Asia, for example, required the merchant to transport his merchandise over long stretches of territory that were the havens of outlaws, bandits, and other robbers, who had no respect for lawful behavior. Even in the areas protected by the Mamluk soldan, which included Syria and Egypt in addition to Arabia, caravans with armed escorts were occasionally attacked by Arab gangs.

The armed protection provided by the soldan, however, came at a price. For the privilege of crossing his territory, the soldan levied a heavy tax on the merchants and their caravans. Other rulers of crucial harbors and territories also extracted what they considered their fair share of the wealth passing through their lands. Nonetheless, everyone seems to have profited mightily.

The relationship between the Venetians and the Muslims was a delicate matter. Care had to be taken to avoid offending the other side. On one occasion, a Venetian captain, named Piero Marcello, thinking he had been wronged by the Muslims, lured ten of the Muslims on board his ship, seized them, sailed off with them, and sold them to some Turks as slaves. The Venetians, so as to placate the understandably outraged soldan, immediately sentenced Marcello to death by hanging. They also sent a delegation of high-ranking officials to meet with the soldan, who in the meantime had seized a group of Venetian merchants in retaliation. In time, an agreement was worked out.

Although mindful of the tact required when dealing with the Muslims, the Venetian merchant, when abroad, lived in a very comfortable style, carrying with him all the amenities of home. In Alexandria, Egypt, one of the most important cities for the buying and selling of spices, the Venetians maintained two palaces for their own use. The palaces contained private bedrooms, baths, and kitchens. They also contained storerooms, shops and facilities for packing and loading the spices. The palaces were surrounded by pleasant gardens, and functioned as self-contained communities.

In the fifteenth century, Venice was the keystone of the commercial economy of Europe. Some European cities, such as London, Paris, Amsterdam, Madrid, and Lisbon, were important to their national economies. Other, smaller cities played a similar role for the economies of their particular regions. But on the world scale, all were secondary in importance to Venice.

In all the cities, trade flourished, aided by bankers with newly invented instruments of credit. Money was lent, borrowed, exchanged and invested. Throughout Europe, a commercial revolution was under way. The medieval feudal system was giving way to a capitalist system with its market driven economies. As world trade became a vital factor in the economies of Europe, the importance of Venice as the gateway to the East multiplied. In the Rialto, the financial center of Venice, bankers and merchants engaged in commercial transactions on a scale and complexity unknown to any previous age. All Venetians gloried in the pursuit of wealth. "The desire to grow rich," claimed one, "is as natural to us as the desire to live." "Riches," he continued, "contribute ... a marvelous dignity to every activity."

Nearly all the highly valued goods of Asia entered Europe through Venice, at the initiative of Venetian entrepreneurs. The city was aided by its geographical location. But more importantly, the Venetian government vigorously supported the commercial community. The whole city acted as a single enterprise, with one goal: to engage in profitable trade. As a result, the Venetian population prospered tremendously.

Thus the Rialto became the Wall Street of fifteenth century Europe – the center of a flourishing network of trade that reached east to China and north and west to the limits of the known world.

Merchants of other nations maintained residences and warehouses in Venice. German merchants, for example, lived and worked in the Fondaco dei Tedeschi a combination warehouse-hotel close to the Rialto. (The word *fondaco* derives from *foundouk* – the Arabic word for inn or trading post. Tedeschi is the Italian word for Germans.) These merchants bought most of the Venetians' spices and other products of Asia. The Signoria required every German merchant to deposit his goods, and to reside at the Fondaco dei Tedeschi. No German was allowed to trade with anyone other than a Venetian. The intent of this rule was to prevent Germans from dealing directly with Eastern suppliers. Venice was determined to keep, in its own hands, the monopoly of trade with Asia. To force compliance with this policy, agents of the Venetian government kept the German merchants under constant surveillance. No deviation was allowed.

In return to agreeing to this restrictive policy, the German merchants were allowed to buy and sell in Germany without Venetian competition, for the Signoria forbade any Venetian merchant to trade in Germany. Since Venice controlled non-German trade by similar and other means, the Venetian monopoly was maintained. As a result, Venice became the principal trading center in Europe. To the Fondaco dei Tedeschi, the German merchants brought iron, hardware, a cotton-linen textile known as fustian, and silver currency to be exchanged for spices, silk, cotton, wool and cloth. Everyone profited. Although the Venetians profited more than anyone else.

The Venetians could see no obstacle before them. In the words of Fernand Braudel, "Venice slept the sleep of the rich."

As the fifteenth century drew to a close, the Venetians thought they had found the key to everlasting prosperity. As the Republic approached its most perilous epoch, the Senate was mainly concerned with frivolous matters. The Senators were particularly distressed at the extravagant sums spent by women on clothing. In a fit of frugality, the members of the Senate condemned the "useless expenditure by women ... in order to show off." The august patricians then proceeded to decree that women must "be content" with old fashions. "No female dress shall be worn ... of any fashion other than that in use at present," said the lawmakers, all of whom by the way were men. To discard perfectly good, but unfashionable dresses, said the Senators, would do "considerable harm to the fortunes of our gentlemen and citizens."

The Senators, as puritanical, humorless, and cheap as any founder of Massachusetts Bay, seemed unable to understand the fashion statement being made by Venetian women. The new fashions said the Senators are even "uglier, and more dishonest" than the former ones. In a statute that tells us as much about women's clothing styles as about the attitudes of the lawmakers, the members of the Senate outlawed slashed robes, multi-colored sleeves, embroideries, fringes and sleeves edged with cloth of a different color. From a land that in time would give the world Prada and Pappagallo, Armani and Versace, these were bold words indeed.

But the Senate would soon be dealing with matters more weighty than women's fashions. In the summer of 1499, devastating news reached the city. The disaster relayed in the news, exclaimed Girolamo Priuli, a prominent merchant-banker, is "of greater importance to the Venetian state than the Turkish war, or any other wars which might have affected her." "In this I ... see the ruin of the city." "The wisest heads," he continued, "take it to be the worst piece of information we could possibly have." So dreadful was the news that Signor Priuli in a moment of despair declared emphatically that "Venice is ruined."

Along the Grand Canal, the gondoliers glided their functional, but beautifully designed, gondolas hither and yon as they had done for hundreds of years, carrying passengers and goods up and down the waterway, which curved gracefully through the heart of the city. The shouts of the gondoliers maneuvering their crafts mingled with the noises of commerce as ocean going galleys were unloaded of their cargoes and vendors sold their merchandise and produce in the city's marketplaces.

The vessels on the waterway were of all shapes and sizes. Some of the gondolas were simple craft, used for hire, like a taxicab of today. Others, obviously private and owned by patricians, were opulent with enclosed cabins. In addition to the well-formed gondolas, wide and bulky sailing barges crossed the gray-green water of the Canal. And everywhere were the galleys, with their masts and sails and rigging.

In this summer of 1499, the city would have had its usual large number of pilgrims, who were traveling from all of Europe to Venice to take passage on a galley bound for the Holy Land. While awaiting the departure of the galleys for the four to six week journey, the pilgrims, like all tourists, would have visited the marketplaces. In those marketplaces were sold all the articles of fifteenth century trade: spices, gold, silver, ivory, wild animals, jewels, paintings, silk, wine, ebony and every variety of fine cloth. Venice at the end of the fifteenth century was as much a treat for the tourist as it is today.

At the edge of the Canal, white marble palaces sparkled under the hot and brilliant sun, casting their reflections upon the murky water. Everywhere it seemed, the Venetian flag, a golden lion emblazoned on a scarlet background, flew proudly and defiantly. As the fifteenth century approached its end, Venice was the most powerful and prosperous state in the world. Its navy controlling the sea-lanes was the largest in the world.

Signor Priuli's statement therefore seemed, at first, a nonrational statement from a cautious banker not usually given to over-reaction.

The news Signor Priuli had just heard in that summer of 1499 was that a Portuguese navigator named Vasco da Gama had sailed a fleet of ships around the southern end of Africa into the Indian Ocean and had reached India, where he had bought spices directly from Asian suppliers. The power and prosperity of Venice, Signor Priuli realized, were dependent upon its monopoly of the spice trade, from which its citizens made outrageous profits. The loss of the spice trade, he said, "will be like the loss of milk to a new born babe." "There is no doubt" he continued, "that the Hungarians, Germans, Flemish, and French, and those beyond the mountains who formerly came to Venice to buy spices with their money, will all turn towards Lisbon."

In the banking houses on the Rialto, Venice's commercial center, the merchants fervently discussed the threat. The merchants, dressed as usual in fine, multi-colored silk clothing of the best quality, asked each other what he had heard. The news was garbled and inaccurate. Initial reports had stated that the navigator was a man named Columbus. Nevertheless, if true, the shock to the Venetian way of life would be devastating. As the gondolas and barges traversed the traffic-laden canals, under the hot summer sun, nothing seemed changed. It seemed like a day just like any other. Yet everything had changed.

The Venetian monopoly of the spice trade was broken. No longer could the merchants of Venice control the sale of pepper, ginger and the other spices, which provided zest to the appetites of the Europeans and wonderful profits to the bank accounts of the Venetians.

Now, the Venetians feared, any maritime nation could become a competitor in this lucrative trade by sailing a fleet of ships from Europe to Asia, buying there the spices at the same low prices paid by the buyers for the Venetians, and returning to Europe to undercut the merchants now gathered on the Rialto and on the Piazza San Marco. Those Venetian merchants could imagine no greater calamity.

One of the first responses of the Signoria to the news of the Portuguese achievement was to send a spy to Lisbon. He was named Leonardo da Ca'Masser. For two years, Ca'Masser gathered information on Portuguese voyages, deliveries and commercial organization. He learned of their efforts to eliminate the Arabian competition from the Asian spice trade. He discovered that east of India, spices were even cheaper than in Calicut, where the Portuguese had landed. All this, he reported to the Venetian leaders. He then added his own analysis of Portuguese capabilities. It proved to be remarkably perceptive.

The Portuguese, Ca'Masser said, did not have sufficient resources to close off completely and permanently all sources of supply of spices to Venice. To succeed in such an endeavor, the Portuguese would need more ships and men than they could ever muster. Nevertheless, concluded Ca'Masser, the Portuguese indeed were capable of inflicting serious damage to Venice's control of the spice trade and thereby to Venice's economy. Nothing was going to be as easy as it had been before. The Republic of Venice which had for centuries been blessed with unparalleled prosperity now had to fight for its very economic survival. With this information, the Doge and the members of the Signoria pondered what to do. Never had the Serene Republic faced a greater threat.

Chapter 6: The Unknown Seas

The age of oceanic discovery that culminated in Vasco da Gama's historic voyage to India began with the vision and drive of one man. He was Prince Henry of Portugal. So important was the contribution of this man to the course of history that he has come to be called simply Prince Henry, the Navigator. All other possible appellations are overused, and none other could do justice to his achievements, anyhow. He was the third born son of King John and Queen Philippa. Of his two older brothers, Duarte was born in 1391, and Pedro was born in 1392. Henry himself was born in 1394, two years after Pedro. As the third in line to inherit the Portuguese throne as a young man, and even further back in line to inherit the throne after the birth of Duarte's son, Afonso, Henry was free to leave to his older brothers the boring and tiresome tasks of governance of the kingdom. He himself could pursue other interests, and thus was able to change the world.

In the one painting we have of him, Prince Henry wears a simple russet-colored cloak with no jewelry or ornamentation of any kind. He was described as a man of good height and broad frame with big, strong arms. Although his stern expression inspired fear on first meeting, his personality was calm and dignified. In his personal habits, he was frugal, scholarly and religious. He spent little money on himself, and lived in a modest house that in no way reflected his status as a prince of an important European monarchy. In his youth he drank wine in modest amounts, but he gave up even this indulgence when he grew older.

Some detractors described him as egotistical, unmethodical, impulsive, habitually tardy and a spendthrift on causes that interested him. Considering the amount of money he spent on oceanic exploration, the latter charge, at least, may be true. He lived the life of a monk. Such was the man who almost single handedly changed the course of European civilization and put it on the road of discovery and economic expansion.

Other countries on other continents, though, also had the opportunity to grab the leadership in exploration and its attendant benefits. Prince Henry was not alone in looking at the sea and wondering what lay beyond the horizon.

On the other side of the globe during Prince Henry's lifetime, China was ruled by an emperor named Zhu Di.

Zhu Di was a cruel, mean-spirited man. He frequently executed people who were so rash as to disagree with him. Under his reign terror was an active instrument of state power. His one redeeming character trait, though, was his vision of China as a country vigorously engaged with the nations of the world. This policy of openness, however, was strongly opposed by the intellectual and religious leaders of the country. A China openly trading with the peoples of other lands was heresy to orthodox followers of Confucius. To these traditionalists, foreigners – that is non-Chinese – were heathens who could only dishonor the purity of the Chinese people.

Thus, they believed that all contact with foreigners should be avoided.

Moreover, the orthodox Confucians believed that merchants were an ignoble class of scavengers that preyed upon society out of greed and for villainous profit. Confucians ranked merchants below prostitutes in status and value to the community. To the Confucians only farmers performed an esteemed trade.

Zhu Di had no use for the Confucians. He ordered an admiral named Zheng He to build a fleet of great ships to open trade with other countries of Asia and Africa. Interestingly, though, neither Zhu Di nor Zheng He was interested in Europe. Europe was too poor and offered nothing of value that could be used in exchange for China's silk, porcelain, and fine jewelry.

Zheng He had the same thirst for exploration as did Prince Henry. Moreover, Zheng He had the resources to venture into the unknown oceans. The Chinese, at this time, built ships that were bigger and more seaworthy than the ships built in any European nation. Between 1405 and 1432 Zheng He sailed these vessels west into the Indian Ocean on voyages of exploration that went farther and farther. Zheng He probed the Persian Gulf and explored the eastern coast of Africa. The Chinese were on the verge of becoming the first modern people to round the southern coast of Africa.

But after Zheng He and the emperor Zhu Di died, their successors had no interest in pursuing the quest for new discoveries. China turned inward. China facing no sea-going enemies, allowed its navy to deteriorate. After

Zheng He, Chinese ships never again probed the unknown.

Many factors played a role in China's naval decline. The government was corrupt. The naval fleet was a drain on tax resources. And China's principle enemies were the land-based Mongols to the north.

But the greatest factor in China's naval decline was the return to power of followers of traditional Confucian values. China once again became a closed society in which association with the heathen was considered an immoral act.

Historians have often wondered why it was the Europeans who discovered the sea routes to the East, and why the Asians did not find the same routes to the West? Why were the Europeans, and not the Asians, destined to discover America? Certainly, the Asians did not lack technical capability, an area in which they equaled or exceeded European expertise. Nor did they lack in economic incentives. The prospect of new wealth applied to all peoples. The fortunes and misfortunes of geography, wind and weather, likewise, affected all peoples equally.

Perhaps, the reason for the success of the Europeans is that the kingdoms of the East after Zheng He simply lacked a Prince Henry the Navigator. In sending his country's small ships into the unknown seas, Prince Henry set the way for Vasco da Gama's voyage to Asia, and Columbus's discovery of America.

For our purposes, there is no need to get into a discussion as to who really discovered America.

Nevertheless, brief mention of some intrepid souls is warranted.

The first European to sail west towards America rather than to hug the European and African coastlines may have been St. Brendan, an Irish monk who journeyed forth from the Emerald Isle in the sixth century. Brendan's voyages of discovery were described as oral history passed down from one generation of Irish to another. Two centuries after the voyages this history was written down in a Latin text titled *Navigatio Sancti Brendani Abbatis.*

Although much of the *Navigatio* is clear fantasy, some passages such as the description of a volcano that can only have been on Iceland have to be true.

Navigatio describes Brendan's sailing vessel as a wood frame covered with oak-tanned oxhide and caulked with ox-tallow. The boat was thus similar to the curragh – the Irish fishing vessel that dates back to before the time of Julius Caesar.

Brendan with seventeen fellow monks and seamen sailed the Atlantic for seven years. He discovered Iceland and sailed far enough north to encounter icebergs. He also sailed south as far as the Azores. Given the smallness of his boat, the long distances traveled, and the adverse weather encountered, Brendan's voyages were a remarkable achievement.

In the tenth century westward exploration was continued by the Norse Vikings. They reached Labrador and Newfoundland by way of Iceland and Greenland. No permanent Viking settlement survived, however.

Columbus may not even have been the first European to reach America after the Vikings. A plausible case has been made that Basque fishermen were exploiting the Grand Banks off the coast of Canada long before Columbus set forth on the *Santa María*. For centuries preceding Columbus, the Basques from the region of the border of France and Spain supplied much of Europe with salted cod. Yet the source of their cod – a cold water fish – was a secret. The Basques saw no reason to tell the competition where their highly profitable product came from. But since the Basques did not fish the fishing grounds known to other Europeans, the only possible source was the North American fishing areas. If the Basques did fish the Grand Banks, they would inevitably have found what are now the maritime provinces of Canada. The Basques would have also needed a place to land in order to salt and dry their fish.

In support of the argument that the Basques had beat Columbus to America by many years, historians cite a statement of Jacques Cartier, the explorer who claimed Canada for France a few decades after the Columbus voyages. While sailing about Nova Scotia, Cartier counted the presence of one thousand Basque fishing vessels. It appears that the continent Columbus claimed to have discovered was already well known to many Europeans.

Yet, from the perspective of later developments, the discovery of America means the voyages of Christopher Columbus. It was his discovery – or rediscovery if you will – that was publicly proclaimed in a loud voice to the peoples of Europe. The voyages of Columbus to

America have historical meaning that is lacking in the voyages of his predecessors.

And the road to Columbus's discoveries begins with Prince Henry the Navigator.

At Sagres, a small sea coast town at the southwestern corner of Portugal, where the country juts out into the Atlantic, Prince Henry established an academy for the study of navigation. Sagres also functioned as the command center for the exploration of the southern lands and seas. The region of Portugal in which Sagres is located is remote and neglected. It is far from the commercial capital of Lisbon. Along the coast of this most southern province of Portugal sandstone cliffs directly confront the Atlantic Ocean, whose high swells, unbroken in their long journey across the open sea, crash upon the rocky shore.

From his room at the academy, Prince Henry looked out at the Atlantic. Through the Moorish style windows, which were open to the wind and weather since they contained no glass, Prince Henry saw the ocean stretch unimpeded to the horizon. Here he spent many hours brooding and wondering what lay beyond that horizon. On a calm summer's day, the view of the sea is a beautiful sight. The azure blue of the sky mingles at a distance with the gray blue of the sea. Along the coast the countryside is fertile, and farms with green fields and abundant orchards flourish. Small harbors tucked among the sandstone cliffs allow access to the sea. From these harbors, valiant fishermen had gone forth for countless generations. From these same harbors, over a half-century before Columbus, Prince Henry would send forth ships with the sole mission of exploring the unknown.

Prince Henry's motives in sending his ships out on their voyages of exploration are unclear. He never stated that the discovery of a sea route to India was his goal. We do not know if he even realized that India could be reached by sailing around the southern tip of Africa. Maps that were highly regarded by the Europeans of this period show Asia and Africa as one continuous landmass, encircling a land-locked Indian Ocean. Certainly, the traditional medieval European believed that Asia could not be reached by way of the sea.

Prince Henry, however, had frequent contact with the north African Jews and Arabs. From the Portuguese port of Sagres, north Africa is a short sail down the Atlantic coast and across the Straits of Gibraltar. The Jews and Arabs of north Africa had more accurate information on the true shape and size of the continents than did the Europeans. As itinerant merchants and traders, the Jews acquired substantial geographical knowledge of Africa, and were beginning to grasp an understanding of the continent's true shape and immense size. In 1375, Abraham Cresques, a Jew from Majorca, prepared a map for the King of Aragon that indicated that a sea route to India existed around the southern tip of Africa. Many Muslims had also traveled overland to the Indian Ocean, and had described in detail their journeys.

More important than their travel observations, though, were the ancient libraries retained by the Arabs. By a curious circumstance, the Arabs possessed most of the existing manuscripts of ancient Greece. These thousand year old writings, containing the books of the first learned Europeans, had been safeguarded through the centuries by the Arabs who had recovered them in the waning days of the Roman Empire. Ironically, these same books, carefully preserved by the Arabs while Europe wandered somnambulant through the Dark Ages, would spark the European Renaissance in the Fifteenth Century.

From these Arab libraries, Prince Henry would have been able to obtain copies of books by the ancient Greek authors Herodotus and Strabo. In the fifth century B.C., Herodotus wrote of a few Phoenicians who had sailed from Egypt south into the Indian Ocean from the Red Sea, and who had returned three years later by way of the Mediterranean, indicating that they had circumnavigated Africa. Herodotus did not believe some of their statements, namely, that in the southern hemisphere the sun appears in the north, the opposite direction from which it is seen in the Mediterranean region and everywhere else in the northern hemisphere. The sun appears in the north when observed from below the equator. The fact that the sailors were right, despite Herodotus's disbelief, shows that ancient navigators had at least traveled far south of the equator.

Five centuries after Herodotus in the first years of the Christian era, Strabo, an academician, also expressed knowledge of the true shape of Africa. He wrote in a guide for Red Sea sailors that at a certain point in the south, the unexplored coast curves to the west and the waters mingle with the Western Ocean, meaning the Atlantic.

Although Prince Henry could have read the books by Herodotus and Strabo, there is no evidence that he did. Nor do we know if he was informed by scholars that the ancients believed that a sea route to Asia existed.

If Prince Henry did not begin his quest of discovery in the hopes of reaching Asia, he may have been motivated by the more limited objective of reaching the fabled wealthy kingdoms of western Africa. Chief among these was the kingdom of Guinea, which was located in much of the area now made up of the countries of Guinea, Ghana, Liberia, Mali and their neighbors. From Arab sources, the wealth of Guinea was well known to the Portuguese.

In his conversations with the Arabs, Prince Henry would have also learned about the wealth of the city of Timbuktu. Timbuktu is not a legendary place. It is located in present day Mali near the most northern part of the Niger River, which flows from there east and then south to the Atlantic Ocean. Timbuktu, itself, is 800 miles from the Atlantic. Just to its north is the Sahara Desert. In the fifteenth century, Timbuktu existed as a vibrant community with a thriving cultural life and a well-established university. It was an important west African trading center. The city was a marketplace where the traders crossing the Sahara in desert caravans met the merchants from the south. Here ivory, slaves, and gold were traded for salt and textiles.

The Portuguese could not reach Guinea or Timbuktu by overland routes, however. These routes, of necessity, ran through the Sahara Desert, which was impenetrable by European travelers. In addition, the Sahara was occupied by hostile and warlike tribes, ready to defend their country against any intruders from the north.

If the Portuguese were to reach the Kingdom of Guinea, they had to go by sea.

The ships used by the first Portuguese explorers were called caravels. These were excellent vessels for exploring an unknown coastline. They were of shallow draft, which meant that the bottom of the boat was not deep in the water. A vessel with a shallow draft, such as a caravel, obviously was well suited for reconnoitering an unknown coast, where hidden reefs and unseen rocks could instantaneously rip through a ship's hull. The caravel by design was also highly maneuverable, and could sail into the wind. Ships of more cumbersome design could go forward only when the wind was from the ship's rear or stern quarters.

Sailing ships such as the caravel could sail into a head wind because they incorporated significant technological advances in hull, sail and rigging design. A modern sailboat, designed for racing, can point to within forty degrees of the wind. Getting a boat to point high into the wind involves many factors including the design of the ship, the shape of the sails, and the ability of the captain and the crew.

The caravel could point higher than any other sailing ship of the time. Since the explorers of the African coastline faced into the prevailing wind about half the time, the ship's ability to point high was of crucial importance if they ever expected to return to Portugal. One major improvement was the addition of a large triangular sail called a lateen sail. The lateen sail, which originated in Arabia, was a major breakthrough in sail design and allowed a ship to sail into the wind.

The caravel evolved from ocean going fishing vessels. By modern standards it was a small ship. It was only around seventy feet long. To visualize the length of one of these ships, imagine placing the stern on home plate of a baseball diamond. If so done, the bow would not even reach first base. The width of the ship was about twenty feet. In these vessels, the explorers set out on voyages that would take them thousands of miles into uncharted waters. Two of the ships used by Christopher Columbus, in his 1492 voyage of discovery to America, were caravels. These were the *Niña* and the *Pinta*. The *Santa María*, Columbus's third ship, was of a different design.

The caravel had one major deficiency, however. It had insufficient cargo space to be a profitable trading ship. When commerce replaced exploration as the ship's chief purpose, the caravel was replaced by vessels designed to carry cargoes of valuable merchandise, even though the cargo carrying ships lacked the caravel's desirable sailing characteristics.

Another problem the mariners of this era faced regardless of their type of ship was knowing where they were. They had no Global Positioning System's triangulating electronic satellite signals to give them their positions to the nearest meter. As they crossed unknown oceans, they had only primitive instruments and their innate knowledge of the sea to determine their coordinates. To find their latitude – the distance north or south of the equator – the captains would measure the height above the horizon of a celestial object, such as the sun or the North Star. If they accounted for the time of day and the time of the year, they could determine fairly accurately, though not precisely, their latitude. The instruments used did not allow for precise measurements. The mariner had to simultaneously sight the celestial object and the horizon from the deck of a ship rolling with each wave—not an easy task. Moreover, a small observational error resulted in a large error in the calculation of the actual position.

The first instruments for measuring latitudes were no much more than rulers held vertically at arm's length. In 1595, a full century after the age of discovery began, John Davis, for whom the Davis Strait in Canada is named, invented the backstaff, a device that greatly increased the accuracy of latitude measurements. The invention of sextant, however, with its double reflecting mirrors did not occur until 1731 when John Hadley presented his design to the Royal Society.

The determination of longitude—the east-west position of a ship or geographical point—was even more difficult. Until the eighteenth century mariners calculated their longitude by dead reckoning, that is, by estimating their distance covered each day. Unfortunately, the estimates were just that, estimates only. Moreover, the mariners had to account for unseen and unknown factors such as oceanic currents. Scientists realized though that if an accurate timepiece could be invented that would work on a moving ship, longitude could be calculated by observing the position of a celestial object, such as the North Star, and referring to a mathematical table that gave the longitude for that object at that particular instant. In the eighteenth century John Harrison, an English clock maker, invented such a timepiece that he called a chronometer.

During the lifetime of Prince Henry, though, the inventions of the sextant and the chronometer were far into the future.

When Prince Henry committed Portugal to the voyages of exploration, the means of determining a ship's position at sea had not changed in a thousand years. A primitive tool to find latitude, dead reckoning to find longitude was all the mariner had. While these means worked fairly well in the familiar waters of the Mediterranean and European Atlantic coast, they were ill-suited to the trials that lay ahead as the ships ventured into the untraveled seas.

Prince Henry began his pursuit of oceanic exploration and economic expansion by colonizing Madeira and the Azores, and by attempting to seize the Canary Islands. These island groups, seven hundred miles from Portugal, extend in an arc from due west of Lisbon down to the coast of Africa.

When the Portuguese landed on Madeira, the closest island in the chain, it was covered with trees and brush so thick that they had to use machetes to cut a path to the interior. Yet they were not the first Europeans to discover the island. In the undergrowth much to their surprise, they came upon a small stone chapel with a Latin inscription that said: "Here came the Englishman Machin, borne by a storm, and here lies the woman who came with him." The Englishman who wrote the inscription was Robert Machin, a gentleman, and, as his knowledge of Latin indicates, a man of learning. The woman was a lady named Anne Dorset. Nearly a century before the coming of the Portuguese, Robert and Anne, in a moment of passion, fled England, when Anne's father, disapproving of Robert, betrothed her to another man. Leaving England for France, they were blown out to sea by a sudden storm. By pure chance their boat washed up on this island of Madeira, two thousand miles from their home. Anne soon died. Robert, according to one story, also died shortly afterwards. According to another story, he fashioned a boat out of a tree, and sailed to Africa.

For the Portuguese, the island of Madeira became a source of wood and sugar. Wood was always in short supply and at that time prior to the development of competitive plantations in America sugar was a rare and expensive commodity. The original sugar cane on Madeira had been brought there from Sicily. The sugar cane flourished, and in the fifteenth century, Madeira sugar and its resultant confectionery delights became a much desired addition to the dining tables of prosperous Europeans. The sugar industry thrived on Madeira until lower cost producers in Brazil and the Caribbean ended its virtual monopoly. Faced with economic ruin, the planters turned their cane fields into vineyards, and produced instead the wine we call Madeira.

Although the vineyards thrived on Madeira, and thrive to this day, the Portuguese learned a lesson in ecology on a small neighboring island called Porto Santo. On the ship that brought the Portuguese to Porto Santo, they had taken a female rabbit and her litter. When they arrived, they let the rabbits loose on the island. The result was a disaster. "The rabbits multiplied so fast," wrote one observer, "that before long they covered the whole island and the men could plant nothing which was not at once eaten or destroyed." A century later, the island still belonged to the rabbits.

The Portuguese had better luck in the Azores. These uninhabited islands, far out in the Atlantic and a good part of the way to North America, were discovered in 1431 by explorers who had been ordered by Prince Henry to sail west and see if by chance any land existed out there where man had never been.

Another group of islands, the Canary Islands, off the coast of Africa, had been discovered and colonized by the Spaniards. Or, to be more precise, they had been rediscovered and recolonized by the Spaniards. The Canaries were known in Roman times and had been settled by people from North Africa. But as the Ancient world disintegrated, contact with the Canaries was lost.

When the Spaniards came, in the fifteenth century, the islands were inhabited solely by an indigenous tribe known as the Guanches. For a hundred years, the Guanches fought the Spaniards. But it was an uneven battle. These primitive inhabitants with their simple tools were annihilated by unfamiliar infectious diseases and superior Spanish weapons. The Canary Islands were potentially important supply bases for ships traveling south. Prince Henry's efforts to seize the Canaries from Spain, however, were not successful. The issue was finally determined when the Spaniards decisively defeated a Portuguese invading force in a crucial battle in 1477.

Beyond the Canaries, though, the seamen of Prince Henry faced an obstacle more troublesome than the Spaniards. South of the Canary Islands explorers of the west coast of Africa soon reached a natural barrier that had blocked southern voyages since European man first learned to sail. The barrier was Cape Bojador, a point west of the Sahara, where geographical conditions create unusually heavy seas and strong currents. In addition, it is an area of reefs and shallow water. To make matters worse, persistent northerly winds at Cape Bojador made it difficult for a European sailing vessel to return home. Portuguese seamen called the area beyond Cape Bojador the "Green Sea of Darkness," and believed anyone venturing into its fold would never see Portugal again.

Prince Henry was determined to shatter the assumption that Cape Bojador was an impenetrable barrier to southern exploration. He was convinced that the caravels of the latest design could sail through Cape Bojador and return safely. To prove his theory was correct, he asked one of his best captains, a man named Gil Eannes, to undertake the task of attempting to sail past the dreaded cape, and to return.

In 1433, Eannes and his crew set out for Cape Bojador, full of confidence in their ability as seamen to overcome any obstacle. As they approached the fearful cape, though, they lost their nerve. They turned around, raided the Spaniards on the Canary Islands, and returned home. Prince Henry was not pleased. He bade them to make another attempt to push past Cape Bojador, and promised them honors and profits if they succeeded. With this inducement, Eannes and his sailors set out again the following year. This time they made it. The barrier was breached. The jinx was broken.

They sailed several miles past the cape, and landed on the barren coast. There was no sign of any inhabitants. In such a desolate place, there was little Eannes could do. He picked some common wildflowers called by the Portuguese roses of St. Mary, returned to his ship, and sailed back to Portugal.

When Eannes presented to Prince Henry the handful of wildflowers picked from the desolate land south of the Cape, all knew that a momentous event had occurred. The barrier to southern exploration no longer existed. "This feat was, perhaps, Prince Henry's greatest achievement," writes the distinguished historian, C. R. Boxer, "since it was only accomplished by patient determination and a readiness to expend large sums of money on voyages from which no immediate return could be expected."

No sooner had Gil Eannes returned to Portugal in 1434 with the news that he had successfully broken through the Cape Bojador barrier than Prince Henry ordered more voyages down the west coast of Africa and past Cape Bojador. The knowledge that Cape Bojador no longer was an obstacle to exploration spurred Prince Henry to find what lay beyond.

Although several exploratory expeditions were sent out in the next few years, it was not until 1441, eight years after Eannes traversed Cape Bojador, that the next significant event occurred: the capture of the first natives. In 1441, Antão Gonçalves and his crew sailed a caravel 200 miles beyond the cape. One night they went ashore. They found a path and followed it. They soon came upon a naked man driving a camel. The Portuguese attacked the poor fellow. Although he defended himself vigorously, he was quickly subdued, and became the first Portuguese captive of a black African. As they returned to their ships Gonçalves and his men captured a second African, a black woman. Then several more Africans were taken before Gonçalves decided to return to Portugal and present his prizes to Prince Henry.

When the black Africans were brought to Europe, the Portuguese immediately realized that there was a ready market for the sale of the blacks as slaves. When the owners of other ships saw the profits to be made from trading in slaves, they quickly pointed the bows of their ships south. No one pretended that these were voyages of exploration. Nor did anyone have moral qualms about capturing and selling human beings. These voyages, all agreed, were simple commercial ventures to capture Negro slaves for sale at a profit. Prince Henry, himself, received one-fifth of all the slaves captured. The remainder was divided between those with shares in the voyage. Gomes Eannes de Zurara, the Portuguese historian, who chronicled the events, described one such division in 1444, which split black families arbitrarily to achieve the correct number of slaves in each share:

"On the next day, which was the 8th of the month of August, very early in the morning, by reason of the heat, the seamen began to make ready their boats, and to take out their captives and carry them on shore, as they were commanded. And these, placed together in that field, were a marvelous sight, for amongst them were some white enough, fair to look upon and well proportioned, others less white like mulattoes; others again were as black as Ethiops, and so ugly, both in features and in body, as almost to appear the images of a lower hemisphere.

"But what heart could be so hard as not to be pierced with sorrowful feeling to see that company? For some kept their heads low and their faces bathed in tears, looking one upon another; others stood groaning grievously, looking up to the height of heaven, fixing their eyes upon it, crying out loudly, as if asking help of the Father of Nature; others covered their faces with the palms of their hands, and threw themselves upon the ground; others made their lamentations in the manner of a dirge, after the custom of their country. And though we could not understand the words of their language, the sound of it well accorded with the measure of their sadness.

"But to increase their sufferings still more, there now arrived those who had charge of the division of the captives and who began to separate one from another in order to make an equal partition of the fifths; and then it was needful to part fathers from sons, husbands from wives, brothers from brothers. No respect was shown either to friends or relatives, but each fell where his lot took him.

"And who could finish that partition without great toil, for as often as they had placed them in one part, the sons, seeing their fathers in another, rose with great energy and rushed over to them; the mothers clasped their other children in their arms, and threw themselves flat on the ground with them, receiving blows with little pity for their own flesh, if only they might not be torn from them.

"The Infant (Prince Henry) was there, mounted upon a powerful steed, and accompanied by his retinue, making distribution of his favors, as a man who sought to gain but small treasure from his share; for he made a very speedy partition of the forty-six souls that fell to him as his fifth."

Regretfully, this first result of the discoveries by the Portuguese explorers was the establishment of a trade in slaves.

But as the Portuguese plundered the African coast of its human wealth, the black Africans learned quickly that these white Europeans with their big ships did not come on voyages of friendship. The native Africans began to fight back.

One such counterattack took place in 1446. Captain Nuno Tristão and his crew in a caravel were sailing south of Cape Verde. As they sailed south, they could see the changes in the vegetation on the mainland. The barren soil of the Sahara gave way to grassland and then to forest. Along this forested coast, they came upon an unknown river. The river invited exploration. They launched the ship's boats, and began the journey inland. The river was winding, mysterious, and beautiful. The men were fascinated by the peaceful, yet forbidding, scene unfolding before them.

Then suddenly, the tranquility was shattered. The peace and calm became unrelieved chaos. A shower of arrows, fired from an unseen enemy on the shore, descended upon the boats. The Portuguese sailors turned and fled back towards the ship. As they did so, they discovered a more severe problem.

The arrows were covered with a deadly poison that was so lethal that four men died before even reaching the caravel. On board the ship, the men who had been struck by the arrows died one by one. Their bodies including that of Nuno Tristão, the captain, were buried at sea. Only three youths, a slave, and a servant were not wounded. Of those wounded, only two survived. Miraculously, these seven survivors sailed the caravel back to Portugal.

As successive Portuguese explorers pushed farther south, they came upon fertile lands where slaves could be easily purchased. Here, the Portuguese had no need to capture the slaves themselves. For a price, African chiefs and headmen were quite willing to make war on neighboring tribes in order to capture fellow members of their own race for sale to the Portuguese.

To pay for the slaves, the Portuguese brought to the Africa of the Senegal, products that had never been seen before in the land south of the Sahara. Cloth and textiles were brought from England, Ireland, France and Flanders. Brass pots and utensils were carried from Germany. Wheat was transported from Morocco and northern Europe. In exchange, the Portuguese received Negro slaves. Between 1450 and 1500, it is estimated, 150,000 slaves were sold to the Portuguese, who in turn sold them mainly to the Spaniards and Italians. After the discovery of America, most African slaves were sent to the Portuguese and Spanish colonies in the new world.

The Age of Discovery brought little good to the people who lived south of the Sahara. The black African tribes, although lacking knowledge of writing, maintained an oral history of their people. Each generation recited the history to its descendants. One of their oral statements, describing the events from the Negro perspective, went this way: "One day the white men arrived in ships with wings, which shone in the sun like knives. They fought hard battles with the Ngola (one of the tribes) and spat fire at him. They conquered his salt pans and the Ngola fled inland to the Lukala River. Some of his bolder subjects remained by the sea and when the white men came they exchanged eggs and chickens for cloth and beads. The white men came yet again. They brought us maize and cassava, knives and hoes, groundnuts and tobacco. From that time until our day the whites brought us nothing but wars and miseries."

Since the slaves were the hapless captives of inter-tribal warfare, the slave trade also proved profitable for the rulers of African tribes, and thereby set off a period of armed conflict between the tribes that lasted for centuries. The only redeeming feature of this warfare was that an enemy tribesman was worth much if taken alive, and nothing if killed. This simple fact of economics mitigated most of the savagery common to warfare.

The excitement of discovering new lands, however, still amazed the Portuguese explorer. One of these brave men, named João Fernandes, set out alone on an expedition into the interior of Africa, near the Sahara. He spent a year with the Tuareg people, traveled the desert with them, and lived as a guest of their chief.

Later, he gave the following report to Prince Henry:
"The heat is very great and so is the dust from the sand.
Most of the people travel on foot, but a few ride on
horseback, and others on camels. Though the grazing is
scanty, there are great numbers of camels of all colors.
The men of rank own captive Negroes and possess
much gold, which they bring from the land of the
Negroes. There are in that land many ostriches and
deer, gazelles, partridges and hares. Swallows which
depart from Portugal in the summer come to this land
of sand, but the storks pass over to winter in the land of
the Negroes."

Despite the adventure of seeking new lands, the
prospect of exploration for its own sake attracted few
Portuguese. It was the quest for wealth that brought the
Portuguese to Africa. In addition to the slaves, the
Portuguese traded for gold. They had heard stories of
massive amounts of gold being used as a medium of
exchange between the African kingdoms. One of their
captives, a man knowledgeable of the trade within
Africa, told the Portuguese that he had personally seen a
caravan of three hundred camels, each laden with many
bags of gold. The gold was traded for salt and other
commodities with an unknown people. He did not
know with whom the commerce was transacted, for the
entire exchange was done by what was called the "silent
trade," a procedure in which the buyers and sellers
never met.

In practicing the silent trade, the seller would leave his
goods in a location established by custom, and go away.
The buyer would come and examine the goods. If he
wanted the articles, he would place beside the goods,

the amount of gold he was willing to exchange. The seller would return. If the gold were of sufficient quantity, he would take it and leave. If not, he would leave the goods and gold untouched in expectation of a better offer.

This went on until the deal was completed or until one side broke off the "negotiation." But the buyer and seller never met. Yet they trusted one another not to steal both the gold and the goods. Absolute honesty was essential for these transactions to take place.

The silent trade was the traditional means of exchange between the African kingdoms. Nearly two thousand years earlier, the Greek historian, Herodotus, had described the same procedure.

The Portuguese did not have to resort to the silent trade. They traded directly with the African chiefs with whom they came in contact. To facilitate the commercial relationships, the Portuguese built a permanent fortified trading center on the island of Arguim, below Cape Blanco. Here the Portuguese and Africans met and traded horses, brass pots, cloth and corn for gold, slaves and ivory. The general rate of exchange was six slaves for one horse. Depending on the condition of the horse and the slaves, the number of slaves per horse would vary.

Trade and scientific discovery were unquestionably the dominant factors behind the Portuguese voyages of exploration. Religion, though, was another important factor. Prince Henry was a devout Catholic and was driven by a mission to bring Christianity to the people below the Sahara. He had also heard tales of the existence of an isolated Christian kingdom that was said to be somewhere in eastern Africa. This kingdom, which no European had ever seen, was rumored to be ruled by a priest named Prester John. The search for Prester John was an element in Prince Henry's drive to explore the unknown lands and seas.

Prince Henry died in 1460. After his death, the Portuguese continued their voyages down the western coast of Africa. It is not clear if they were searching for a route to the Indies, or if they were simply seeking to find what lay beyond the unexplored horizon. Afonso V succeeded to the throne of Portugal. Afonso did not have Prince Henry's intellectual vigor or scientific interest. For his exploits he was called "Afonso the Erratic" by his people. One of his countrymen said he "raged around Africa like a hungry lion roars around some guarded fold."

Nevertheless, the policy of exploration was not diminished. Portuguese explorers continued to sail farther and farther down the western coast of Africa, and the continent little by little revealed its mysteries and immense size. In the twenty years following the death of Prince Henry, nearly two thousand miles of additional coastline were unveiled to European eyes. The Portuguese sailors explored Sierra Leone, then the lands we now know as Liberia, Cote d'Ivoire, Ghana, Benin, Nigeria, Cameroon, and Gabon. These lands and their people, though, were poor, and offered few goods with which to trade.

In 1481, King João II ascended the throne of Portugal. He brought with him a fresh interest in achieving the dreams of Prince Henry to discover new lands. King

João was a monarch who intended to actively promote the search for a sea route around the southern tip of Africa. He directed Diogo Cão, an experienced seaman, to lead a new expedition. This first effort, though, was not encouraging.

Cão sailed south in the spring of 1482 and reached the River Congo. There he met "black men with frizzled hair" who came to trade ivory for cloth. He sailed on further, going where no European had ever gone before. But he ran short of supplies and was forced to return home. Although he did not know it, he was still over fifteen hundred miles from the Cape of Good Hope. In 1485, he set out again. This time he reached around 700 miles further down the coast than he did on his first voyage. But again, due to limited supplies of food and water, he could not continue. He returned to Portugal. He had reached as far as the country we now call Namibia.

The problem of supplying food and water for the crews of the ships proved to be a major hurtle to overcome. The limitations of available food and water imposed a severe restriction on the length of the exploratory voyages. The caravels, built for maneuverability and speed, had little cargo carrying capacity. Thus, the need to carry food, fresh water and other drinkable beverages for a long voyage was a significant problem. In the tropics, especially, the need for fresh water to prevent dehydration and heat stroke was foremost in the minds of all captains heading south.

The sailors, however, were not deliberately denied a healthful diet. Government regulations specified what the crew members were to be fed. They were, said the regulations, to be served meat and wine on Sundays, Tuesdays and Thursdays. On the other days of the week, something similar to porridge was to be the main dish. On all days, the meals were to include cheese, onions or sardines. Prunes and figs were allowed to be substituted for the wine. We do not know how rigidly these regulations were followed. In times of scarcity, of course, adjustments had to be made. Frequently, crews were forced to survive on hardtack—a baked mixture of flour and water. Nevertheless, the Portuguese ships of exploration left port carrying a full load of meat, fish, wine, flour, cheese, lentils, plums, almonds, garlic, mustard, salt, sugar and honey.

But even as the Portuguese ships pressed south, some people raised doubts that the venture would have a successful outcome. While Diogo Cão was making his unfruitful search for the southern tip of Africa, one such detractor, an outspoken and presumptuous Italian seaman, showed up at the Portuguese court. He was seeking royal support for a totally different approach to the task of finding a sea route to India. You Portuguese have it all wrong, he told the court. Sailing around Africa is not the easiest way to the Indies. Rather than sail south and east down the coast of Africa, he explained, sail due west, and the land of Cipangu, as he called the Asian country of legendary wealth, will be reached in ninety days. The Portuguese thought the Italian was somewhat mad, and sent him away. The Italian's name was Christopher Columbus.

Chapter 7: Christopher Columbus

The sequence of events that brought Christopher Columbus to the Portuguese court was unplanned and can only be deemed one of those tricks that the fates occasionally throw at mankind. Columbus literally washed up on the Portuguese shore, emerging from the sea after abandoning a sinking ship. He was twenty-four years old.

Columbus grew up in the Italian city of Genoa. His father and grandfather were weavers of wool cloth, a humble but honorable trade. As a weaver Domenico Colombo, Columbus's father, was an independent tradesman. He was not the employee of another man. He owned his own looms. He bought raw wool, spun the wool into yarn, and wove the yarn into cloth with the help of apprentices. He then sold the finished product to tailors and other customers. He was also a merchant, in a small way, of cheese and wine. But despite his energy and willingness to undertake new business ventures, Domenico appears to have spent most of his life only one step ahead of his creditors. Even his son-in-law, who had married his daughter Bianchinetta, had to sue Domenico to receive payment of the promised dowry. In his old age, he had to lease his garden and most of his house to a shoemaker to make ends meet.

Columbus was not interested in following his father's trade as a weaver. Living in the seafaring city of Genoa, he naturally looked to the sea as a source of a livelihood. He probably worked as a fisherman in the Mediterranean Sea at an early age. He undoubtedly sailed to the nearby seacoast towns of Nervi, Portofino, Rapallo, Cogoleto and Savona. As he grew older, he may have acted as an agent for his father, and as a trader for his own account, sailing to the major coastal cities to buy wool, wine and cheese, and to sell his father's cloth. We do know that as a young man he acquired considerable sailing experience.

In May, 1476, Columbus signed on as a common seaman on a trading ship bound for Portugal, England and Flanders. The ship joined several others to form a convoy, and thereby gained some measure of protection in a sea afoul with pirates and naval ships of warring states. The convoy, however, did not succeed in its purpose. Within days of passing through the Straits into the Atlantic, the little fleet was attacked by ships of the French navy. Columbus's ship was sunk. He grabbed a piece of floating wood, and began the six mile swim to shore. Although exhausted from the ordeal, and his energy drained by a wound he received when the French attacked, he reached land. He dragged himself out of the sea near the Portuguese town of Lagos, which coincidentally was not far from the town where Prince Henry the Navigator had sent forth his ships of exploration only a few decades earlier.

The people of Lagos treated Columbus and the other survivors of the wreck with generosity. Columbus recovered and made his way to the Portuguese capital of Lisbon, where a colony of Genoese citizens offered familiar food and language and much needed assistance.

His arrival in Lisbon was the pivotal event in his life. If his ship had not been sunk by the French off the coast of Portugal, Columbus would have probably lived and died an obscure Genoese seaman. The Americas would have had to wait many more years for their discovery by a post-Viking European. Columbus had to experience Lisbon, if he were to proceed with his life's task.

Lisbon in 1476 and in the years thereafter was the most exciting place a sailor could be. News of the Portuguese discoveries along the coast of Africa opened the mind to new possibilities. The return of Portuguese ships laden with African slaves of exotic physical appearance, and with goods, previously unknown, stimulated seamen to think of what lay beyond. Already the possibility of reaching the Indies by sailing around the southern tip of Africa was being discussed. Some were also suggesting that the Indies could be reached by sailing due west into the unknown sea.

Only two years before Columbus's fateful shipwreck, learned men proposed to the Portuguese king, Afonso V, the possibility of sailing west to the Indies. The most highly regarded of these advocates of a western route was Paolo Toscanelli, a physician who amused himself in the scholarly pursuit of mathematics and geography. Toscanelli lived in Florence. He carefully studied the writings of the ancient mathematicians and geographers. He was also greatly influenced by the book written a century and a half earlier by Marco Polo, whose account of his journey to China created in European minds dreams of heretofore unknown extravagance and riches.

In 1474, Fernão Martins, a canon at the Cathedral of Lisbon, told King Afonso about Toscanelli. Martins, who was later made a cardinal, had met Toscanelli in Italy and regarded him as one of the great scholars of the day.

King Afonso requested Martins to ask Toscanelli the simple, but most important question: What is the shortest route to the Indies?

Toscanelli was delighted to respond. The shortest route to the land of the spices, said he, is to sail west. Cipangu (Japan) lies only three thousand miles beyond the Canary Islands. Sail west and the abundance of the East will be within one's grasp. To make sure that King Afonso fully understood the measure of Asian wealth, Toscanelli described the riches of Asia in his reply to Father Martins. "The noble island of Cipangu," wrote Toscanelli, "is most fertile in gold, pearls, and precious stones." The Asians are so wealthy, he continued, using Marco Polo's book as the source of his information, that the "Japanese cover their temples and the royal residences with solid gold. ... And the land of the Great Khan is as rich as any which may be found, and not only can great profit be obtained there and many things, but gold and silver and precious stones and all kinds of spice can be obtained in great abundance, which are never brought to these, our regions."

Despite the attractiveness of the western route, King Afonso did not act on Toscanelli's advice. The Portuguese were convinced that the only feasible way to the Indies remained the route around the African continent. Perhaps they realized that Japan was not three thousand miles west of the Canaries. Perhaps they understood that the true distance was 10,600 miles.

Columbus, meanwhile, was establishing himself in the Portuguese capital. His younger brother, Bartholomew, had already set up a shop in Lisbon to sell sailing charts and books. Columbus became a partner in

Bartholomew's store, and spent much time in preparing the charts to be sold. Chart making in those days was an occupation for the entrepreneur. No government printing office existed to sell, for a modest fee, accurate maps of the coastlines and seas. The chart maker had to rely on his own resources to get the data for his maps. To gather the information needed to prepare the charts, Columbus spent many hours talking to Portuguese sailors about their African voyages, about winds and currents, and about the unknown lands, the unexplored oceans. In Lisbon, in the 1470's, the imaginative mind could dream of unlimited possibilities. New ideas were everywhere.

Columbus did not remain long in the chart making trade, though. He was not made for such sedentary pursuits. He returned to the sea. He sailed north to Greenland, Iceland, and Ireland, and west and south to Madeira and the Canaries. He even sailed down the African coast. To earn a living, he resumed his occupation as a merchant, buying and selling sugar with modest success.

And he read books. Although he was not a well-read man, he read a few books again and again. The most important of these was *Imago Mundi* by Cardinal Pierre d'Ailly, who had written the book around the year 1410. Cardinal d'Ailly had been a scholar at the Sorbonne University in Paris. *Imago Mundi* was a compendium of ancient texts on world geography. One can tell from the abundant margin notes in Columbus's copy that Columbus studied the book assiduously. Other books that led him to believe that the Indies were within sailing distance to the west were *Historia Rerum* by Cardinal Piccolomini and the *Travels of Marco Polo*.

The next significant event in his life was his marriage to the daughter of a Portuguese aristocrat. He met his future wife at the chapel of the Convento dos Santos, where he had gone to hear Mass. Her name was Dona Felipa Perestrello e Moniz. At the time they met she was living as a student at the convent, which maintained a prestigious boarding school favored by Portugal's best families for the education of their daughters.

The marriage of the daughter of a Portuguese noble to an impoverished Italian seaman, a weaver's son, who had literally washed up on the beach only a few years earlier has been a subject of discussion ever since Columbus's life became the focus for examination. Such marriages across class lines did not often take place in the structured society of fifteenth century Portugal. Columbus's son, Ferdinand, said Dona Felipa was struck by Columbus because he was "a man of fine presence" and "behaved very honorably." That may have been true. Other factors, though, may also have been at play. Dona Felipa's father was dead. Her widowed mother, although a member of an aristocratic family, may not have been able to afford a dowry. Even aristocratic families occasionally fell on hard times. The impoverished nature of Dona Felipa's family fortune may be further surmised since there is no mention of a dowry in the records.

Another factor influencing Dona Felipa's choice of a husband was, perhaps, her age. When she first met Columbus, she was twenty-five years old, which in the fifteenth century was rather old for a woman who was not a nun to be unmarried. Whatever the reasons, she must have been having enough fears of permanent spinsterhood to make an Italian seaman, the son of an indigent weaver, look attractive. After the marriage, she could dress him up and improve his table manners.

We can also wonder why Columbus chose to attend Mass in a chapel where he knew he would meet the daughters of influential families. As a man of high ambition, he certainly knew the importance of the right marriage. Most likely, he and Dona Felipa, for all these reasons, were meant for each other.

The marriage of Christopher and Dona Felipa was actually a significant event in the chain of events leading to the fifteenth century discovery of the Americas. Dona Felipa's deceased father had played an active role in the Portuguese exploration and colonization ventures. His widow, Dona Felipa's mother, noticed her new son-in-law's interest in navigation and in the location and shape of distant lands. She captivated him with stories of past voyages of exploration. More importantly, she let Columbus examine her late husband's writings and sea-charts. These were, of course, invaluable sources of information on winds and currents and the general knowledge of the sea.

Possibly through his mother-in-law, Columbus also learned of the letter written by the Florentine geographer Toscanelli to the Portuguese king. Columbus at once wrote to Toscanelli, expressing his hopes for a westward voyage, and asking advice. Toscanelli replied graciously. "To Cristobal Columbo," he wrote, "I see your great and magnificent desire to go where the spices grow, and in reply to your letter I send you the copy of another letter which I wrote a long time ago to a familiar friend and servant of the Most Serene King of Portugal." Toscanelli thereupon enclosed a copy of the letter he had sent to King Afonso.

In a second letter to Columbus, Toscanelli added further encouragement for the voyage. Approving of the proposed journey and beckoning the prospects of material enrichment, Toscanelli wrote: "So that when the said voyage is made, it will be to powerful kingdoms and most noble cities and provinces, very rich in a great abundance of all kinds of things very necessary to us, as well as in all kinds of spices in great quantity and jewels in great abundance."

The Toscanelli letters were not immediately important. Columbus needed no inducement of spices and jewels to further the enterprise. A few years later, though, when he sought financial support for his undertaking, the letters from the esteemed geographer provided an element of credibility to a venture that otherwise would have appeared to be the fantasies of a lunatic.

In 1481, about the time Toscanelli and Columbus exchanged letters, King Afonso died. The new king of Portugal was João II, the son of Afonso. King João was young and energetic. He listened to new ideas. It was he who sent Diogo Cão to explore the unknown coast of the African continent. As the new monarch, King João instructed an informal group of advisors, known as the *Junto dos Mathematicos*, to examine Columbus's proposal. The advisors met and subsequently reported to the King that Columbus was vain and boastful, and that his plan for reaching Cypango was "simply founded on imagination." Portuguese funding of the enterprise was denied.

It was not the only tragedy to beset Columbus. His wife, Dona Felipa, died, leaving to his care their small son. In 1485, no longer having family ties or royal support in Portugal, and probably being broke as well, Columbus dejectedly left Lisbon for Spain with the uncertain hope of finding a monarch who would take seriously his vain and fanciful idea of sailing west to the Indies.

Chapter 8: Asia, At Last

King João, the king of Portugal, did not believe that
Columbus could succeed in his proposed venture to
reach the Indies by sailing west. Nevertheless, the mere
knowledge that people from other countries were
seeking a sea-borne route to Asia lent a sense of urgency
to Portugal's efforts to reach Asia. A new undertaking
had to be launched soon to determine if ships could
reach India by sailing around the southern tip of the
African continent. For the new venture, King João
chose Bartholomeu Dias, an aristocrat in the royal
court. The expedition would consist of two caravels and
a much larger supply ship, carrying food. The addition
of the supply ship was an effort to overcome the
problem, encountered by Cão, of running short of food
before reaching the hoped for destination.

This little fleet of three ships left Lisbon in August,
1487. For most of the way, Dias followed the course
taken by Diogo Cão five years earlier. As Dias and his
men approached the point where Cão was forced to
turn back, however, they ran into strong opposing
winds and currents, from the south, against which the
ships could make no headway.

Cão had previously met the same conditions, and had
reported the nature of the adversity to the
cartographers, mathematicians, technical advisers, and
other academicians at the Portuguese court. We can
easily imagine the discussions touched off at the royal

palace by Cão's revelations. If the opposing wind and currents were so strong in the southern latitudes that even a caravel could not make headway against them, then the whole venture might fail, even if the southern cape was nearly in sight.

Someone, probably one of the academicians in the court, proposed a possible solution. The solution drew on the knowledge acquired from countless sea voyages.

Mariners knew that at the latitudes of the Azores and Portugal the prevailing winds blow from the west. Portuguese navigators had discovered many years earlier, though, that south of the Azores at the lower latitudes along the African coast near the equator, the prevailing winds shift and blow southward. The reason for this shift in direction, we now know, is that the winds are circulating clockwise around an oceanic high pressure system that is usually present in the mid-Atlantic above the equator.

Portuguese seamen, returning home with their cargoes of Negro slaves, soon learned to avoid the northern headwinds along the African coast by sailing northwestward away from the continent. This tack led them deep into the Atlantic where they were far from land, but away from the fierce headwinds of the coast. When they reached the Azores they turned east and caught the high latitude prevailing westerly winds that practically carried their ships into Lisbon harbor. The journey was much longer in distance than the most direct route, but much shorter in time due to the advantageous use of the direction of the prevalent winds.

A scholar at the royal court noted, perhaps, that the Azores are about as far north of the equator as the southern tip of Africa was believed to be south. Was it possible, he may have suggested, that the wind systems in the southern hemisphere are the mirror image of those of the northern hemisphere – circulating counter-clockwise rather than clockwise. If such were the case, a ship sailing southwestward, out to sea, away from the African coast, would pick up a westerly wind that would propel the ships around the southern cape.

We do not know, if one of the learned men in the royal palace was the first to suggest sailing out to sea when faced with contrary winds and currents along the southern African coast, or whether Bartholomeu Dias, acting without counsel, decided on such a tack himself. We do know that Dias, making no headway against the wind and current, ordered his two caravels to turn to the southwest and sail away from the African coast and into the open sea where the ships would be out of sight of land. He ordered the supply ship to remain where it was. They would, they hoped, rejoin it later.

It was a high risk decision. No European had ever sailed the Atlantic Ocean of this region. Indeed, it is unlikely that anyone had ever sailed these waters. Moreover, Dias did not know how far south the African continent extended. They sailed southwest for many days, when, as they had gambled, the wind swung to the west. The crews of the two caravels turned the ships eastward, and with the wind on their backs, sailed back towards Africa, hoping that with their maneuver out to sea, they had not sailed so far south as to miss landfall entirely.

After sailing eastward many days without sighting land, Dias ordered the ships to turn north. Soon land appeared. The sailors anxiously sought to determine the bearing of the coast. If it ran north to south, the African landmass would still stand between them and the Indies. They would have failed, after all their efforts, to find a sea route to Asia.

With great joy, they realized the coast did not run north to south. It ran from west to east with a slight bend to the north. They had possibly, although not certainly, sailed around the southern end of the five thousand mile long African continent. They made landfall in a sheltered cove. It was a pleasant summer day. From their ships, the mariners could see a sandy shore, and beyond the shore, groups of small, dark-skinned men watching over herds of grazing cattle. The native Africans, frightened by the sudden appearance of ships of a size and kind they had never seen before, fled into the bush. Dias named the cove *Angra dos Vaqueiros* – Bay of the Cattlemen – after the herdsmen tending the grazing cattle. It is today called Mossel Bay.

Dias resisted the urge to turn for home, and instead continued eastward along the coast. After several days sailing, the coast turned sharply northeastward, indicating that they had rounded Africa, and that Asia lay open before them. Only now, with food in short supply, did Dias turn his ships about and begin the long journey back to Portugal.

It was January, 1488, and Dias and his crews had been at sea for over a year. They had sailed where no Europeans had sailed before, and had proven the feasibility of a sea-borne trade route between Europe and Asia. As he passed the southern cape, the search for which had taken so long, Dias named it *Cabo Tormentoso*—Stormy Cape, indicative of the region's usual weather. But back in Portugal, King João did not like the name *Cabo Tormentoso*. He renamed this southern most piece of land *Cabo de Boa Esperança*, Cape of Good Hope, because it promised the high hope of fulfilling the Portuguese ambition of sailing to the Indies.

King João died in 1495. He was only 40 years old. Although he had vigorously pursued the enterprise of reaching India by way of the Cape of Good Hope, the goal was unattained at the time of his death. Bartholomeu Dias's 1488 voyage, which reached a point a little beyond the southern tip of Africa, was the farthest the Portuguese had gone during King João's reign. Being the father of no legitimate children, King João was succeeded on the Portuguese throne by his nephew, Manuel.

Grandiose and pompous, Manuel ruled with an extravagant and ostentatious style. Moreover, his ambitions were larger than Portugal, itself. Soon after becoming king, he cast his eyes on the Spanish throne of Ferdinand and Isabella. Well aware that Isabella's brother Juan, the heir to the Spanish throne, was in poor health, Manuel proposed marriage to the eldest daughter of Ferdinand and Isabella. If consummated, the marriage would significantly increase the possibility of Manuel becoming at some point king of both Portugal and Spain. The kingdom of Spain, itself, had only recently come into being with the marriage of Isabella of Castile to Ferdinand of Aragon.

Before Isabella would consent to the marriage of her daughter to King Manuel, however, she demanded that certain conditions by met. Foremost among these was the requirement that all Portuguese Jews be either baptized or expelled from the country.

Isabella was motivated by the purest of motives. She fervently believed she was doing God's work in advancing the cause of the Church of Rome. The modern belief that God might listen to prayers in Hebrew, Arabic and English, as well as to prayers in Latin, was utterly beyond her comprehension. Spanish monarchs who reigned after her were also convinced that they were performing God's mission on earth. Nearly a century later, Philip II sent the Invincible Spanish Armada against Protestant England and its heretic queen, Elizabeth I. When the Armada was resoundingly defeated, Philip II spent the rest of his days wondering why God had chosen to give victory to the faithless heathens. The fact that the English seadogs out-gunned and out-maneuvered the Spanish grandees was irrelevant from Philip II's viewpoint.

Isabella was obsessed with the idea that only believers in the true faith should be allowed to live in her kingdom. Her obsession was to result in much hardship for the Spanish Jews, and later, in even worse hardship for the Portuguese Jews. Isabella's first concern, however, was to drive the Moors from Spain. For centuries, these Muslims had controlled a large part of the Iberian peninsular. They were in retreat, though, before the forces of Christianity. On January 2, 1492, Granada, the last Muslim stronghold, surrendered to Isabella's troops. With the Muslim presence eliminated from Catholic

Spain, Isabella could now turn her attention to the elimination of the Jewish presence, and thereby achieve total Catholic purity. On March 30, 1492, less than three months after the victory over the Muslims, Ferdinand and Isabella ordered all Jews either to convert to Christianity or to leave the country within four months.

More than 200,000 Spanish Jews were affected. Nearly all chose to remain true to their faith and to leave Spain. To do so meant they had to leave the country where they and their ancestors had peacefully lived since before the coming of Christianity. To do so also meant selling their property at distressed prices. One fine house was exchanged for a donkey. A vineyard was bartered for several yards of cloth. Most of the exiles were reduced to poverty. But still they left. Many went to Portugal. The rest went to France, Italy, North Africa and Turkey. The Jews who chose to convert to Christianity and remain in Spain were called Marranos. The depth of their conviction to Christianity was questioned, though, with much justification. Most Marranos secretly continued to practice their old religion.

August 2, 1492 was the last day the Jews could remain in Spain. On that day, in the seacoast town of Palos, the harbor was full of ships carrying these tearful and desperate people into exile, leaving behind most of their possessions and the country in which they had lived their entire lives. But on that day at one side of the harbor were three ships with a different mission. The day after the last Jews left, Christopher Columbus ordered these three ships, the *Niña*, the *Pinta*, and the

Santa María, to raise anchor and to set sail on a westerly course.

Because King Manuel wished to placate Queen Isabella, the Jews of Portugal received the same treatment as they did in Spain. On December 25, 1496, an edict was issued ordering the Jews to convert to Christianity or to leave the country. As in Spain most chose to leave. They roamed the Mediterranean looking for a safe haven. Of those who survived the ordeal, most eventually found homes in North Africa, Turkey, and Palestine. Known as the Sephardic, these Jews in time prospered as merchants in the Islamic countries to which they migrated.

The Portuguese Jews who became Marranos by converting to Christianity did not fare well. They were blamed for every dire event, including a plague brought on by a bad harvest. On April 19, 1506, a violent maniacal mob surged through the streets of Lisbon killing Jewish men, women, and children wherever they were found. In one particularly gruesome incident, young women were thrown from the upper stories of a building and caught on spears by those standing below. The mayhem went on for three days, and resulted in the deaths of between 2,000 and 3,000 Marranos.

Despite the turbulent state of his kingdom, King Manuel resolved to continue the Portuguese tradition of exploration. To command the next expedition, he chose Vasco da Gama, a young, well-borne sea captain from the town of Sines. Before authorizing Vasco da Gama to renew the effort to find a sea route to India, though, King Manuel asked his Council for advice on whether to proceed.

Most of the members of the Council were against the undertaking. Some believed that the risks and costs were too great. Even if the venture succeeded, they said, the expense of maintaining the far-flung fortresses necessary to protect the trade routes would bankrupt the kingdom. Others believed success would only create other problems. Neither the Sultan of Egypt nor the Republic of Venice, they pointed out, would passively sit by and watch the Portuguese undermine the source of their wealth.

Nevertheless, with Bartholomeu Dias already having gone beyond the Cape of Good Hope, and with Christopher Columbus recently having returned to Spain, convinced that he had discovered a sea route to the Indies, King Manuel had a powerful incentive to complete the task of exploration begun by Prince Henry.

No record exists of Portuguese voyages for the period from December, 1488, when Bartholomeu Dias returned from the voyage to the Cape of Good Hope, to July, 1497, when Vasco da Gama left Lisbon for his historic journey. The Portuguese government was very secretive about its oceanic ventures for obvious reasons, and the archives of the period were destroyed in a disastrous earthquake and fire long before any historian had an opportunity to examine the records.

It is unlikely, though, that no voyages of exploration took place during this nine year period. In all probability, the Portuguese navigators continued to probe the south Atlantic, seeking the best route to the Cape of Good Hope. Since sailing ships are dependent upon winds and currents, the best route may not be the straightest course, which can be beset with contrary winds and opposing currents. The argument that the Portuguese never ceased to actively explore the south Atlantic finds support in the route ultimately taken by Vasco da Gama. In his epic 1497 voyage, da Gama did not follow the African coastline. Rather, like Bartholomeu Dias, he swung far to the west, almost touching South America, before turning south and then east on a heading for the southern tip of Africa. Such a course optimized prevailing winds and currents. It is not likely that he just happened on that route.

Three years later, in 1500, another Portuguese explorer, Pedro Alvares Cabral, actually reached South America by coming upon Brazil, where the country's present province of Pernambuco bulges into the Atlantic, a few degrees below the Equator. Some historians, assuming continuous Portuguese exploration, have speculated that the real Portuguese discovery of Brazil was possibly made a decade earlier than Cabral's 1500 voyage and that the Portuguese, therefore, found the New World a year or two before Columbus landed at San Salvador. Since all records of this period were destroyed in 1755 in a Lisbon earthquake, theories of Portuguese discovery of America prior to Columbus must remain in the realm of speculation.

That the Portuguese carefully planned Vasco da Gama's voyage can be seen in the design of his ships. In designing new ships, the Portuguese clearly had studied the failures of the earlier voyages, and were ready to make innovative changes to improve the chances of success. The main problem encountered by Cão and Dias was insufficient supplies. The caravels were too small to carry enough food and water to complete the journey. To remedy this deficiency, the caravel would not be the ship of first choice to be used by da Gama. Instead, a new design would be used for the main ships of the expedition. The new ships would be twice as large as the caravels.

Bartholomeu Dias, aware of the limitations of the caravels from his voyage to the Cape of Good Hope, was asked to be the naval architect of the vessels for the planned voyage. Calling upon his experience at sea, Dias designed the new ships to be longer and wider than the old caravels. He gave up the maneuverability of the caravel, but gained room for additional supplies. Two such ships, the *São Raphael* and the *São Gabriel*, were built. They were to be the main ships of Vasco da Gama's fleet. To them he added a caravel, named the *Berrio*, and a storeship, which was larger than any of the other three ships.

The four ships of Vasco da Gama's fleet left Portugal on July 8, 1497. In January, 1498, they rounded the Cape of Good Hope, and began the journey up the east coast of Africa, where no European had gone before. The supply ship, its usefulness ended, was broken up and destroyed. In March, the fleet reached Mozambique, a port city of obvious affluence. The houses there were built of white stone. Between the houses were gardens and groves of palm trees. Here the Portuguese entered the land of Islam. At anchor in the harbor were four large ships, manned by Arabic speaking sailors. Da Gama soon learned that these Arabian ships carried cargoes of pepper, cloves, ginger, silver, gold, and gems, including pearls and rubies.

When the Muslims recovered from the shock of discovering that the new arrivals were Europeans, who had sailed around the southern tip of Africa, they immediately decided to defend their faith and wipe out these Christian dogs. Fortunately, da Gama learned of the impending attack, and the small Portuguese fleet made its escape. With the aid of a captured pilot, the three ships sailed on to India, and arrived at the city of Calicut on May 21, 1498 ten months and two weeks after leaving Lisbon. The goal of sailing to Asia, begun in the early years of the century, with Prince Henry's cautious probes down the north African coast, was achieved.

Shortly after entering Calicut, Vasco da Gama arranged to meet the Indian maharajah—the first meeting ever of an Asian prince with the representative of a European monarch. One of da Gama's lieutenants accompanied da Gama, whom he called the captain-major, on this fateful encounter. Describing the events of that day, the lieutenant wrote:

"The captain-major was deposited at the house of a man of rank, while we others were provided with food, consisting of rice, with much butter, and excellent boiled fish. The captain-major did not wish to eat, and when we had done so, we embarked on a river close by, which flows between the sea and the mainland, close to the coast. The two boats in which we embarked were lashed close together, so we were not separated. There were numerous other boats, all crowded with people. As to those who were on the banks, I say nothing; their number was infinite, and they had all come to see us. We went up that river for about a league, and saw many large ships drawn up high and dry on its banks, for there is no port here."

Presently, they reached the palace, and were ushered into the presence of the maharajah. The lieutenant described the scene:

"The king was in a small court, reclining upon a couch covered with a cloth of green velvet, ... upon this was a sheet of cotton material, very white and fine, more so than any linen. The cushions were the same fashion. In his left hand the king held a large gold cup. ... Into this cup the king threw the husks of a certain herb that is chewed by the people of this country because of its soothing effects. ... On the right side of the king stood a basin of gold, so large that a man might just encircle it with his arms; this contained the herbs. There were likewise many silver jugs. The canopy above the couch was all gilt. ..."

"The king ordered that water for our hands should be given us, as also some fruit, one kind of which resembled a melon, except that its outside was rough and the inside sweet, whilst another kind of fruit resembled a fig, and tasted very nice. (This latter may have been a banana.) There were men who prepared these fruits for us; and the king looked at us eating, and smiled; and talked to the servants who stood near him supplying him with the herbs referred to."

Da Gama thereupon addressed the maharajah, stating that he had come from Portugal, a rich and powerful country in Europe, and that the king of Portugal wished the friendship of the Indian leader. The maharajah was polite and gracious, and the meeting came to an end.

The next day, though, things did not go as well. Da Gama had neglected to bring from Portugal gifts worthy of an Indian prince. All he had was four scarlet hoods, four strings of coral, six hand washbasins, a case of sugar, two casks of oil, two casks of honey, and some other odds and ends. The Indians were insulted by this meager showing, and said that the gifts were of such modest value that the Portuguese kingdom could not be nearly as rich as da Gama had stated.

Relations did not improve, and three months later da Gama and his fleet of three ships began the yearlong return journey back to Portugal, where on September 18, 1499, the voyagers made a triumphal entrance to Lisbon.

Although the maharajah was not impressed with da Gama's gift of washbasins and honey, da Gama had determined that huge profits could be made in the spice business. At Venice in 1499, pepper sold for as much as 80 ducats per hundred-weight. In Calicut, the same pepper could be bought for as little as three ducats per hundredweight. Thus in the journey from Asia to Venice, the price of pepper increased more than twenty-five fold. So high was the price of spices in Europe that at Antwerp one and a half pounds of pepper cost more than an entire butchered sheep purchased at a slaughterhouse. In comparison, a pound and a half of pepper today costs less than a few large lamb chops. In Germany a pound of nutmeg cost as much as seven fat oxen.

Of course, the price difference did not become pure profit. Costs of transporting the spices over deserts and seas were high. Periodic wars between potentates along trade routes disrupted supply. Moreover, kings and princes along the way were always ready to extract their tax. The problems of land transportation, though, simply increased the profit potential of the ocean route around Africa's Cape of Good Hope.

Realizing that a good thing was at hand, King Manuel quickly moved to create the infrastructure needed to support the commercial enterprise. He ordered new wharves and warehouses to be built in Lisbon. He also ordered the construction of new ships.

In the spring of 1500, less than six months after da Gama returned from the first European voyage to Asia by sea, King Manuel readied a fleet of thirteen vessels to sail to India and bring back spices. The fleet was under the command of Pedro Alvares Cabral. It was during this expedition that Cabral discovered Brazil. He stumbled upon the South American continent while sailing west to pick up the favorable winds and currents of the south Atlantic. After discovering Brazil, though, his troubles began. Five of his ships sank by the time he reached India. At Calicut, itself, he was met with armed resistance from the Muslims, who correctly regarded the Portuguese as a threat to their end of the spice trade. When the Muslims sent out a fleet to sink Cabral's remaining ships, the Admiral made a hasty withdrawal from the Asian continent.

Only five of his ships were fit to make the return voyage to Europe. Of these one was lost on the homeward bound journey, leaving four ships, out of the original thirteen, to make the journey to India and return. These four ships, though, returned loaded with spices. At Lisbon, 2000 hundredweight of pepper, 600 of cinnamon, and 400 of ginger were off-loaded for profitable sale. The seamen of the *Annunciada* also brought back a strange bird, completely unknown to Europeans—the parrot. To their amazed countrymen, the sailors also told stories of other strange animals—elephants and rhinoceroses and crocodiles.

Subsequent voyages by Portuguese explorers led to more discoveries in that part of the world where Europeans had never been.

One traveler, upon returning home, recalled with amazement his first sight of the actual spice growing plants. "It is to be observed," he wrote, "how all spices grow in India. Pepper grows like grapes in clusters, just as do elderberries. At times they bring to us green peppers just as they come from the tree. Cinnamon quills come also from large trees resembling the willow tree growing here. They have leaves that are broader than those of the willow tree, and when the time comes the cinnamon bark is peeled off and is dried. That is cinnamon bark, and afterwards the tree must stand two years until it grows a new bark again."

The traveler also observed other spice plants. "The greater part of ginger," he noted, "is found to grow at Kandinor, not far from Calicut. This is at times imported to Lisbon; it consists of roots, and has leaves like wide-bladed grass. I have seen it to be sure."

The traveler concluded his report with a description of still other spices, luxury items, and good things to eat: "The buds of cloves and nutmeg blossoms are obtained from Malacca which is located 700 miles beyond Calicut. How this spice grows even they do not know.

From there is also obtained the largest supply of drugs and precious gems. Pearls are sought in an island located in the Persian Gulf. They are also sought at a place called Kayl located on the continent. From there they bring many strange things, such as oriental rugs. Also large cocoa nuts are imported from there; they are called metzen and are good to eat."

However, it was the Asian animals that made the greatest impression upon the Europeans. In 1514 in a public relations gesture that affirmed the Portuguese discoveries, King Manuel sent to Rome what may have been the world's first traveling circus of wild animals. Before the Pope and Roman populace, the Portuguese paraded leopards, a panther, an elephant and many colorful parrots. A rhinoceros had been captured, but the poor beast died before reaching Rome. Of all the animals, the elephant was the biggest hit. He bowed down three times before the Pope. Then he sprayed the awe struck dignitaries with water from his trunk. Europeans who had never even heard of such animals were fascinated.

But King Manuel was thinking of more serious matters than an elephant that bowed and sprayed water from his trunk. Although the Europeans were amused by the Asian beasts, King Manuel, in 1502, was not amused by the Muslim attempt to attack Cabral's fleet. Even though the attack had been aborted, the Muslims clearly intended to hurl back the Portuguese from any Asian foothold. The Muslims, King Manuel believed, had to be taught a hard lesson.

Chapter 9: The Portuguese Challenge

Despite Cabral's successful voyage to India, King Manuel was incensed that the Muslims had planned to attack Cabral's ships, and had forced the Portuguese fleet to flee ignominiously for safety. King Manuel did not intend to back down before the Muslim opposition. No Catholic king could tolerate defiance by a Muslim foe. The issue was about more than religious differences. The future control of the spice trade was at stake. The Muslims correctly saw that the Portuguese intended to grab a large share of this highly profitable business. A confrontation was inevitable.

In response to the Muslim challenge, King Manuel at once sent a new fleet to India. The fleet was heavily armed and was ordered to establish a Portuguese military and naval presence in the East. The fleet consisted of twenty-five vessels. It was commanded by Vasco da Gama now making his second voyage to Asia. This armada rounded the Cape of Good Hope in the late summer of 1502.

On this journey through Indian waters Vasco da Gama left behind a trail of blood and ashes. Off the Malabar Coast, the Portuguese captured a large sailing dhow loaded with Muslims, including many women and children. They were returning from a pilgrimage to Mecca. When the Muslim pilgrims refused to turn over to the Portuguese all their wealth, da Gama ordered the dhow set afire, and then watched impassively as the Muslim women held their children on the blazing deck and cried for mercy. Wrote one observer: "Each woman grabbed her small child, raised him in her arms, and pleaded for mercy for the innocent children." Another seaman wrote, in a matter of fact tone, "We took a Mecca ship on which were 380 men and many women and children. We took from it 12,000 ducats, and goods worth at least another 10,000. Then we burned the ship and all the people on board."

Da Gama sailed on to Calicut, where he seized several hapless traders and fishermen. He hanged them. Then he cut off their heads, hands, and feet, threw the body parts into a boat, and let it drift ashore. Reportedly, da Gama attached a note, written in Arabic, to the boat, advising the maharajah to use the body parts to make a curry. Before leaving India, he bombarded Calicut. He returned to Portugal, where the king conferred on him enough riches to make him one of the wealthiest men in the land. He was still unhappy, though. Only when the king made da Gama a member of the nobility, and proclaimed him Count of Vidigueira, was the explorer satisfied.

In 1505, King Manuel created the post of Viceroy of India. The viceroy was to be stationed in India, and would have absolute authority to govern. Since communication with Portugal required a voyage of over six months by a sailing ship, the viceroy was, of necessity, given undisputed power to rule. The first viceroy was Francisco de Almeida.

Almeida's first task was to establish Portuguese control over the region. Da Gama's reign of terror had temporarily subdued the Muslim and Hindu populations, but such a policy could not be effective for long. Portugal could only support a force of less than ten thousand men in Asia. Against the total populations of India and the countries further east, this force had to be used with much ingenuity.

Almeida's policy was to rely upon sea power as the key. He established only a few land bases in all of Asia. He carefully selected the locations of these land bases for their ability to control the trade routes and for their ability to be defended with comparatively few men. Almeida then planned to use naval power to support these fortresses built at the landed strong points. Almeida foresaw that only the navy could defend the far flung empire. Individual land fortresses would always be vulnerable to attack by overwhelming hostile forces.

Everything would depend upon sea power. In formulating this policy in his very first months as viceroy, Almeida devised the strategy that would be used by every western power down to the present day. Sea power formed the basis upon which the British Empire was built. Today, aided by air power, Almeida's strategy remains, even in the nuclear age, a vital element of American defense policy.

In 1509, Almeida was succeeded as viceroy by Afonso de Albuquerque, a farsighted and capable administrator, who was also an aristocrat with family ties to the royal house. His policy, in these early years of the formation of the Portuguese Empire, was to establish naval bases at Goa, Malacca, Aden, and Ormuz. Goa was an important trading city in India. Malacca commanded the sea-lanes to Japan and to the eastern spice islands. Aden and Ormuz controlled the entrance to the Red Sea and the Persian Gulf.

The fortresses controlling the entrance to the Red Sea were strategically situated to interdict the spices being transported to Venice. King Manuel wished to make clear to the Asian spice merchants that henceforth the Portuguese would be their only customer.

In furtherance of that policy, the Portuguese soon after reaching the East established a trading colony at Goa, on the western coast of India. At the time of the Portuguese arrival, the city with its well-protected harbor was already a prosperous trading center for Arabian horses, which were brought there by Muslim merchants to be sold to Indian potentates, who coveted the horses for their strength and speed.

The city was even then known as Golden Goa for its wealth. Yet, for all its wealth, it was not a desirable place to live by western standards. A European traveler to the city noted that "all the houses are made of straw, and are very small, having no opening except a low and narrow doorway. The furniture consists of a few rush mats, on which people lie down to sleep or take their meals." Straw houses or not, the Goa was vital to the Portuguese, and in 1510, Albuquerque, seeking a secure base for Portuguese operations, seized control of the city from the Sultan of Bijapur.

To make permanent Portuguese control of Goa, Albuquerque sought to create an indigenous population that would be loyal to Portugal. To accomplish this task, he encouraged Portuguese men to marry Indian women and to raise children, whose allegiance, at least in part, would be to Portugal. To add to the attractiveness of marriage, Albuquerque offered a dowry. Portuguese soldiers who married were also released from military service, and were left free to pursue whatever commercial ventures that interested them. Since most of the Portuguese who sailed for India were soldiers from the poorest class, the prospect of making a new beginning in Goa held for them great appeal, and many readily accepted Albuquerque's offer.

For most of the Portuguese soldiers and seamen who reached Goa, the opportunity to start life afresh in India was the first break they had ever been given. Many were not only poor. They were also convicts, who had been pardoned on condition that they enlist for the long and highly dangerous voyage to the Far East. This practice of pardoning convicts who agreed to labor on a ship bound for far off lands was a frequent recourse of many countries at this time. It was a practice that obviously solved many problems. It emptied the prisons. It removed from the home country thugs and other reprobates who threatened the public safety. And it provided a labor force willing to undertake dangerous tasks for little pay.

At least one pardoned convict, Bartolome Torres, sailed as an able seaman on Christopher Columbus' flagship, the *Santa María*, on the 1492 voyage that resulted in the discovery of America. Senor Torres, it appears from the record, had killed a man in a brawl. He was sentenced to be hanged, but had the good fortune to be pardoned in time to participate in the world's most famous ocean voyage. Fortunately, few other crewmen on Columbus' ships had the colorful character of Senor Torres. The same cannot be said of the Portuguese sailors and soldiers sent to India. Yet, they became the force that allowed Afonso de Albuquerque to create the Portuguese Empire in Asia.

With control of Goa firmly established, the Portuguese set out to bring into being the empire that would dominate Asian trade. In addition to Goa, Albuquerque built fortress cities at Ormuz, which commanded the Persian Gulf, and at Malacca, which controlled the straits through which ships, sailing to the spice islands of Indonesia, had to travel.

The Portuguese also gained control of Ceylon, the large island nation, now named Sri Lanka, off the southern coast of India; the Moluccas, the chain of islands between the Philippines and Australia; and Macao, the Chinese city near Hong Kong. With these and other strongholds, complete control of Asian trade with Europe appeared to be within the Portuguese grasp.

In establishing political domination over this vast area, the Portuguese met with surprisingly little resistance from the Asian emperors. Since the total Portuguese force, at its height, consisted of a few thousand men and a small number of ships, in lands thousands of miles from home, an aroused Asian population, properly led, would have had little trouble annihilating these European intruders.

The Portuguese, however, were able to exploit many advantages. First, their will to prevail was strong, and the Asian government leaders' will to resist was weak. Also, under the command of Afonso de Albuquerque, the Portuguese had a vigorous and decisive commander, who aggressively used his limited number of men and ships to maximum advantage. In addition, Albuquerque possessed the formidable ability of being able to recognize and take advantage of the petty political differences between the various Asian princes. By selectively providing military support for Asian kings in disputes with other Asian kings, Albuquerque subdued the opponents and made the victors dependent upon, and respectful of, Portuguese arms.

Albuquerque was particularly adept at exploiting the long standing animosity of Hindu and Muslim sovereigns towards one another. In this manner, the Portuguese supported the Raja of Cochin in his little war with the Samorin of Calicut. Likewise, in east Africa, the Portuguese allied themselves with the Malindi tribe in a dispute with the neighboring Mombasa tribe. By rising above the petty quarrels of the native population, Portugal became the dominant power in Asia.

The Portuguese also had better ships than their Muslim and Hindu opponents. The Portuguese ships were designed for the rigorous, often storm bashed, voyage from Europe to the Far East. Their ships, accordingly, were stoutly built. In contrast, most of the vessels thrown against them were oared galleys and similar fragile craft that were designed for sail under the placid conditions of the Indian Ocean and Red Sea. Moreover, the Portuguese were better equipped and better trained with ship-borne cannon.

The issue of Portuguese dominance of Asian trade was decided in 1509 in a battle at Diu. At Diu the Muslims assembled a fleet to defeat the European intruder. In the battle Portuguese ship-borne cannons annihilated the Muslim flotilla. Lacking sophisticated weapons, the Muslims never had a chance.

Not surprisingly, after Diu and for the remainder of the sixteenth century, the Portuguese were the masters of the Indian Ocean. In time, they would lose their dominance of the region to other world powers possessing still greater resources. The two peoples who would ultimately defeat the Portuguese were the English and the Dutch. But for the century following da Gama's historic voyage, the Portuguese faced no serious rival in Asia.

Unfortunately, the Portuguese ruled with a brutal hand. Cruel and inhuman treatment of the native people was accepted without reservation. So rare was the contrary true that the historian K. G. Jayne had to make special note that "here and there, men ... might rise to a saner and kinder humanity." The same historian, writing of Afonso de Albuquerque, lamented that "he never shook himself free from the inhumanity of his age."

The mistreatment of native population was still being practiced a century later, when Jean Mocquet, a Frenchman, visited Goa. In a book published in 1645, he described what he saw:

"As for the slaves, it is pitiful what cruel chastisements the Portuguese give them, making them suffer a thousand kinds of torment. For they put them in double sets of irons, and then beat them, not with twenty or thirty blows of a staff, but with as many as five hundred. ... The master, a Portuguese or half-caste, standing by, and counting the strokes on his rosary.

"While I was lodging at Goa, I heard nothing but blows all night long, and some weak voice which could hardly sigh; for they stuff their mouths with a linen cloth, to keep them from crying aloud, and scarce allow them to breathe. After they have well beaten them in this sort, they slash their bodies with a razor, then rub them with salt and vinegar, lest they should mortify.

"One woman had a slave who was not alert enough, nor prompt to rise when summoned; her half-caste mistress caused a horseshoe to be nailed to her back, so that the poor creature died some time after. ... Another, for not being wide enough awake, had her eyelids sewn to her brows. ... Another there was, who was hanged up in a room by the hands, for two or three days together, and that for a very small matter, to wit for having let spill about a pint of milk. ... The master of the lodging, having one day bought a Japanese slave girl, chanced, while conversing with his wife, to remark that the girl had very white teeth. The woman said nothing then, but biding her time until her husband was out of doors, she caused this poor slave to be seized and bound, and all her teeth to be torn out, without compassion."

Yet, despite the barbarity of the Portuguese behavior, the economic consequences of the creation of the Portuguese dominion were immense. They quickly established near total control of the spice trade. An abundance of wealth poured into the Portuguese coffers in Lisbon. Portuguese colonies in Africa and Brazil added to the overflowing supply of valuable products. Gold came from Guinea, sugar from Madeira and Brazil, silk and porcelain from China, cotton textiles from the Indian towns of Cambay and Coromandel.

Spices were available from India and many of the Asian islands. Ceylon exported cinnamon, Indonesia and Malabar produced pepper. The spice islands in the Moluccas were especially bountiful. Mace and nutmegs were grown on Banda; cloves on the volcanic islands of Ternate, Tidore, and Ambon which with their deep, loamy, well-drained soil and warm, rainy climate were well suited to cultivation of the plant.

With this great geographic area within the Portuguese sphere of influence, the Portuguese seemed to possess the means to totally control the spice trade. Such a stranglehold on the flow of spices to Europe would obviously be to the great detriment of the Venetians, who were still dependent upon the desert caravan for the transport of the spices that they were able to procure.

The first effect of the Portuguese discovery and exploitation of the new trade routes upon the Venetian economy was immediate and drastic. Spices virtually disappeared from Alexandria, Cairo and Beirut, the cities where for centuries Venetian merchants had purchased the spices from the Arabian traders who had brought the precious commodities by desert caravan from Asia. Meanwhile, the spices flooded into Lisbon. The price of pepper at Lisbon fell by one-half. The price of the little pepper reaching Cairo rose to nearly ten times the Lisbon price.

The collapse of the overland trade routes also devastated the economy of Egypt. So angry was the Egyptian Sultan at the precipitous decline in his income that he informed the Pope that Egypt would bombard the Holy Places of Jerusalem if the Portuguese did not cease their activities in India. It was an empty threat. The Holy Places were a popular destination for Christians making a pilgrimage to Jerusalem. The money derived from these pilgrims was considerable, and the Sultan, after thinking about the effect the destruction of the Holy Places would have on his royal treasury, decided to seek other means of thwarting the Portuguese advance. He decided to send a large naval armada to India to defeat the Portuguese at sea. The Portuguese, anticipating such an Egyptian response, however, were well prepared and destroyed the Egyptian fleet. After that, the Egyptians never again challenged the Portuguese. The Portuguese control of the spice trade was nearly absolute.

Most of the Portuguese spices were sold to the Germans, with whom a profitable exchange was soon established. The German merchants supplied the goods that were needed by the Portuguese. The Germans were the main suppliers of the silver, copper and lead produced in Europe. These metals were much in demand in India, and facilitated there the purchase of the Asian spices. The German merchants also provided shipbuilding materials, such as wood, pitch and tar that were in short supply in Portugal.

Within a few years of da Gama's first voyage to Asia, the Portuguese had eliminated all challengers for the control of the spice trade. Although the control was not complete, other buyers of spices had to scramble to find spices that had somehow escaped the Portuguese net. In 1504, the Venetian galleys sailed to Alexandria, as they had done for centuries, to buy from the Muslims the spices transported by desert caravans from Asia. The

Venetians to their dismay found not a single sack had reached Egypt. Not a single peppercorn.

In the decade following 1505, nearly eighty percent of the spices entering Europe, entered through Lisbon. Between 25,000 and 30,000 hundredweight were imported each year at Lisbon. In contrast, imports at Venice averaged only 7,500 hundredweight per year during the same period. Spice supplies from the traditional overland routes became so scarce that in 1514 Venetian merchants themselves had to buy supplies at Lisbon to meet their commitments to customers in eastern Europe. In 1509, the Venetians were forced to discontinue direct sale of spices in France, England, and Holland. Sales in those countries by Venetian merchant galleys were not resumed for twenty-five years.

Nevertheless, the Venetian merchants, such as Signor Priuli, who prophesied the imminent collapse of Venice's economy, were overly pessimistic. The success the Portuguese had in the first years of their presence in Asia was mainly achieved by disrupting the established trade patterns. Within two decades, the Muslim middlemen were able to re-establish their dominant position throughout most of Asia. New channels of supply were developed to circumvent the dislocation caused by the Portuguese presence.

As a result, after the period of initial turmoil subsided the Venetians were almost always able to obtain spices in sufficient quantity to remain an economic force, albeit often a much reduced economic force, in European trade. The spice growing regions in Asia were too large and too dispersed for the Portuguese to control to the extent of completely cutting the supply line to Venice. Moreover, the Portuguese quickly realized that they could maximize their own profits by keeping the prices of spices high. Accordingly, they refrained from entering into a ruinous trade war with the Venetians.

In time, the market sorted itself out. Portugal became the principal supplier to those European countries facing the Atlantic, and Venice retained most of the trade within southern Germany, Turkey, and the rest of eastern Europe. Scholars who have studied sixteenth century economic history agree that Venice continued to profit greatly from the spice trade down to 1570 despite Portugal's opening of the sea route to India.

Moreover, like all successful entrepreneurs, the Venetians quickly learnt that a clever marketing strategy was always useful. In this regard they enhanced their position by spreading the rumor that the Portuguese spices deteriorated in quality while exposed to sea air in the holds of ships. Only by being carried on the backs of camels through the Arabian Desert, the Venetians assured the cooks and housewives of Europe, could spices retain their freshness and flavor.

In fact, the spices sold by the Portuguese often were of inferior quality to those sold by the Venetians. The Venetians purchased their spices from Muslim middlemen, who dealt directly with the Indian suppliers. The Portuguese dealt with the same suppliers as the Muslims, but unlike the Muslims, the Portuguese were inexperienced in the trade, and were not knowledgeable about the variation in quality of the spices. The Indians, recognizing an unparalleled opportunity of facing an innocent, but avaricious buyer, unloaded on the Portuguese all the spices that did not meet the standards demanded by the Muslims. Whatever the reasons, the price of pepper remained high, and the spice trade for Portuguese and Venetian alike remained highly profitable.

To enforce Portuguese government control of the spice trade, King Manuel established the *Casa da Índia* to act as the bureaucratic agency overseeing and controlling trade policy. The first duty of the *Casa da Índia* was to make sure that the king got his twenty-five percent share of the imported goods. A second responsibility was to fix the price of the spices. No merchant was allowed to sell below the price established by the *Casa da Índia.*

The fixed prices not surprisingly allowed for a generous profit margin. In 1505, the purchase price of pepper in India was three ducats per hundredweight, the selling price in Lisbon, 22 ducats, a 733 percent markup. For cinnamon, the respective prices were 3.50 ducats and 25 ducats, a markup of 714 percent. The markup for cloves was 800 percent, for ginger, 2500 percent, and for nutmeg, an extraordinary 7500 percent. Even allowing for transportation costs, spoiled cargo, and ships lost at sea, the merchant realized a net profit of, at least, 150 percent. With luck, the net profit reached 400 percent.

The common seamen did not so benefit, however. Upon returning to Portugal, the seamen were searched for contraband goods. The *Casa da Índia* was very concerned that the poorly paid sailor, who had served his king and country at great personal risk, might try to smuggle into Portugal some untaxed goods. The bureaucrats at the *Casa da Índia* were particularly distressed at the thought that a returning seaman might smuggle into the country a few jewels hidden in his clothing or personal belongings. After 1507, though, each seaman was allowed to buy in India a certain quantity of jewels and spices for resale back home. The amount allotted to each seaman depended upon his rank and grade.

The *Casa da Índia* was housed in a large, luxurious building specially constructed for its use. But although the building was completed in 1514, so rapidly did the spice trade grow that a new and larger building was needed by mid-century.

Working closely with the *Casa* was a separate agency reporting to an administrator called the "provedor." He acted as a modern day Secretary of the Navy. He was responsible for outfitting, provisioning, and arming of the fleets, for recruiting the crews, and for providing the required navigational instruments and charts. In time, he also acquired responsibility for the waterfront and wharves.

The Portuguese government also established an agency in Antwerp, a city, which due to its location, became the principal marketplace for the sale of spices by the Portuguese to the merchants of Europe.

Portugal, though, despite the wealth of its trade, did not to become a dominant power in Europe. In their determination to create an empire encircling the world, the Portuguese overextended themselves. In addition to colonies in Africa and Asia, the Portuguese also established, in the Americas, the colony of Brazil, which was a land of unlimited resources and potential.

To support this far flung empire, the Portuguese did not have enough men or ships. In population, Portugal was one of the smallest of all the countries of Europe. Portugal had far fewer people than her competitors— Spain, Britain, France, and Holland—in the emerging race for empires. In the sixteenth century, the exodus of young, Portuguese men to Brazil and to the Far East, where they hoped to make their fortunes, so depleted the number of experienced sailors available for manning the ships that the Portuguese often had to rely upon seamen from other nations simply to get the ships to sea.

The ships themselves were also in short supply. Building a wooden ship, capable of voyages of over a year in duration, was a labor intensive enterprise. In a country with a labor shortage, the number of ships built was of necessity restricted. To make matters worse, Portugal lacked readily available forests of oak and pine from which to obtain the wood to build the ships. Many of the oak and pine forests that Portugal did possess were in the mountains, where few roads existed. Thus, getting the trees from the forest to the seacoast was a task in itself. Much of this shipping deficiency was alleviated, though, by building ships in India, where abundant stands of teak provided an excellent wood for the construction of sea-going ships.

The Portuguese were also hampered in their ability to monopolize the spice trade by the enormous obstacles their ships had to overcome in making the voyage around the African continent and across the Indian

Ocean to the Asian ports, and finally in returning to
Europe. The voyage from Lisbon to Goa was nearly
fourteen thousand miles, which was about three times
as long as the journeys Columbus made from Spain to
America. The number of ships lost at sea was
extraordinary by any standard. Even Columbus, on his
maiden voyage to America with three ships, lost the
Santa María off the coast of Hispaniola in the
Caribbean.

Making the voyages from Portugal to India still more
hazardous was the fact that over this entire distance few
friendly ports existed to provide a safe haven from a
storm or a secure place to repair a damaged ship. Once
out of sight of the European coast, the Portuguese
seamen and travelers were alone for most of the
duration of the voyage, which would take over half a
year. Any mishap was likely to have tragic
consequences. Adding to the perilousness of the
voyages was the problem that the simple wooden ships
of the period had not been designed to endure such
long journeys.

Thus, the high probability of disaster at sea was the ever
present threat on every voyage to Asia during the
sixteenth and seventeenth centuries. Shipping records
indicate that for every two ships leaving Portugal for
India during this period, only one returned. Of course,
not all that failed to return were shipwrecked. Many
safely reached their Asian ports, but were in a too
distressed condition to venture to return. Others were
diverted to trade solely between Asian ports.
Nevertheless, numerous were the vessels that came to
an untimely end by smashing upon unseen reefs and

shoals off the African coast, after which the ships were pounded to pieces by the remorseless waves while their surviving crewmen and passengers, if any survived, struggled to reach the hostile and barren shore, where new hardships awaited them. The sea took a grievous toll.

The Portugal to India journey was dependent upon the seasonal strength and direction of the winds, and, in the Indian Ocean, upon the monsoons. The best time for a ship to leave Lisbon was in late February or early March. A ship departing at this time would round the Cape of Good Hope in June and reach Goa, the Portuguese outpost in India in September or October. It was a voyage of seven months. For the return voyage, late December was the best time to depart, resulting, if all went well, with an arrival at a home port in Portugal in mid-summer, a year and a half after first leaving. A ship leaving late in either direction would face violent and terrifying storms of hurricane magnitude at the Cape of Good Hope.

The Cape of Good Hope is one of the most fearsome places on earth for mariners. At its latitude cold Antarctic wind and ocean currents collide with hot winds and tropical oceanic currents funneled south by the African continent. At the boundary of these sharply contrasting climatic systems, ferocious storms develop frequently. They are a source of concern for today's seaman. In the sixteenth century, sailors on small wooden ships, driven only by cloth sails, faced a horrific ordeal in these storms. For good reason was the Cape of Good Hope originally named *Cabo Tormentoso*— Stormy Cape.

For the Portuguese returning home, the island of St. Helena in the south Atlantic offered a welcome haven and a place for recovery and celebration after having survived the grueling ordeal of sailing around the Cape. One such traveler, believed the island to be a gift of a loving and Roman Catholic god. "The island of St. Helena," he wrote, "serves, on the passage from one world to another, as a resting place for the sea-borne European, and it has always been a hospitable inn, maintained by divine clemency in the middle of immense seas for the Catholic fleets of the East."

The Portuguese allowed pigs, goats and fowl to populate the island so that the voyagers would be assured of finding provisions. Unfortunately for the Portuguese, this haven was not to last. By the end of the sixteenth century, English and Dutch raiders had discovered that St. Helena was an excellent place to capture the spice-laden Portuguese merchantships returning from Asia. At the hands of these pirates from the north, the Portuguese suffered greatly. So it came to pass that the island of St. Helena did not offer "divine clemency for the Catholic fleets of the East" after all. In 1592, the King of Portugal forbade any of his nation's ships to stop at St. Helena.

The caravel, the type of ship used by Prince Henry the Navigator for the first Portuguese expeditions down the African coast, was not equal to the task of sailing to India and back. Although its maneuverability and shallow draft allowed the caravel to sail close to the coast, thereby making it an excellent vessel for exploration, its small size and light construction made it a poor choice for the long voyages in heavy seas that were the essential characteristics of the journey to India. Above all, the caravel simply did not have enough cargo capacity to economically justify its use in the trading voyages to the Far East.

The type of ship chosen for the spice trade was called a *nao*, a word that literally means a large ship. These ships were also known as carracks. The word carrack is of Arabic origin, and means cargo ship. The carracks were up to five times larger than the caravels, and were more strongly constructed. They were built heavy and wide so as to survive the storms of the Cape of Good Hope. They had more masts than the caravels, three as against two, and carried much more sail. Their main advantage was that they were big. The carracks were the supertankers of the sixteenth century. Between seven and fourteen of these ships sailed every year from Lisbon for India.

Although the carracks were the biggest ships of their day, they were not pleasant ships on which to sail. The living conditions on board were very disagreeable. Except when on deck, seamen and passengers spent their time in the dark spaces below deck. Since the ships had no portholes, the only light and fresh air to penetrate the dank interior came through the open hatches. Of course, when the weather was bad, the hatches were closed. Besides the lack of light, there was a lack of space. Rats, cockroaches, lice, and other vermin abounded, and the general lack of cleanliness created an awesome stench that was impossible to remove.

Preparing hot food was difficult. Since these were wooden ships, a fire on board would have devastating

results, and was a seaman's worst fear. Accordingly, on
small ships, hot food was only prepared in a firebox
located on the deck. To minimize the risk of fire, the
firebox was placed against the lee rail, where the wind
would most likely blow overboard any wayward sparks
and embers. As an added precaution, a bucket of water
was always nearby. On large ships, a galley with a
fireplace was placed in the hold at the bottom of the
ship. A lead-lined chimney rose through the decks
above and vented the smoke and heat.

Despite their seaworthiness, the carracks frequently met
with disaster during their voyages. The toll in lives was
of tragic proportions. Few of those on board a
shipwrecked vessel survived the ordeal. Most drowned
without the barest chance of reaching shore. Those who
did reach land often died of exposure or starvation, or
from injuries received in their flight. On a few
occasions, however, some of those shipwrecked were
able to reach safety and to return to Portugal, where
they wrote of their experiences. The tales they told
make gristly reading.

One such shipwreck, where a few people survived to
tell of their ordeal, was the wreck of the *Santiago* on
August 19, 1585. The ship left Lisbon for India on April
1, about one month later than was considered prudent
by most seamen. On board the ship were 450 people.
Three days out of Lisbon, the *Santiago* ran into a violent
storm, which nearly caused the ship to go down in
home waters. But the storm abated and the ship
continued on its way. As it approached the equator, it
was becalmed for sixteen days.

Aboard the vessel, the passengers and crew endured a heat wave that was "so intense and burning," wrote one mariner, "that the heat of Alentejo seemed like the climate of Norway in comparison." The wind, in time, picked up and the ship continued south. Despite its late start from Lisbon and the delays enroute, the *Santiago* rounded the Cape of Good Hope without difficulty. The worst of the voyage appeared to be behind them.

August 19 was hot and sunny. The ship sailed northeastward, past the coast of Mozambique. A series of treacherous shoals called the *Baixos da Judia* was known to be nearby. By nightfall, the captain estimated the ship's position at a point past the dreaded Baixos. Although the shoals had not been sighted, the captain believed that the crew had simply failed to observe the shoals while passing them. The captain was wrong. The shoals were directly in front of them. During the night, after most of the passengers and crew had gone to sleep, the ship smashed into the reefs. The ship foundered on the submerged rocks, but did not sink. The hull was broken. The mainmast had snapped at its base, and lay in shambles on the deck.

In the darkness of the night, people screamed, or cried, or wandered about helpless and confused. As the sky brightened with the coming of the dawn, the seafarers could see the extent of the disaster that had befallen them. The ship was damaged beyond repair. It had broken into three sections, and had come to rest on a coral reef, which was a few miles long at low tide. At high tide, little of the reef remained above water. The coral was of many colors; white, and brown, and pink and red. The red coral was as sharp as glass, and quickly cut a person's skin on contact. Beyond the reef, no land could be seen. These shipwrecked souls, of course, had no means of communicating their need for help to anyone on shore. They were alone. Every passenger and crewman said confession, and prepared to die.

The captain and around fifty others got into the only undamaged lifeboat. As they pushed off from the stricken ship, the captain, whose incompetence had caused the wreck in the first place, told the four hundred stranded survivors that he and the others in the lifeboat were only making an exploratory trip and would return shortly. Needless to say, they never did.

The castaways who remained on board the *Santiago* desperately began to seek a means to save themselves. Some tried to gather up the ship timber that had washed unto the reef. But most who attempted this strategy were swept into the sea by a fierce undertow, and drowned. Others still on the *Santiago* repaired a damaged launch and built rafts. At high tide, the two dozen or so who could get into the launch or onto the rafts cast away, leaving the hundreds on the ship to their inevitable fate. One of those on the launch described the scene:

"The day's spectacle was the saddest and most heart rendering that could be seen. The reef was full of people who had been refused entrance by both the launch and the rafts; the tide was coming in and there was no longer footing for them; those who could not swim began to drown.

"And those who could swim postponed their death but for a short time, because they too were destined to drown. A number of men swam in the water, some after the rafts, others after the boat, and they all drowned. ... Those who were traveling in the boat looked back at the ruins and the broken quarterdecks of the ship and saw that there still were many people on them, and all of them had red tasseled bonnets on their heads and they were wearing jackets like those of reapers cut out of scarlet cloth as well as some colored silks that they had found on the ship; it would have been a beautiful sight at a happier time."

The wreck of the *Santiago* was not an isolated incident. The carracks were often built larger than could be done safely, using the construction knowledge of the time. As the size of a ship increased, stresses on various structural members increased exponentially. The points of failure would only be discovered on a trial and error basis. Unfortunately for the Portuguese, failure was likely to occur in the midst of a violent storm in the emptiness of the Indian Ocean hundreds, even thousands, of miles from a friendly port.

As the builders of the biggest ships, the Portuguese were the first to learn that big size can bring big problems. In an effort to reduce the number of disasters at sea, the King of Portugal decreed in 1570 that no ship should be built larger than 450 tons, which was roughly one-fourth the size of the largest carracks. The limit was later raised to 600 tons. Nevertheless, the decrees were widely ignored. And the shipwrecks continued.

In 1554, only one ship in a fleet of five reached Lisbon after sailing from Goa. In other years, the casualty rate was similar.

In 1589, the *São Thomé* was one of those lost. A Portuguese chronicler named Diogo do Couto later described the *São Thomé's* last moments:

"The wind was whistling on every side, and it seemed to be saying to them, 'Death, Death' ... Within the ship there could only be heard sighings, sobs, screams, weeping, and cries for mercy. ... Between the decks it seemed as though the spirits of the damned had been turned loose with the noise of all the things that were floating in the water and banging against each other, and they rolled from one side of the ship to another in such a way that to those who descended beneath decks the scene seemed like the last judgment."

The toll in human lives was appalling even for those ships breaking up within sight of land. The *São Bento* was one such case. It had been called "the biggest and best vessel sailing on the Indies route." In 1554, it was wrecked just off the African shore. One survivor described the experience:

"The sea was curdled with crates, spars, barrels, and every diversity of things which appear at the untimely hour of shipwreck; and as they were floating in the water all mixed up with the people who were swimming to land, it was a fearful thing to see, and it is a pitiable thing to tell of the carnage that the fury of the sea caused among them.

"All of them suffered a different torment: in one direction there were some persons who, being able to swim no more, struggled in the sea giving great and painful gasps from the quantity of water they had swallowed; there were others whose strength was even more exhausted and they commended themselves to the will of God, letting themselves with the last cry go silently to the bottom; there were other swimmers who were killed by the crates and boxes which pressed against them and stunned them so that the waves could finish them up by sledging them against the rocks; others were pierced in various parts of the body by the spikes in the spars or pieces of ship on which they tried to push their way to shore; and everywhere the water was stained as red as the blood itself which ran from the wounds of those Portuguese whose days thus came to an end."

A contributing factor in most of the shipwrecks was the overloading of the vessels. With only a dozen or so ships making the voyage to and from India every year, the tendency was to cram every space with salable cargo. The fault was with the merchants, who wanted to maximize their profit despite the risk, and with the captain, officers, and crew, who had their own private hoard of salable merchandise.

Such overloading substantially reduced the maneuverability and seaworthiness of the ships. It was clearly a factor in the wreck of the *São Bento*, as the survivor, quoted above, relates:

"As soon as dawn began to appear, we turned in the direction of the beach to look for some clothing to cover our nakedness. The beach we found completely covered with dead bodies, with such ugly and deformed expressions that the painful manner of their death was very clear. Some were stretched out on the rocks and others beneath them, and for many of them there were only arms or legs or heads; some had their faces covered with sand or boxes or one of a hundred other things.

"And the space occupied by the infinity of lost cargo was not a small one, because as far as one could cast his eyes from one end of that beach to another, it was full of odoriferous drugs and an unimaginable diversity of possessions and precious things, many of them lying alongside their owner, to whom they could be of no assistance in his present state, and indeed though they were dearly treasured by him during his lifetime, they were with their weight the cause of his death."

For the Portuguese, who were able to safely reach the African shore, the ordeal was not over. They were now cast up on a desolate and sparsely populated land, far from any European outpost. The natives were not friendly, and were too poor to offer much assistance, anyhow. Of those supposed lucky Portuguese who survived the wreck and made it ashore, only one in ten lived to see Portugal again.

Wealth from trade with Asia was not to be achieved easily nor without much human suffering.

Despite the maritime difficulties in establishing a powerful presence half way around the world, the Portuguese continued to engage in activities designed to disrupt the Venetian source of supply. If the spices did not reach Venice, the Portuguese could charge high prices and not worry about the competition. All in all, such a prospect offered a vision of a most profitable future.

The spices that made their way to Venice began their oceanic journey on the coast of India, from whence they were transported by Muslim shippers across the Arabian Sea to ports on the Red Sea. The Portuguese resolved to destroy this Arabian Sea trade route. To this end, they built the fortresses at Malacca, Ormuz, and the other vital geographical points and sent forth ships, armed with cannon, to interdict the Venice bound spices.

But the fortresses were expensive to maintain, and they could not be built everywhere. In addition, large numbers of expensive warships, with the costly requirement of crews, armaments and supplies were needed to have a sizable impact on the amount of spices reaching Venice. Although the spice trade was enormously profitable, the Portuguese could not afford the expense of eliminating the Venetian competition.

The Portuguese tried to cut the Venetian supply line, but that effort was not successful. Aside from the expense of interdicting the spices headed for Venice, the first problem encountered by the Portuguese was the counter-measures taken by the Muslim traders. Determined to maintain their own profitable business, the Muslims vigorously defended their ships and supply depots. Although the Muslims were not able to defeat the Portuguese, they were able to inflict heavy casualties upon the Portuguese and to hold onto a substantial portion of the spice trade.

The second problem faced by the Portuguese was the corruption of their own officials. Poorly paid and open to temptation, the Portuguese military commanders charged with enforcing the Portuguese policy were frequently induced to place self-interest ahead of government interest. One Venetian representative, in fact, noted that the spices that were carried to Egypt had been "allowed to pass by the Portuguese soldiers who govern India, for the soldiers in that region can only make a living by selling cinnamon, cloves, nutmeg, mace, ginger and pepper for their own profit, against the commands of their king."

Another source of spices to the Middle East was provided by the Portuguese themselves through a confused political path. The Portuguese were faced for various reasons with the political necessity of supporting the Persians. The Middle East being the Middle East, Middle Eastern political alliances in the sixteenth century were no less complex than Middle Eastern political alliances in the twentieth-first century. The Portuguese supported the Persians in a war against the Turks, because the Portuguese were also at war with the Turks. The form of the Portuguese aid to the Persians was the granting of a share of the spice trade. The Persians, in turn, sold the spices they received to the Venetians, who sold them, with the usual middleman's markup, to the Germans, French and English in competition with the Portuguese, who had supplied the spices in the first place.

For these reasons, the Portuguese were not able to greatly reduce Venice's participation in the spice trade, except during the first decade or two. Scholars who have studied the effects of Portuguese competition upon Venetian trade find that Venice's trade in the main recovered during the sixteenth century. For a few years in the 1560's, the quantity of spices sold by the Venetians even equaled that of the pre-discovery years. By mid-century, Venetian merchants had reestablished themselves as the favored suppliers of spices to Germany, Italy and most of France.

Thus the Portuguese were able to diminish but not eliminate the supply of spices to the Venetians. The vastness of the spice growing area, the frequent Portuguese losses due to catastrophes at sea, the corruption of the Portuguese officials, and the vagaries of political alliances, all played a role in insuring that Venice retained a good portion of the European spice trade. Loss of the spice trade did not cause the economic collapse of Venice.

Even so, Venice had other problems to worry about.

During the first decades of the sixteenth century, the Venetians were most concerned, not with the endangered spice routes, but with an intractable war against neighboring European states. In 1508, France, Spain, the Vatican, the German states of the Holy Roman Empire, Hungary, Savoy and the Italian states of Mantua and Ferrara formed an alliance in opposition to Venice. This alliance, known as the League of Cambrai, opposed the expansion of Venetian power on the Italian mainland.

The Vatican was particularly outraged at Venice's seizure of papal land. After Pope Alexander VI died in 1503 and before a new pope could be chosen, Venice occupied the papal territories of Forli, Cesena, Rimini, Faenza and Imola. These were fertile agricultural territories and could supply Venice with a reliable source of wheat and other grains.

Julius II, who became pope in 1503 after the brief papacy of Pius III, was not pleased. He allied with

France and the other states aggrieved by Venice to form the League of Cambrai. The decisive battle of the resulting war occurred on May 14, 1509 at the town of Agnadello, around thirty kilometers east of Milan. By the end of the day, the Venetian army had been decisively beaten. In the months that followed, the Venetians were driven from most of the territories that they had occupied.

The defeat was experienced with shock and dismay in Venice. Girolamo Priuli wrote in his diary, "No one ever imagined that the mainland territory of Venice could be lost and destroyed within fifteen days, as we have now seen."

These were bleak days for the Serene Republic. Along with the first effects of the Portuguese disruption of the spice trade, the defeat at Agnadello resulted in economic depression, little money, and few ships venturing forth in trade.

Nevertheless, Doge Leonardo Loredan was optimistic. Venice still had a large army. The tide would turn. And it did. Over the next eight years, primarily by playing one opponent off against its other enemies, Venice recovered most of the lost territory.

But even as the war against the League of Cambrai and the challenge of the Portuguese competition for the spice trade preoccupied the minds of the merchants of Venice, the Serene Republic had to face economic storms from other directions. Reduction in its share of the world spice trade was only one factor causing Venice's decline as an economic power. Venice still faced a stew of economic problems.

Yet, the problems of the spice trade and the wars with neighboring European states notwithstanding, Venice was about to enter the most vibrant period in its long history. Over the next century, Titian, Jacopo Sansovino, Andrea Palladio, Baldassare Longhena, Antonio Vivaldi and Galileo Galilei would immeasurably enrich the cultural, artistic and scientific heritage of Venice and the world.

Chapter 10: Venice in the Age of Jacopo Sansovino

By 1500 the Portuguese voyages of discovery had opened the spice trade to sea-borne competition. In time the new spice trade routes to Asia would adversely affect Venetian prosperity. All that, however, was decades into the future.

A traveler in Venice as word of the Portuguese discoveries filtered through the merchant community would not have noticed anything unusual. In the Doge's Palace the Portuguese venture was just one more problem to be resolved. On the Piazza San Marco merchants still engaged in their customary activities. For most people life was unchanged.

Yet if we could look back to Venice in 1500 as the Republic stood on the eve of its most challenging era we would notice a much less familiar place. In physical appearance, Venice looked quite a bit different in 1500 than the Venice one sees today. San Marco's Basilica of course was already old as was the Doge's Palace. Many important churches and palazzos had also been built. But in the main, most of the grand buildings one sees in present day Venice were built in the century after the Portuguese became competitors in the spice trade.

In 1500, Venice's golden age was still ahead of her. Contrary to what most people are taught, Vasco da Gama's journey around the Cape of Good Hope was not the beginning of Venice's decline. In art and architecture Venice was about to flourish.

One way to visualize late fifteenth century Venice as the merchants mulled over the future of the spice trade is to look closely at the paintings of that era.

The most noteworthy painting of the period is Gentile Bellini's *Procession of the True Cross in the Piazza San Marco*. Here we have a view of the Piazza San Marco as it existed in 1496. The Basilica, Campanile and Doge's Palace are as they are today. But the other buildings surrounding the piazza are older and less attractive than the present structures.

The Procuratie Vecchie and Procuratie Nuovo which today comprise the north and south sides of the piazza were yet to be built in 1496. The Torre dell'Orologia – the Clocktower – that one sees today also was not yet built. The piazza itself was paved for the first time in 1267 with reddish bricks laid out in a herringbone pattern. The elegant design of stone paving that every visitor walks on today would not be put in place until 1723.

A second painting that allows us to grasp a sense of Venice at the beginning of the sixteenth century is Vittore Carpaccio's *Miracles of the Relic of the True Cross*. This painting shows the Rialto Bridge as a wooden structure lined with shops. The present stone bridge would not be built until 1588.

The style of the fourteenth and fifteenth century buildings is known as Venetian Gothic. It was greatly influenced by architectural developments in France and Germany. It also contained elements of Byzantine and Islamic architecture acquired from Venice's neighbors to the east. The style had to be modified to fit Venetian conditions however.

The Venetians were forced to change the Northern Gothic form of construction so as to be structurally lighter and less massive. The pilings pounded into the mud and sand of the lagoons simply would not support the heavy stone structures that were typically found in the north. The Venetian buildings were thus made mainly of brick and had roofs of wood.

The distinguishing features of Venetian Gothic are the pointed arch window and the quatrefoil – or four-leaf clover – tracery motif. These features reappear repeatedly in Venetian palazzi.

The quintessential gothic landmark is the waterfront facade of the Doge's Palace. Although the Doge's Palace was built and rebuilt over the centuries, the waterfront facade was designed in 1340. The visitor can easily observe the pointed arches and ornamental motif of quatrefoil tracery.

The Doge's Palace also contains decorative elements such as the rooftop cresting and the patterned brickwork of the facade that find their heritage in the cultures of the eastern Mediterranean.

Outstanding examples of fifteenth century palaces are Ca' d' Oro, Palazzo Giustinian, Ca' Foscari, and Palazzo Bernardo. The patricians who built these palaces copied many of the motifs of the Doge's Palace. By this means the noblemen not only created structures of great beauty, but also made the subtle statement that they were members of the ruling class.

Ecclesiastical structures of the period such as San Stefano, Santi Giovanni e Paolo and the Frari are less grand on the exterior than their secular counterparts, but richly interplay light and color inside in their naves and chapels.

The Venetians of the fifteenth century were very content with their modified Gothic-Byzantine-Islamic architecture, even though, in Florence, not far to the south, the Renaissance was beginning to flourish. The Venetians cared not for Brunelleschi's dome on the Santa Maria del Fiore.

Historians have a number of theories as to the Venetians early reluctance to embrace the Renaissance. One is that the Renaissance in the fifteenth century was a Florentine thing, and the patricians of Venice were not about to concede artistic preeminence to their counterparts in the neighboring Italian city. A second theory is that Venice traded with the east and north and would naturally have been most influenced by the artistic developments in the cultures of those regions.

Nevertheless, the Renaissance came to Venice, and it came at the same time as Venice's loss of monopoly power over the spice trade.

The blow rendered to the Venetian economy by the Portuguese discovery of the sea routes to the riches of Asia should have crippled Venetian artistic and architectural development. It didn't. One reason was that the adverse effects of trade competition in spices were much less that is commonly supposed. Another factor is that textile manufacturing, shipbuilding and commercial shipping continued to be prosperous and significant sources of wealth for the Venetians.

Whatever the reasons, Venice in 1500 was about to enter the century of its greatest artistic and architectural achievement. One can observe the vitality of the sixteenth century directly in the Piazza San Marco, which is surrounded on three sides by buildings of the sixteenth century and later.

The Gothic period of Venetian architecture came to a graceful close. The Renaissance style that had long flourished in the rest of Italy finally reached Venice.

Opposite the Doge's Palace is the Libreria – the Library of San Marco – a magnificent building in the Renaissance style. When completed it was called "the richest, most ornate building since Antiquity." It was designed by Jacopo Sansovino the architect most responsible for the sixteenth century transformation of Venetian architecture.

Sansovino was not the first architect to bring the Renaissance style to Venice. His most prominent predecessor was Mauro Codussi, a stonemason who was born near Bergamo in 1440. Codussi moved to Venice as a young man, undoubtedly hoping to find opportunities in the Serene Republic that were not available in his native region of Lombardy.

Codussi's masterpiece is San Michele in Isola, a lovely, small church with a simple, unadorned facade of white, Istrian limestone.

At San Michele, Codussi introduced to Venetian ecclesiastical building the use of classical forms, such as the rounded arch and the triangular pediment. The use of white limestone for the facade instead of the traditional dark colored brick also reinforced the classical idea of a Greek temple, and endowed San Michele with the image when seen from afar of a heavenly apparition sitting upon the water. With its purity of form and shimmering whiteness, San Michele on which construction began in 1469 undoubtedly influenced Palladio a century later when he designed San Giogio Maggiore and Il Redentore.

In 1536, the Venetian government commissioned Sansovino to design a new mint or Zecca. A year later, he received a commission for an even more majestic building, the Libreria, to be built facing the piazzetta across from the Doge's Palace. The Zecca was placed beside the Libreria. Every visitor to Venice walks by these magnificent buildings many times.

The Libreria is one of the great buildings of the Renaissance. Sansovino's design invoked the masterful use of the Doric and Ionic classical orders, harmonious balance and elegant proportions to create a building that is sumptuous without being overbearing.

The Libreria was designed as a place of scholarship and learning. That it was built in the center of the city in Venice's most prominent public place is in itself a statement of the importance the Venetian state placed upon intellectual values.

Thus the buildings of the Piazza San Marco represent what the Venetians considered most worthy. The first is San Marco's Basilica, the center of religious life. The second is the Doge's Palace, the seat of government.

And the third is the Libreria, the cornerstone of the Venetians' respect for scholarship and education. The Venetians were men of business. They were also men who examined the arts, the sciences, and the state of their existence beyond the counting house.

Yet, in the sixteenth century, the area around the Libreria thrived with the activity of daily life. Vegetable, fish and meat vendors sold their products from open stalls on the Piazzetta. The ground floor of the Zecca was occupied by a seller of cheese and salami. On the north side of the Piazza in the Procuratie Vecchie, cobblers, engravers, tailors and painters rented shops open to the public concourse.

In 1538, Sansovino was asked to build another structure, a Loggetta – a meeting place for nobles – to be located at the base of the Campanile in the Piazza San Marco. No expense was spared on its construction. In it Sansovino used an abundance of red, white and dark green marble. It was decorated with bronze statues.

Sansovino's services were also requested by the wealthy merchants, who like their government, spent lavishly during these years. During this period, he built the Palazzo Dolfin and the Palazzo Corner, private residences that equaled in grandeur all previously built mansions.

Venetian painting of the period was also transformed by the humanistic, more natural style of the Renaissance. The most significant painter of the early sixteenth century was Giovanni Bellini.

Giovanni Bellini was the son of a highly regarded painter and the younger brother of another. As an innovator and master of the new ideas of the Renaissance, though, Giovanni was markedly superior to his father and brother and to all other Venetian painters of his day. He brought light, atmosphere and color to painting. Moreover, as a teacher, he inspired Giorgione and Titian, Venice's two greatest painters, to experiment with color, drama and emotional feeling as artistic expression.

His most important works can be seen in the Frari, the Gallerie dell'Accademia, Santi Giovanni e Paolo, and San Giovanni Crisostomo, a church designed by Mauro Codussi.

Chapter 11: Venetian Ships and Forests of Oak

The sixteenth century was an exceptional era for Venetian art and architecture. Money flowed into the construction of monumental churches, government buildings and private palaces. Titian and Veronese, Sansovino and Palladio, were leading Europe's artistic development. Yet the economic well-being of the republic was on shaky ground. Ironically, Venice reached its period of unquestioned artistic greatness at a time of gradual but nonetheless sustained decline in its most important industries, especially in the last decades of the century.

Venice was not ruined by the loss of its monopoly of the spice trade. At least, not in 1499. Nor in the decades immediately following the voyages of Vasco da Gama. The Portuguese quickly became vigorous competitors. But because the Portuguese demanded the highest possible prices for their spices; and because the voyages between Europe and Asia were costly in lives and ships; and because the Portuguese officials charged with enforcing Portuguese naval policy were underpaid and corrupt; and because the Portuguese government, itself, bowed to the political necessity of supplying spices to the Persians, who resold them to the Venetians, the quantity of spices reaching the Venetian merchants remained large, and in some years even returned to the same level as had existed prior to the Portuguese discovery of the sea route to Asia.

Spices reaching Venice by way of the traditional land routes continued to provide the Venetian merchants with a highly profitable commodity for sale. International trade in spices continued to be a prosperous sector of the Venetian economy. The opening of the sea route to the east, rendered Venice a staggering, but not a fatal, blow. Moreover, the trade lost to the Portuguese was made up in trade of other commodities such as cotton and wine.

But if Venice was not ruined by the Portuguese capture of a share of the spice trade, its economy nevertheless was no longer thriving in a state of vigorous expansion. Merchants and workers dependent upon the spice trade were hit hard. In addition, sectors of the Venetian economy not dependent on the spice trade were being clobbered by competition from countries with lower production costs.

Even before Vasco da Gama rounded the Cape of Good Hope, Venetian manufacturers with no connection to the spice trade had major problems with low cost foreign competitors.

One industry to suffer was shipbuilding. Venice thrived on commerce. Venetian merchants were the primary transporters of goods among the ports of the Mediterranean. This trade, besides being profitable in itself, had in earlier years generated hefty profits for the shipbuilding industry, which in fifteenth and sixteenth century Venice was a major source of employment.

As we have seen, the ships used for trade were of two different types. The first was the merchant galley. The merchant galley, or great galley as it was often called, was long, low and narrow. It used both sails and oarsmen as sources of power. These ships were used for the transport of spices and other commodities of high value. The use of both sails and oarsmen provided unique advantages. The sails captured the wind. The oarsmen provided a means of moving the ship forward when the wind died, and of maneuvering the ship into harbors when the wind was calm or blowing from land to sea. The oarsmen were also a fighting force capable of defending their ships and cargoes against armed attack by pirates.

With these characteristics, the merchant galley was well suited to the transportation of valuable goods in the Mediterranean, where the wind was often light and capricious, and a lightly defended ship was a much sought after prize by outlaw pirates. The merchant or great galleys were thus both fighting ships and carriers of high value cargoes. These great galleys were built by the state at the government shipyard called the *Arsenale*.

The second type of merchant ship was the round ship. It was a more typical sailing transport. It carried no oarsmen. It was high, wide, and much larger than the galley. The round ship was used to transport bulky, low value products, such as grain, olive oil and lumber. Few of these round ships ventured beyond the Adriatic, though some sailed to Syria for cotton and alum, to Crete for wine, and to other ports in the Black Sea and Mediterranean for grain, oil, salt. For the most part, the round ships were privately owned and privately built.

The building of these ships employed a large number of Venetian workers. Unfortunately, these workers did not prosper. Even before Vasco da Gama's historic voyage to India, the Venetian shipbuilding industry was in decline. The additional loss of a large portion of the spice trade to the Portuguese in the first decades of the sixteenth century had a further devastating impact upon the Venetian merchant galley fleet and upon the men who built and maintained the spice trade vessels.

For different reasons, the number of round ships being built was also sharply reduced. The Venetian shipyards, where the round ships were made, although not involved in the building of the galleys for the spice trade, faced for the first time competition from lower cost producers in other seacoast cities on the Adriatic.

This low cost foreign competition in the construction of round ships was another blow to the Venetian economy, already staggering from the decline in the spice trade. The emergence of low cost foreign competition in the shipbuilding industry actually preceded by a generation the Portuguese discovery of the sea route to Asia. In the 1460's, the Adriatic port of Istria became so successful in the low cost manufacture of barges and small ships that the Venetian shipbuilding industry fell into a recession. Within a few years the city of Ragusa on the Dalmatian coast became another competitor. Cities such as Istria and Ragusa had the advantages of lower labor costs and better access to timber. Because of this low cost competition, the Venetian shipbuilding industry was in a depressed state two decades before the Portuguese even reached India. And shipbuilding was vital to the prosperity of Venice.

The Signoria of Venice responded by providing large subsidies to those who built their ships in Venice. The subsidies were a heavy drain on the Venetian treasury, however, and were discontinued.

The Signoria further tried to prop up the shipbuilding industry by outlawing the use of ships owned by non-Venetians in Venetian trade. But the economic advantages of building ships in ports such as Ragusa and Istria rather than in Venice were so great that merchants evaded the law by any ingenious means. Venetians themselves could still legally buy Ragusan and Istrian ships, and they did. Ragusians and Istrians also established citizenship in communities within the domain of the Republic of Venice, and thereby became eligible to trade just as if they had been native born Venetians.

When the deterioration within the Venetian shipbuilding industry did not stop, laws were passed to close the loopholes. These new laws still sought to forbid from Venetian trade the use of ships built by non-Venetians. But the laws were easily evaded. A ship built elsewhere could be refitted in Venice and thus qualify as a Venetian ship. In addition, owners requested exemption from the law due to the scarcity of building materials, or to the need to import grain in times when the local harvest failed. As the sixteenth century progressed only very large ships, which required the labor of skilled tradesmen, continued to be constructed in Venice.

Although the foreign shipyards benefited from lower wage rates, their main advantage was access to abundant and low cost ship timber. This was an advantage that the Venetian shipbuilders did not have for the forests that supplied the Venetian shipbuilders were being stripped of their best and most accessible trees. The depletion of the Venetian forests thus became a leading factor in the collapse of Venice's shipbuilding industry. The simple availability of wood allowed other countries, such as England and the Netherlands, which had better access to ship timber to become the commercial carriers of Europe.

Ships were built of oak, larch, fir, elm and walnut. Oak was used for the basic structure of a ship—the hull, ribs and keel. It was also used for the outside planking. Larch, an inexpensive wood, was used for interior planking and cabins. Fir, strong and light, was the best wood for the masts and spars. Elm was superior for capstans and mastheads, as was walnut for rudders.

For the continued viability of the Venetian shipbuilding industry, however, the depletion of the forests of oak was especially serious, since oak was the best wood to use for building the basic framework of a ship. In the age of wooden ships, there was no effective substitute for this kind of tree. The advantages of oak were that it was strong, but not too heavy. It was tough, it was resilient, and it was durable. In addition, its tannic acid provided natural protection against wood boring worms and dry rot.

By the end of the fifteenth century, the number of oak trees sufficiently large for use as ship timber was declining at an alarming rate in the regions most accessible to Venice. The oak that was available became very expensive. Moreover, the Venetian naval authorities, concerned that the use of the remaining trees by builders of merchant vessels would not leave enough of the wood to meet the needs of the navy ships, placed severe restrictions on the cutting of the valued trees.

As early as 1470, the Signoria acted to halt the deforestation of the oak groves. It decreed that no oak, whether on public or private land, could be cut without prior approval from the Arsenale. But to meet the objections of villagers living near the forests, local authorities were allowed to give local residents the right to cut trees for houses, mills, bridges, and other necessary structures.

Needless to say, this local exception virtually negated the rule. Moreover, if legal authority to cut was denied, little could be done to prevent illegal cutting. Despite the need to preserve the trees for the future defense of the Republic, mighty oaks were still being felled for use in barrels and as firewood.

The cold and hungry peasant had more immediate needs for the wood than did the Signoria. The peasant, also needing the land for pasture and farmland, found ways to get rid of the trees.

Nevertheless, the Signoria, perhaps the world's first organization of conservationists, did accomplish many goals. To prevent cattle and sheep from wandering among the trees and eating the seedlings, barrier ditches were ordered dug around the oak groves. In addition, to prevent erosion seedlings were required to be planted in vulnerable areas. Inspectors were also appointed to force compliance with the law.

The effect of reserving the wood for naval ships, though, forced the builders of merchant ships to purchase oak timbers in foreign countries.

The purchase of ship timber in foreign countries, however, was only a short step from the more obvious remedy, the purchase of entire ships built in foreign countries. This quickly occurred. By the end of the seventeenth century, two of every three large Venetian merchant ships were foreign built. Most of these foreign built ships were constructed in Holland, where the Dutch had easy access to the abundant forests of Scandinavia.

The forests of Scandinavia, in addition to being bountifully endowed with fine oak, had the advantage of being infiltrated with many deep rivers and streams. Use of these waterways provided the only effective means of removing the large timbers from the forest, which rarely contained anything wider than mountain trails.

The forests of the Mediterranean, like the forests of the north, lacked usable roads. But the Mediterranean forests were also deficient in navigable waterways. Along with this accident of topography, the waterways of Scandinavia had the further advantage of being fed by heavy rainfall, which swelled the rivers and allowed continuous removal of the trees. In contrast, the rivers and streams of the Mediterranean region often dried to a trickle during the summer droughts. Thus even climate and the shape of the land conspired to give the Dutch and other northern shipbuilders an advantage over their Venetian counterparts.

By the seventeenth century, the Venetian merchant had little choice but to order ships from the Dutch. Since the Dutch by then were major competitors of the Venetians for the most lucrative commercial markets, the merchants of Venice were in the unhappy position of having to rely on a competitor for the very ships needed for the competition.

Chapter 12: Venetian Textiles and English Wool

With both shipbuilding and the spice trade in decline Venice faced an uncertain future.

Fortunately, the Venetians had other valuable sources of wealth. Besides the traditional industries that had made Venice rich, the manufacture of textiles and fine glassware added to the prosperity of the Republic. During the sixteenth century, as the shipbuilding industry and spice trade were hard hit by upstart competitors, the textile and luxury glassware industries expanded at a rapid pace. Yet, as in the shipbuilding industry, the low cost northern competitors – England and the Netherlands – would see the opportunity for profit in those areas where Venice was at a comparative disadvantage.

In the sixteenth and seventeenth centuries, the manufacture of textiles was as vital to a country's prosperity as the manufacture of steel, automobiles and semiconductors would be in the twentieth-first century. In some regions of Europe one worker out of every four worked in the textile or clothing trades. Only agriculture employed more people.

In the sixteenth century—that is in the century following the Portuguese discovery of the sea route to the spice producing regions of Asia—textile production in Venice more than made up for the loss of income from the diminished share of the spice trade. The boom in textiles, especially luxury textiles, propelled the

Venetian economy to new heights. Venice became the leading producer of textiles in Europe.

The textile merchant-entrepreneur of the Late Renaissance did not run a factory as is done in the modern sense of the word. Rather he hired independent tradesmen to perform specific tasks in their own homes and shops. These tradesmen – the spinners, weavers and dyers, who performed the essential textile manufacturing operations – usually owned their own equipment, such as the looms and spinning wheels, and functioned more as independent sub-contractors than as wage earning employees. The tradesmen, in turn, hired apprentices and helpers.

By modern standards the manufacture of cloth was very labor intensive. In Venice in the sixteenth century the average daily production of a silk-loom was less than four feet of cloth. A silk-loom set up for gold velvets produced on average less than fifteen inches per day of the costly fabric. But looms weaving less luxurious fabrics such as satin and damask still made only a yard and a half of finished cloth. In England at the same time, productivity was not much better. In Yorkshire, fifteen people typically worked for a week to weave a cloth twelve yards long and less than two yards wide.

One effect of the low productivity by our standards was that clothing was expensive. Most people owned only the clothes they wore. Even among the nobles and people of wealth, one's clothing was a status symbol worthy of being ostentatiously displayed.

Like the industries of current times, the manufacturers of textiles in the sixteenth century had to compete in the international market against producers from many counties. Also, like current times, some countries were newcomers to the field, able to undercut the established manufacturing nations with better products and lower prices, and ready to exploit any niche in the market left uncovered by the arrogant and over-confident established producers.

Venice proved to be highly vulnerable to these in-roads of foreign competition. During the first half of the seventeenth century—that is, during one man's lifetime, the textile industry in Venice went from a position of international dominance to a position of near total collapse.

The manufacture of cloth in Venice had a long history. At the time that the Portuguese were making the discoveries that would ultimately undermine the spice trade, the textile industry in Venice was of little importance. But as the spice trade slumped, the textile industry boomed.

The growth of woolen cloth production in Venice in the first half of the sixteenth century was phenomenal. Production rose three fold in the five years between 1516 and 1521. It doubled again by 1544. And doubled again by 1565. In the fifty years proceeding 1570, production of woolen cloth increased at an average rate of about nine percent per year. If a Wall Street stock analyst had wandered through Venice in the mid-sixteenth century he would have rated the textile industry a strong buy.

The robust expansion of the industry did not continue after 1570, however. Production grew slowly until the end of the century. In 1590, the number of woolen pieces produced was only slightly higher than it had been twenty five years earlier. In 1602, the peak was reached. After that, the trend was downward. During the decline, some years were better than others. There were upturns and revivals. There were periods when an upswing of several years gave the weavers and shop owners reason for optimism. The hope, however, was misplaced. The unmistakable long term trend of production during the seventeenth century was down. On average about two percent fewer pieces of wool cloth were produced each year of the seventeenth century than the year before. By 1700, production was one-tenth the level it had been a century earlier.

The Venetians sold their cloth in Germany and in the countries of the eastern Mediterranean. It was a high grade product made from the best English and Spanish wool. A particular grade of scarlet cloth was especially popular. In establishing a thriving textile industry in the early sixteenth century, Venice benefited from the turmoil ravaging other cloth producing cities. In terms of natural resources, though, Venice was ill suited to maintain a large cloth producing industry. Textile production was most easily achieved in areas that provided ample space for the weaving operations and quick running rivers to cleanse the cloth. Venice had neither ample space nor quick moving rivers. What Venice did have was political stability at a time when other textile producing centers were being devastated by war and internal upheaval.

In the first decades of the sixteenth century, the period in which the Venetian textile industry took hold, most of the cloth sold in European markets was produced in the cities located in the northern Italian mountains. However, during this period, these normally prosperous regions were plagued with misfortune. In the Lombardy region, persistent warfare was a disaster for the weavers of Milan, Bergamo and Pavia. In Brescia, military devastation reduced cloth production by eighty percent. In Como, the textile industry was crippled by a war between France and the Germany states, which disrupted Como's markets and sources of wool supply. Even Florence, in Tuscany, suffered from the depredations of the period.

Into this void, stepped the Venetians, ever ready to turn a profit when opportunity presented itself. Isolated from the warfare that afflicted the rest of northern Italy, Venice was quick to expand its cloth producing industry.

As the industry entered its mature phase in the last decades of the sixteenth century, the Venetians met increasing competition from other Italian states as the political situation in those states became more stable.

After 1570, the wars and civil discord in northern Italy ended, and the cities of Lombardy and Tuscany rebuilt their commercial enterprises. In Florence, Como and Bergamo, the textile producers rapidly expanded their businesses.

Venice felt the sting of competition. The competitors hit hardest in the markets of the eastern Mediterranean that were vital to Venetian interests. In 1578, a Venetian representative in Constantinople noted the change in the trade patterns, and warned that "there have appeared in this city cloths brought here by the Florentines. They are of excellent material and fine colors. ... There is, therefore, reason to fear that, owing to this competition, our own industry will lose both its reputation and its profits. Our merchants are very worried."

As the sixteenth century ended the demand for Venetian cloth changed from slow growth to steady decline. Within a century the industry that had once employed a large portion of Venice's working people would virtually disappear.

Competition from other Italian city-states was one of the factors contributing to the collapse of Venice's cloth producing industry. But a greater problem came from competitors far north of the Italian peninsular. Countries that had never been significant exporters of cloth became major players in the international market. The new competitors were England and the Netherlands.

In England, the weaving of cloth and the raising of sheep for wool had always been a pursuit as vital to the well-being of the local community as the growing of grain and the cutting of firewood. Before the Tudor Age, though, most of the cloth produced was of a utilitarian quality, good for local consumption, but not of sufficient quality to interest foreign buyers. Wool was spun into yarn, and yarn was woven into cloth by the inhabitants of the villages and towns for local consumption. The woolen cloth was mainly used for clothing in the region where it was manufactured. Some of the bolts of cloth were traded in the marketplaces and fairs of English cities. A small number made their way to the fairs of France and the Netherlands. Thus, until the fifteenth century, English cloth was not a major factor in European trade. In the Middle Ages, little English cloth entered the stream of international commerce.

England's role in Europe's textile industry during this early period was that of a supplier of raw wool. England raised sheep. A lot of sheep. There were more sheep in Britain than people, and English wool was a valuable product needed by foreign producers of textiles.

In medieval times, wool exports made up such a large portion of England's foreign trade that the wool became an inviting target for taxation. The export of wool, in fact, nearly undermined the development of the British parliamentary system. In the fourteenth century, the English kings were desperate for cash. The kings did not want to ask noisome Parliaments for money, however. Parliament was emerging for the first time as a political force, and consistently refused to grant taxes without receiving royal concessions in return.

As a way around this predicament, the monarchs ever hopeful that Parliament would simply disappear entered into private agreements with the wool merchants. In return for a customs duty on the exported wool, paid directly into the royal treasury without the meddling oversight of the members of Parliament, the kings authorized the merchants to form a monopoly to control exports. Everyone got something. The kings got their money, the wool merchants got the monopoly power to set prices, and the members of Parliament got angry. It subsequently took nearly half a century for

Parliament to assert control over this arrangement between the royal house and the merchants of wool.

The raising of sheep for wool had been a profitable undertaking in England since early times when villagers acquired the right to allow their sheep to graze on common lands. Any villager could buy some sheep and simply let the animals feed on the grass of the open fields. The raising of sheep became especially profitable in the central regions of the country.

In the fifteenth century, though, large landowners began to fence off their lands, evict their tenants, and raise sheep with the help of a few shepherds. A shepherd did not even require a monetary wage, for he was often paid by being given the right to keep several of his own sheep with the master's flock. The shepherd might also have received such non-monetary compensation as the rent-free use of a house or land, and gifts of lambs and firewood.

The process of fencing off the land and prohibiting its use by the tenants was known as enclosure. It was of great advantage to the landowner, but often an economic catastrophe for the tenant, who was displaced from the land that his family may have farmed for generations.

The process of enclosure was, of course, bitterly resisted by the tenants. The English agrarian system of the time retained vestiges of the feudal age. Most of the land was owned by a relatively small number of barons. The peasants leased their fields from the landowners under long term agreements. Much of the land was not leased, but was used in common as pasture by both the landowner and the tenants. On these commons, peasants let graze their cows and horses and sheep. To prevent overgrazing, many villages imposed limits on the number of animals any individual tenant could own.

The use of the commons was as important to the tenants as the leased fields on which they grew grain and vegetables. In the horses that grazed on the commons, the peasants possessed a necessary beast of burden to pull the plow. From the cows, the tenants obtained milk, butter and cheese. From the sheep, meat and wool. The right to graze their animals on the common land was thus indispensable for the tenants' survival.

The battle of enclosure began with the commons. The landowners, unable to seize the land under long term lease, attached instead the common land. The landowner simply fenced off the commons with hedges, ditches, or other devices and then allowed only his own sheep to graze on it.

The legal status of the commons was not clear. The tenants claimed that the ruling principle was the "custom of the manor," and that therefore the landowner could not arbitrarily fence off the commons for his own purposes. Under the custom of the manor, the tenants claimed that they had as much right to the commons as did the landowner. Not surprisingly, the landowners did not agree. The landlords argued that the use of the commons by the tenants was allowed simply as a temporary concession by the landowners. It was a right, said the landowners, that could be withdrawn at will.

The tenants fought to retain the right to use the commons through legal action. One such case involved the village of Wootton Basset. In 1555 in this hamlet, Sir Francis Englefield, the owner of the manor, fenced off all of the two thousand acre common, except for 100 acres that he left for the tenants. Moreover, on the one hundred acres remaining to the villagers, Sir Francis placed limits on the number of animals that could be grazed. The limits were "to the mayor for the time being two cowes feeding, and to the constable one cowe feeding, and to every inhabitant of the said Borough, each and every of them, one cowe feeding and no more, as well the poore as the riche."

The acreage left for use by the tenants was not sufficient for their survival.

The legal action brought by the villagers, though, was proof of the maxim, "Justice delayed is justice denied." As the suit dragged on without conclusion, the tenants were impoverished and had to abandon Wootton Basset, leaving Sir Francis in possession of both the commons and their farms. All over England, similar communities were reluctantly deserted by their inhabitants. Historians who have studied this period write of empty villages—hamlets that simply ceased to be.

Not all the dispossessed tenants chose legal means to fight the enclosures. In 1549, fifteen thousand peasants in the county of Norwich resorted to violent rebellion against those who were destroying their means of earning a livelihood.

The rebellious peasants led by a tanner named Robert Kett spread out over the countryside destroying all vestiges of the enclosures. The hedges fencing in the common fields were ripped up. The barrier ditches were filled in. The houses of the landowners were vandalized. The guns, swords and other weapons of the gentry were confiscated. Sheep, cows and other livestock were driven off or slaughtered for food. The beginning of the rebellion, in fact, appears to have been a rather festive occasion. While arguing their grievances, the peasants ate well. Reports indicate that thousands of sheep, cattle, swans, ducks, chickens, pigs and deer – most belonging to the landlords – were roasted over open campfires.

Kett established a headquarters at Mousehold Hill in the north of Norwich county. From there he maintained remarkable discipline over what could have been an unruly mob. Although much property was destroyed, no landowner was killed.

The government was slow to react. Only on July 31, several weeks after the rebellion began, did the government move to end the uprising. Even then the government was restrained. The rebels were offered a full pardon, if they would simply return to their homes. The rebels refused. The rebels also became more violent. The next day, they assaulted and seized the city of Norwich.

Only then did the government move to forcefully put down the insurrection. Even so, Norwich was not recaptured until August 24. Three days later, the insurgents made a last stand at Mousehold Hill and were defeated. In bloody fighting over three thousand of the rebels were killed. Kett was captured. He was tried, convicted, and hanged at Norwich Castle. So ended the most serious peasant rebellion against the enclosure of land for the raising of sheep.

The rebellions did not cease, however. Peasants made landless by the enclosures were a persistent source of potentially explosive fury. In 1598, nearly a half century after Kett's Rebellion, an act of Parliament noted that "sundry towns, parishes and houses of husbandry (have) been destroyed and become desolate, by means whereof a great number of poor people are become wanderers, idle, and loose."

In May, 1607, these dispossessed again moved to rebellion. Reported one contemporary writer, "a great number of common persons ... violently cut down hedges, filled up ditches, and laid open all such enclosures of commons and other grounds as they found enclosed, which of ancient time had been open and employed to tillage. These tumultuous persons in Northamptonshire, Warwick and Leicestershire grew very strong, being in some places of men, women and children a thousand together, and at Hillmorton in Warwickshire there were three thousand." Nothing came of these rebellions. As one angry member of Parliament sympathetic to the tenants' cause protested to his colleagues: "The ears of our great sheepmasters do hang at the doors of this House."

Some of the dispossessed peasants left for parts of the country untouched by enclosure. Most sought work in the towns and cities. Many undoubtedly became weavers in the rapidly expanding textile manufacturing industry.

By the end of the fifteenth century, England had moved beyond being predominantly a wool supplier for foreign textile manufacturers, and had become instead a major manufacturer of textiles in her own right. England was shipping less and less of her wool abroad. A century and a half earlier, England had exported 32,000 sacks of wool and 5,000 bolts of clothes. At the beginning of the fifteenth century, the balance had shifted to 19,000 sacks of wool and 37,000 clothes. By the end of the fifteenth century, wool exports fell to 5,000 sacks and cloth shipments rose to 82,000 bolts. Fifty years later, cloth exports reached 118,000 bolts.

The type of cloth first made by the English weavers was called broadcloth. It was a warm, heavy material that was well adapted to the cold, wet English climate. A lighter, cheaper cloth was called kersey. Both broadcloths and kerseys were known as woolens.

A fabric distinct from the woolens was called worsted. The yarn used in worsted fabrics was made in a different manner than that of the woolens. The fabrics were also treated differently after weaving. Most woolens underwent fulling, a process in which the material was immersed in soapy water and then beaten while still damp. The result was a warm, dense, durable fabric, admirably suited to the needs of the Englishman working in a land where a cold rain is the usual state of the weather. Worsted fabrics were not fulled. They were lighter in weight than the woolens, and could be produced in a wide array of patterns. The type of wool used in woolens and worsted also differed. Woolens were best made with fine, short wool, while long, course wool was preferred for worsteds.

The yarn used in both the woolen and worsted cloth was spun by spinners, who were almost always women and children working at home. Typical was the father who "sette his sonnes to scole, and his daughters ... to wool werke." Spinning the yarn was tedious, but undemanding work. On sunny days the spinning wheel would be set up outdoors, the women working together. The resulting yarn was of uneven quality, though. Some was spun too soft, and some too hard.

The uneven quality of the yarn was often used as an excuse by the masters to drive down the wages paid the spinners, who were habitually exploited by their employers. Wrote one observer, "After a poor woman has been laboring twelve hours to earn sixpence by spinning and reeling half a pound of wool ... the putter-out of wool or packman, by the order of his master, deducts three half-pence or twopence out of that hard-earned pittance." "It is a business conducted in so shameful a manner as to call loudly for the attention of the Government," wrote another observer.

Weavers were not much better off. They for the most part worked in their own homes on their own or rented looms. It was a solitary trade in which few weavers ever made much money. Moreover, the hours were long. Fourteen hour days were usual, seventeen hour days not uncommon.

The weaver's main problem was his dependence upon the clothier, who was the entrepreneur who tied together all the elements of the cloth making enterprise. The clothier was the middleman who delivered yarn to the weaver and purchased the newly woven cloth. The clothier traveled around the country with a train of packhorses, buying the cloth for later resale in England or abroad. The trade in cloth was frequently performed in the town marketplace, where on market day people came from the surrounding countryside to sell produce and cloth, and to purchase needed goods.

Often a peddler would be at the market, selling all manner of objects. In 1540, a literary spirit described the peddler's varied but necessary assortment of goods as:

"Gloves, pins, combs, glasses unspotted,

Pomanders, hooks, and lasses knotted,

Broaches, rings, and all manner of beads,

Laces, round and flat, for women's heads,

Medals, thread, thimbal, shears, and all such knackes."

The weaver came to these marketplaces with his cloth, which he needed to sell so as to buy supplies for the coming week. Noting the hand-to-mouth existence of the weavers, one observer wrote that the weavers brought their cloth pieces to market, "being compelled to sell the same at the week-end, and with the money received for the same to provide both stuff and wherewith to make another the week following, and also victuals to sustain themselves and their families till another be made and sold."

The relationship between the weaver and the clothier was often not friendly. Many times the weaver felt badly used by the clothier, who was usually able to set the price of the cloth. The relationship became even more adversarial when clothiers set up young apprentices in their own establishments to compete with the independent weavers.

The weavers' discontent resulted in the enactment by Parliament of the Weavers' Acts of 1555 and 1558. The first act described the burdens that the weavers had to endure. The primary troublesome condition addressed was the competition to the weavers by the clothiers. Said the act: "The weavers of the realm (complained that) the rich and wealthy clothiers do in many ways oppress them, some by setting up and keeping in their houses divers looms, and keeping and maintaining them by journeymen and persons unskillful, to the decay of a great number of artificers which were brought up in the science of weaving, their families and household."

The Weavers' Acts limited to two the number of looms a country clothier could hire out. In the future, a town clothier would be allowed to own only one loom. The Statute of Apprentices, passed in 1563 not long after Queen Elizabeth ascended the throne of England, also restricted the trade of weaver to those who were the sons of weavers or who were the sons of landowners of some wealth. Thus, the Statute of Apprentices closed off the weaving trade to most people looking for a means of earning a living. Such at least was the hope of the weavers.

Clearly the intent of these laws was to restrict competition and preserve the status quo. In practice, however, all these acts of Parliament contained exemptions that effectively nullified the force of the law. What was not nullified was simply disregarded.

Most of the profits of the textile trade were retained by the clothiers. A few clothiers became extremely wealthy. One, a man named Peter Blundell, who was born about 1520 of "very mean parentage," left an estate valued at 40,000 pounds when he died in 1599. In the sixteenth century, 40,000 pounds was an enormous fortune. By way of comparison, in 1610, the largest and most expensive fighting ship in the English navy, the *Prince Royal*, was built and equipped at a cost of 20,000 pounds.

Some of the achievements of the clothiers were even celebrated in verse. Thomas Deloney, a major contributor to the greatness of Elizabethan literature, wrote a laudatory story praising the accomplishments and lifestyle of a John Winchcombe, a fictional character, who nevertheless must have had real life counterparts. Describing in poetry John Winchcombe's textile operation, Deloney wrote:

Within one roome being large and long,

There stood two hundred Loomes full strong:

Two hundred men the truth is so,

Wrought in these Loomes all in a row.

By every one a pretty boy,

Sate making quils with mickle joy;

And in another place hard by,

A hundred women merily.

Were carding hard with joyfull cheere,

Who singing sate with voices cleere.

And in a chamber close beside,

Two hundred maidens did abide,

In petticoates of Stammell red,

And milke-white kerchers on their head:

...

These pretty maids did never lin,

But in that place all day did spin:

And spinning so with voices meet,

Like Nightingals they sung full sweet.

...

A Dye-house likewise had he then,

Wherein he kept full forty men:

And likewise in his fulling Mill,

Full twenty persons kept he still.

Describing Winchcombe's household, Deloney continued:

He kept a Butcher all the yeere,

A Brewer eke for Ale and Beere:

A Baker for to bake his Bread,

Which stood his household in good stead.

Five Cookes within his kitchen great,

Were all the yeare to dresse his meat.

...

This was a gallant Cloathier sure,

Whose fame for ever shall endure.

The poem contains obvious exaggerations. Even in the England of Queen Elizabeth, "pretty maids" did not while preparing wool for spinning sing such that their "voices meet, like nightingals they sung full sweet." The vision of two hundred maidens joyfully singing as they performed their dreary chores does not ring true. The sound of music could not obscure the tedious nature of their work. Yet, despite sounding as if written for the Elizabethan version of the National Association of Manufacturers, the poem describes certain elements of economic change that must have had some basis in reality.

The first new element was the use of a large number of workers in one building owned by a single proprietor. Previously, all textiles had been manufactured in the homes and shops of the weavers. Now, if the poem is correct, more than five hundred men and women worked in one establishment. Such an operation could be described as the world's first textile factory.

A second new element of change described in Deloney's poem is the wealth of the clothiers. Many of these men, even those born of "mean parentage," were accumulating fortunes so large that the people of the established upper classes were becoming threatened by the new order. The traditional upper classes possessed wealth based on the ownership of land, which was passed down from one generation to the next. The rise of mere merchants to positions of substantial wealth upset the established social order. One such clothier, William Stumpe, the son of the parish clerk of North

Nibley in Gloucestershire, was actually elected to Parliament.

The landed gentry, though, were most disturbed by the interest of the new rich in buying land, the traditional measure of one's social standing in Elizabethan England. The established upper class was so outraged by this threat to their system of values that they enacted an act in Parliament, in 1576, which forbade any clothier from owning more than twenty acres in Wiltshire, Somerset or Gloucestershire. The act, however, appears to have been unenforceable.

In time too, the wealthy clothiers wished to forget the source of their riches. Being a clothier limited the man's status, no matter how rich he was. One such clothier, named Thomas Dolman, sold his business, bought an estate, built a mansion, and became a country gentleman, to which the local townspeople rhymed:

Lord have mercy upon us, miserable sinners,

Thomas Dolman has built a new house and turned away

    all his spinners.

Although the export of cloth by the English during the reign of Queen Elizabeth was substantial, the woolen product most often sold had limited appeal in the markets of Europe. The woolens were too heavy, too dull, and too lacking in character for the sophisticated buyer. The woolens may have been perfect for the cold and rainy weather of England, but they were ill suited for the warm, sunny climate of the Mediterranean. If the English merchants were going to expand their markets, they had to develop a better product.

Fortunately, the English textile industry was able to benefit at this time from events occurring on the European continent. Across the Channel in the Netherlands, a country with a textile industry more advanced than England's, discord and religious strife prevailed. One result of this strife was an infusion into England of highly skilled Dutch tradesmen fleeing the warfare in their home country. The new immigrants brought with them knowledge of what the rest of Europe wanted to buy.

For historical reasons related to the inheritance of kingdoms of Europe, the Netherlands in the sixteenth century was under Spanish domination. In 1568, the country erupted in revolution in a war that was to last eighty years. Hatred of Spanish rule was one reason for the rebellion, the religious hostility between Catholic and Protestant was another. In 1648, peace was achieved. The Protestant northern provinces became the separate and independent state of the United Provinces, more generally known as Holland after the name of the largest province. The southern provinces, predominantly Catholic in religious belief, became the country of Belgium. In the sixteenth century, the southern Netherlands was known as Flanders.

The warfare in the Netherlands, which became known as the Eighty Years War, profoundly affected the textile industry. While the war raged Protestant textile workers in the southern provinces fearing religious persecution moved to the northern provinces and to Protestant England. The Flemish workers who crossed the Channel to England brought with them technical skills and marketing expertise unknown in England. This infusion of exiled textile workers from the Netherlands breathed a new spirit into the entire British textile industry.

Suddenly, England was a major factor in world textile markets. As the English industry became more dynamic and competitive, cloth and wool exports comprised, in some years, ninety percent of England's total value of exports. By 1610, the Venetian ambassador to England was able to report to the Signoria that the textile industry formed "the chief wealth of this nation."

Before the beginning of the Eighty Years War, the textile workers of the Netherlands had developed new, high quality fabrics that were lighter than the traditional English woolens. The new fabrics were known as the New Draperies. They came in a bewildering assortment of textures and types. They were often mixtures of different types of yarn. The New Draperies that were called bays, says, and serges combined the wool and manufacturing techniques of worsted and woolens. Calimancoes were processed to resemble satin. Mockadoes and camlets were mixtures of sheep and goat wool. Bombazines were mixtures of worsted wool and silk. Some of the New Draperies were of plain weave. Others were twilled and tufted. They also came in many different colors and designs.

In comparison, the native English products were staid and old fashioned.

A major advantage of the New Draperies was that they could be comfortably worn in warm climates. The countries of the Mediterranean became a natural market for the New Draperies. The Mediterranean market, though, had always been the domain of the Venetian textile industry. The Venetian cloth manufacturers would now, for the first time, have to face significant low cost foreign competition from the English.

The Turkish market was an especially lucrative target for the English. At one time, nearly all textiles imported into Turkey had been made in Venice. By 1635, however, the New Draperies from England had driven most of the Venetian product from the market. In that year, the Venetian representative at Constantinople was forced to report that:

"The English devote their attention to depriving our people of the little trade that remains to them in the mart of Constantinople, as they imitate Venetian cloth and make borders after the Venetian manner; they also have plates and wheels sent from their country, and although there is no market for these it shows that they are trying to imitate everything and despoil our merchants of all of the trade they have left."

A year later, the same representative reported to the Signoria that the English were sending to Constantinople cloth patterned after the Venetian product. The English fabric, in fact, was called "anti-Venetian." Summarizing his observations of the trade in Turkey, the Venetian representative wrote:

"Among the bales of cloth I notice some which (the English) call "anti-Venetian" which means in imitation and for the destruction of ours, a prejudice which is increased by many other advantages which the English have in trading in these parts, both from the Capitulation which they have with the Porte and because their trading is done by means of a company ... They are not only exempt from half the duties which may be remitted to them, but they have a thousand chances of smuggling, which assuredly they do not miss."

In face of these adversities, Venice's textile manufacturers proved resistant to change. They were unwilling to alter age old practices in order to compete against their northern competitors whose lower costs and superior marketing ability provided a great advantage. As a result, the Venetian export trade of cloth deteriorated.

Venetian government policy also contributed to the collapse of the Republic's textile industry. These practices included excessive regulation, inflexible labor policies, and a burdensome tax system that taxed most heavily those producers who faced the strongest foreign competition. Basically, Venice was slow to respond to the foreign challenge. Vested interests and traditional defenders of the status quo opposed any change that would have enabled the republic to abandon outdated public policies. These policies handicapped the Venetian merchants ability to compete against the new competitors in the world market.

In the area of labor practices, unduly rigid work rules adversely affected the textile industry. Workmen with skills in the necessary trades belonged to guilds, which functioned in many ways like trade unions do today. They represented their members in negotiations to set wages, working conditions, and other matters of concern to the workingmen. They were a powerful force in the political structure of Venice.

Unfortunately, the guilds often insisted upon economic concessions that were detrimental to the long term viability of the textile industry. Foremost, they demanded wages that were too high, considering the strength of the foreign competition that the Venetian textile manufacturers had to face. Comparable wages were roughly twice as high in Venice as in England. In addition to their inflexibility on wages, the guilds also demanded the retention of regulations requiring the use of outdated and inefficient production methods, which necessitated more workers than were actually needed. The intent was to keep the current members of the guilds fully employed.

In another way of guaranteeing the livelihoods of their current members, the guilds successfully argued for regulations limiting the number of new people admitted to the trades. By restricting the number of available trained workers, the guilds created an artificial scarcity of tradesmen, and forced the manufacturers to employ the current guild members at wages higher than would have otherwise prevailed.

The Collegio del Lanificio, the association of wool manufacturers, was not hesitant to criticize the restraints placed upon their industry. Like all associations representing manufacturers, the Collegio del Lanificio had its own interests to protect, and its viewpoint undoubtedly was not free of bias. Nonetheless, given the state of affairs that existed, their list of grievances may have had merit. They asked for flexibility in setting wages. "The regulations on wages should be removed," said the employers, so that "the merchant, knowing the worth of his workman, should reward him in accordance with his output and with the amount previously arranged between them." In addition to the issue of wages, the employers had other complaints as to the work attitudes of the guild members. "Apart from the disproportionate wages," wrote one employer, "both punctuality and obedience are lacking. Wool entrusted to hired workers is not safe. Work takes too long and is badly done. The weavers are even more disobedient than the others, and can only be made to work at all by punishments and deductions from their wages. The number of holidays is a third difficulty."

Another burden carried by the Venetian textile merchant-tradesman was the high rate of taxes on his product when compared to the taxes paid by textile producers in other countries. The Venetian Senate taxed imports of raw materials. It also taxed the exports of finished goods. In addition, it had taxes on the use of labor and on the manufacturing process itself. These taxes were established in the days when Venice held a virtual monopoly on trade with the eastern Mediterranean. The result of all these taxes was to transfer the costs of running the Venetian government to the foreign consumers of Venetian products. When Venice held a near monopoly on the production of cloth, the tax structure made sense. The foreign consumers had little choice but to pay. And when they paid, ducats flowed into the coffers in the Doge's Palace.

Unfortunately, the Senate did not adjust the taxes downward when the monopoly ceased to exist and Venice had to confront severe price competition from countries that taxed their merchants at a much lower rate. In Venice, taxes on a piece of cloth came to forty-two percent of the selling price. On a piece of cloth selling for 79 ducats, for example, taxes comprised 33 ducats. The cost of the wool raw material was 12 ducats or fifteen percent of the total. The forty-three percent remaining was made up of labor, overhead, and profits. The French government of King Louis XIV, in contrast, not only had a lower tax rate, but, as a further aid, subsidized export industries such as textiles.

During this critical period, Venice was also engaged in a long and expensive war against the Turks for possession of Crete and control of the Eastern Mediterranean. The war, which in the end was inconclusive, resulted in a huge increase in the size of the Republic's debt. The increased debt carried the burden of increased interest costs, which in time required still higher taxes. These higher taxes further limited the Venetian merchant's ability to compete.

Because of the tax burden on foreign trade, smuggling became an attractive venture for many. At night, when it was easiest to evade the customs agents, smugglers in small boats silently ran great risks to illegally transport goods into and out of Venice. Much of the copper, wood, wool and hides used by the republic's manufacturers entered the city through illegal channels. Customs agents were armed, and small boat owners were regulated, but the smuggling continued unabated, becoming so pervasive that the honest merchant had a difficult time competing against his less principled neighbor.

The policy practiced by some countries, such as France and England, of subsidizing exports at the same time that they were restricting imports also hurt Venice. France, in one such case, placed an import duty of 100 gold crowns on every chest of Italian velvet, making the Italian product prohibitively expensive for a Frenchman. In addition, the policy of the French government of granting a subsidy to French exporters undermined the ability of Venetian manufacturers to compete in what were once lucrative markets. Wrote one Venetian textile manufacturer: "If it is true, as it appears, that the King of France is giving a bounty of a gold doubloon for every piece of cloth which is sent to the Levantine markets, as well as exempting it from all duties, then we need look no further for the reason why it is sold in Constantinople at such low prices."

Still another burden born by the Venetian textile producer was excessive regulation. The regulations were established with the best intentions. They were meant to preserve the reputation as Venice as a manufacturer of high quality goods. For each grade of cloth, woolen producers were required to comply with regulations mandating the quality and weight of wool, the number of threads per inch, the type of dyes used, and finally the length and width of the finished cloth. Only those pieces of cloth meeting all the regulatory requirements were given the valued export permit. A manufacturer who deliberately violated these regulations was likely to find himself sentenced to a galley "with his feet in irons."

Wherever Venetian goods were sold, the mark of San Marco upon an article was the sign of the highest quality. Nearly all products made in Venice, including woolen cloth, silk cloth, books, soap and glassware, were the subject of senatorial regulation to guarantee indisputable excellence. As a result, the seal of San Marco upon an item was greatly valued, and its unlawful use became a means of deceit for those engaged in fraud and the manufacture of counterfeit products.

Although the regulations, in the main, achieved the praiseworthy intent of maintaining high quality, an undesirable consequence was to place sharp limits upon the manufacturer's flexibility to respond to the changing demands of the marketplace. The French, English and Dutch carrying no such regulatory burden were quick to supply finished woolens of somewhat lower quality, but at much lower prices. The rigidity of the Venetian regulatory scheme permitted the underdeveloped countries of northern Europe – England, France and Holland – to establish product niches in the international textile trade that were not served by the manufacturers of Venice. Frequently, these niches became the most important segments of the market.

The statutory requirement placed upon Venetian manufacturers was that the product be of "the old standard." The regulations, defining "the old standard," described in detail the shape, color and quality of the cloth that the Venetian textile manufacturers were allowed to make. Unfortunately, foreign customers wanted cloths in brighter colors and lighter weights than the Venetian producers were authorized to make.

Looking at the competitors product, a Venetian businessman noted accurately, although a bit contemptuously, that the silks made in other countries were "lighter and less well made, deceiving the eye of the purchaser with their colors, and selling cheaper than ours ... while our silks cannot be sold at the same price because they contain more material, are better made, and better dyed—although they cannot compete with the foreign goods in brightness. ... Today it is usual to think that whatever is cheapest is best."

The logical response to the new competitive environment would have been to change the regulations to allow the producer more flexibility. However, whether due to the extreme rigidity of the government of Venice at this crucial time, or to the resistance of the guilds, which found any change in the law to be job threatening, no substantive modifications were made in the regulatory restrictions. As late as 1723, over a hundred years after the problem arose, the Venetian ambassador to Constantinople would still have to advise his countrymen that "the only way to increase Venetian exports to the Levant will be to produce a lighter, cheaper type of cloth, with brighter colors."

Other nations were less rigid in their control of business activity. England, which had emerged as Venice's main competitor, allowed entrepreneurs great latitude. Although the British government attempted to regulate closely business activity, and probably wanted to exert as much control as did the Signoria in Venice, in practice, the English laws proved largely unenforceable.

Despite the ultimate unenforceability of British laws, however, even in England the removal of trade restrictions was not accomplished without a struggle. The most harmful practice was the granting of monopolies by the crown. These monopolies conferred upon the holder the absolute right to sell or manufacture a product. All monarchs of the major

European countries claimed as a royal prerogative this right to grant monopolies.

In England, though, this privilege met its sternest challenge. Parliament listed the granting of monopolies as one of its chief grievances against the crown. The members of Parliament were most incensed at the usual practice of granting monopolies to highly placed members of the King or Queen's court. Queen Elizabeth, for one, favored the dashing Sir Walter Raleigh with several monopolies. The excessive profits to the holders and the increased costs to the consumers were self-evident. Members of the court grew rich at the public's expense.

Yet, Parliament was powerless to act. The Crown would not tolerate interference. Queen Elizabeth, for instance, in 1571, bluntly told the members not to "meddle with ... with matters of state, but such as should be propounded unto them" by the Crown.

A quarter of a century later, she was more tactful, but no more willing to give up this privilege. In 1597, her Lord Keeper benevolently replied to Parliament: "touching the monopolies, her Majesty hoped that her dutiful and loving subjects would not take away her prerogative, which is the chiefest flower of her garden and the principal and head pearl of her crown and diadem."

Parliament would not act. But Queen Elizabeth also faced in one man, a more powerful opponent than all the members of Parliament combined. He was the Lord Chief Justice, Sir Edward Coke. In time, a case invoking the royal prerogative was presented to the high court, presided over by the Lord Chief Justice. The case was brought by Edward Darcy, an Esquire and groom of the Queen's Privy Chamber.

The case, one of the most important in English jurisprudence, had at its crux the mundane subject of common playing cards. Darcy was the holder of a monopoly, granted by the Queen, to make, import, and sell playing cards. Despite this monopoly grant, a man named Allen engaged in the playing cards trade. Darcy, indignant at this affront to the royal prerogative, not to mention the loss to his own bank account, sued. The Queen, he asserted, had an absolute right to grant a monopoly.

Lord Chief Justice Coke did not agreed. The granting of monopolies, said Coke, was against common law, statute law, and Magna Carta.

His arguments to Magna Carta prove to be the most interesting. That great charter's Article 29, upon which Lord Chief Justice Coke relied for his ruling, states that "no freeman shall be ... deprived of his freehold or liberties, or free customs ... but by the lawful judgment of his peers or by the law of the land." Whether the barons who extracted that pledge from King John at Runnymede in 1215 meant that it should apply to the manufacture of playing cards is not clear, but Lord Chief Justice Coke said it did.

"If grant be made to any man," Coke decreed, "to have the sole making of cards, or the sole dealing with any other trade, that grant is against the liberty and freedom of the subject, that before did or might have used that trade, and consequently against this great charter." More importantly, said Coke, "all monopolies are against this charter, because they are against the liberty and freedom of the subject, and against the law of the land." "Monopolies in times past," he added poetically, "were ever without law, but never without friends."

Legal historians have criticized Coke's reasoning in the Case of Monopolies, as *Darcy v. Allen* came to be known. Coke, they say, misinterpreted the law and provided overly broad meaning to an Article of Magna Carta that meant something else entirely. Nevertheless, monopolies were struck down, and English ingenuity was free to develop. The law was as Lord Coke said it was.

Moreover, Coke was not through with his assault on the restrictions to free trade. By an ancient law, the tailors guild could prohibit any non-member from practicing the trade. The lawfulness of this practice was challenged in the high court as the Case of the Tailors of Ipswich. The judges ruled that the Tailors' Ordinance violated common law for no one could be constrained from working at a lawful trade.

Said the Lord Chief Justice: "the law abhors idleness, the mother of all evil ... and especially in young men, who ought in their youth (which is their seed time) to learn lawful sciences, and trades, which are profitable to the commonwealth, and whereof they might reap the fruits in their old age, for idle in youth, poor in age."

With these rulings Lord Chief Justice Sir Edward Coke may have established himself as the first activist judge in an english speaking nation. Of course at the time of

Darcy v. Allen England was the world's only english speaking nation.

The lessening of government interference with trade encouraged English inventors to develop machines to make products cheaper and better.

In Venice, the rigid regulations adhered to by the guilds and by the government stifled most innovations. The leaders of the Republic of Venice were unwilling to tolerate any change that would alter practices that were centuries old.

In England, whether by design or by lack of enforcement power, the government gave the citizens great freedom to tinker, improvise, improve, and innovate.

One man to take advantage of the Elizabethan policy of non-interference was William Lee. He was a clergyman whose mind was apt to wander on to subjects other than the topic of his Sunday sermon. He was an observer of worldly practices as well as a philosopher of Biblical quotation.

Among the tasks that interested him was the hand knitting of socks. Why, he asked, could not a machine be built that would automatically knit socks? That he would even think of such a question was a major advance in itself, since the industrial revolution which established the concept of mechanization was not to occur for another century and a half. In the Elizabethan age, technical progress was slow.

So in the history of modern man, the Reverend William Lee must hold a special place. He may have taken the first step towards the industrial revolution and our technology driven society.

What the Reverend William Lee did, in 1589, was invent a machine that would knit socks six times faster than the most skilled hand knitter. He called his machine the knitting frame. It came to dominate the making of hosiery. When it was adapted to make silk stockings, one observer noted that "the Englishman buys silk of the stranger for twenty marks and sells it him again for a hundred pounds."

Reverend Lee's efforts to receive a monopoly for his knitting frame, however, were unsuccessful. Befriended by a member of the Queen's Privy Council, Lee wrangled an audience with Queen Elizabeth to show the devise to her highness in his quest for a monopoly. She summarily rejected his petition. "Thou aimest high, Master Lee," she imperiously admonished. "Consider thou what the invention could do to my poor subjects. It would assuredly bring to them ruin by depriving them of employment, thus making them beggars. To enjoy the privilege of making stockings for everyone is too important to grant to any individual."

Nevertheless, even without a monopoly the knitting frame found its place in the rapidly changing world of international trade. The economic advantages of the knitting frame were so obvious that English manufacturers had to use every resource to prevent its design from being copied by what one Englishman called, "the nimble spirits of the French, the fertile wits of the Italian, and the industrious inclination of the Dutch."

Like England, France also developed industries capable of competing with Venice. But unlike England, where the government was passive and non-intrusive, the royal government in France provided abundant support for industry, especially industries manufacturing luxury goods. The architect of this royal policy was Cardinal Richelieu, the chief minister to the unimaginative King Louis XIII. For the two decades preceding his death in 1642, Richelieu was, in fact, the supreme power in France.

The manufacture of luxury textiles was one of Richelieu's passions. The making of silk cloth especially interested the Cardinal. Reviewing the accomplishments of the French weavers, Richelieu, perhaps not an unbiased observer, wrote: "Plush of such fine quality is made at Tours that it finds a ready market in Italy and Spain and other foreign countries. The plain taffetas that are likewise manufactured there are sold in such quantities throughout France that there is no need to try to sell them elsewhere. The red, violet and yellow velvets to be found there are finer than those at Genoa. It is almost the only place where silk serge is made; as for the watered silk of Tours, it is as excellent as that obtainable in England, and the gold cloth of middling standard made there is of better quality and cheaper than that of Italy."

Richelieu's policy of active government support for industry was continued by Jean Baptiste Colbert, the chief advisor to King Louis XIV. The most famous factory to receive a state subsidy was the Hôtel des Gobelins, where tapestries rich in color and of unprecedented beauty were manufactured for the palaces of Europe. Other enterprises subsidized by the French monarchy were lace manufacture at Chantilly, Sedan and Aurillac, fine cloth at Abbeville, and glass making at St. Gobain. Many of the products of these companies were specifically designed for the Palace of Versailles, which King Louis XIV was then building in the opulent and extravagant manner that he felt would do justice to his reign.

As a result of these entrepreneurial activities in England, in the Netherlands, and in France, Venice during the seventeenth century was confronted in the markets of Europe and the Eastern Mediterranean by new products manufactured in countries with lower labor costs, greater entrepreneurial skills, and more responsive governments. From the New Draperies of England and the Netherlands to the gold cloth and tapestries of France, Venice was being beaten in the textile markets that the Serene Republic once took for granted.

Chapter 13: The Battle of Lepanto

During the sixteenth century, Venice was challenged economically by England, France and Holland. These countries grabbed a large share of the markets for ships and cloth that Venice had once dominated.

In addition to these challenges from the west, still another menace loomed in the east. In the eastern Mediterranean in 1571, Turkey, once again, threatened to unleash its powerful military apparatus against Venice and the other peoples of western Europe. In the sixteenth century, the Ottoman Empire, as Turkey and the Turkish controlled lands were known, was one of the most powerful states in Europe. The sphere of control of the Ottoman Empire extended north to Hungary and included present day Greece, Bulgaria, Romania, and Croatia. The valley of the lower Danube was in firm Ottoman control.

The Turkish army of the sixteenth century was disciplined, well supplied, and highly trained. Being Muslims for whom alcohol was forbidden, Ottoman soldiers did not drink. This sobriety of the Turkish forces made them an even more fearsome power in the eyes of the Christian Europeans. They were led by Suleiman the Magnificent, an intelligent and cultured man, who was also one of the great military leaders of the age.

In the early years of the sixteenth century, the Turkish army marched north into the Balkans, which contained no Christian army capable of stemming the onslaught by the Ottoman forces. By 1529, the triumphant Turks stood before the Austrian capital of Vienna, the gateway to western Europe. Nothing, it seemed, could prevent Suleiman's Turks from overrunning all of Germany, France, Italy and Spain.

The subjugation of western Europe by a Muslim army from the east seemed inevitable. But it did not happen. Fortunately, for the Austrians and the other Europeans not under Ottoman control, the Turks at this time were attacked themselves by a Persian army on the Asian flank of the Ottoman Empire. An Austrian diplomat at Constantinople reported that "only the Persians stand between us and ruin." The Turks, faced with this diversion, withdrew their forces to meet the Persian threat, and did not press the attack against Vienna. For the moment, Europe was safe.

But the Persian check on the Turkish policy of expansion did not hold, and the Turkish army, free of its tether, moved south and east conquering present day Syria, Iraq, Lebanon, Egypt, and most of northern Africa. Europe's turn would come later.

The Ottoman Empire was a Muslim empire. Suleiman the Magnificent assumed the titles of the Sultan of Turkey and the Caliph of Islam. Some European Christians believed that he was an agent of the Lord sent to punish the unfaithful followers of Christ. "We must not be amazed if God is now punishing the Christians through the Turks," wrote one Protestant clergyman, "as He once punished the Jews when they forsook their faith. ... The Turks are today ... the rod and scourge and fury of God."

In the summer of 1570, the Ottomans seized Cyprus from the Venetians. The island of Cyprus, located in the eastern Mediterranean between Turkey and Egypt, was an abundant source of grain and wine. It was also a safe haven for Christian pirates raiding Turkish shipping. The defenders, however, were no match against the Turks. Except for the fortified port of Famagusta, which would hold out for an entire year, the island was quickly overrun.

As the year of 1570 ended, Christian Europe looked eastward with abject fear upon the Muslim expansion of the Turkish state. The Ottoman advance had not been stopped. With the fall of Cyprus, all of the eastern and southern shores of the Mediterranean were in Muslim hands. If this alien force was not decisively beaten soon, the western Mediterranean countries of Spain, France and Italy would be laid waste, their Christian religion outlawed and destroyed, and their people made virtual slaves to the Sultan of Turkey. Never in the fifteen centuries of its existence had Christendom been in such mortal peril. If the Christian forces failed now the Koran would replace the Holy Bible, and the cross would be torn down from every church in Europe. At least, that was what many Christians believed.

In reacting to this threat, Pope Pius V prevailed upon the Spaniards and the Venetians to join the Papacy in a Holy League to defeat the infidel and save Europe from an Islamic future. They made the decision to combine their naval forces and to sail eastward for a decisive battle.

By the fall of 1571, the fleet of this Holy League was ready. Although Venice contributed more ships than any other power, the fleet was commanded by Don Juan of Austria, who was chosen by the Pope for his firmness and ability to bring together people more used to fighting one another than to fighting as allies. Even so, some of the Spaniards and Venetians, on at least one occasion, got into a violent altercation with each other, resulting in several deaths.

Despite these internal disputes, a fleet of 213 galleys assembled off the coast of Sicily. The fleet thereupon sailed east to confront the followers of Islam. However, it did not go unwatched. One night a Turkish ship painted black and using black sails slipped into the Christian fleet. Sailing silently in the quiet of the night, the black ship, unobserved by any lookout, counted the Christian ships and took note of their armament. Then it sailed away.

The Ottoman fleet, commanded by Muezzinzade Ali Pasha, was numerically superior. It was made up of 274 vessels. This Islamic fleet, the largest ever assembled to that time, rode at anchor in the Gulf of Lepanto, a body of water that is nearly surrounded by the mainland of Greece. On the morning of October 7, the Christian ships entered the Gulf. The sea was choppy. A southeast wind was blowing. The Turks raised anchor and sailed west to meet their Christian adversaries. Both sides had underestimated the strength of the other. The Muslim black ship had failed to count all the Christian vessels. Likewise, the Christian spies had underestimated the size of the Ottoman fleet by over a hundred vessels.

As the fleets approached each other, spread out along parallel and converging lines, sailors and officers on each side looked in awe at the strength and numbers of their opponent. At eleven o'clock, the wind that had been driving the Turkish fleet westward suddenly dropped to a dead calm. Both fleets would now approach each other using only the human strength of their oarsmen. Everywhere there was movement and commotion as 200,000 men in nearly 500 ships endeavored to do their best in this, the most important moment of their lives. Trumpets and horns sounded. Captains shouted orders to speed up their respective crafts and to maintain proper position with the rest of the fleet. Seamen muttered and swore as they bent to their tasks. But as the fleets were about to converge, a silence fell upon the water, broken only by the rhythmic creaking of the oars and the splash as they hit the water, and by the sound of the boats pressing through the becalmed sea. On every ship, both Muslim and Christian, men prayed in their respective religious litany.

On this day, October 7, 1571, the future control of the Mediterranean, and, thereby, perhaps of all Europe, would be decided.

On the nearly 500 vessels, two hundred thousand men were about to engage in a hand to hand battle in which no quarter would be given. The two fleets, formed into the two parallel lines, smashed together, and the bloody ordeal began. The battle lasted four hours. As it began, the Ottomans appeared to have the advantage. They had sixty more ships than the Allies, and forty thousand more men. They were tough, disciplined, well trained, and united. Despite these advantages, the Battle of Lepanto was a disaster for the Turkish forces. They lost 240 ships, while the Allies lost only twelve. More important, 25,000 Turks were killed. The Allied deaths totaled 8,000.

The surprising result was due in large part to the superior use by the Allies of ship-borne cannon. In the sixteenth century, cannon were still relatively new devices, developed after the discovery by Europeans that gunpowder could propel a lethal charge against an enemy's castles and ships. Gunpowder had been invented by the Chinese, when they found, in the ninth century, that the mixture of crushed charcoal with naturally occurring saltpeter and sulfur produced an explosive material.

By the fourteenth century, knowledge of the material and how to make it had reached Europe. It took another century, though, for the Europeans to develop cannons that would effectively use the gunpowder. The first cannon tended to blow up, and were a greater danger to the artillerymen than to their enemy. Many technological advances had to be made in the casting of bronze before cannons played a meaningful role in any battle. Curiously, much of the foundrymen's knowledge of casting cannon was derived from experience in casting church bells.

Nonetheless, the role artillery would play in warfare was obvious. A well fired cannonball could, in an instant, smash through a castle wall that had been impervious to enemy attack for centuries. Yet, faced with this revolutionary means of attack that threatened to upend the way warfare had been waged since ancient times, those in charge of a castle's defense quickly found a solution to the problem posed by the new weapon. They built new walls that were short and thick, replacing the walls that were tall and thin. The cannonballs bounced off the new walls, which were also often built with an angular slope to further deflect the missiles.

The Venetians were the leaders in adapting guns for use on ships. This leadership role in developing naval gunnery was forced upon them by necessity. For a number of reasons, Venice by the sixteenth century was short of men. The resulting shortage of sailors and oarsmen to defend the ships required the Venetians to place great reliance on guns as a means of protection. With great ingenuity, they developed short, light naval guns that could be easily loaded and fired.

The efficiency of the Venetian galley as a firing platform was crucial at Lepanto, where the Turks, with an abundance of men, relied on their age old tactics of boarding an enemy ship and overwhelming its crew in brutal hand to hand combat. As the Venetian and Ottoman galleys closed with each other at Lepanto, the Venetians fired their cannon point blank at the Ottoman decks crowded with Turks ready to board. So effective was this fire that countless Turks were killed or critically wounded before their vessels were even able to grapple with the Venetians.

Yet, the outcome of Lepanto need not have been decisive. The Turks had the resources to build a new fleet, train new sailors and soldiers, and adopt new strategies and tactics. These resources were never used, however. Psychologically, the Turks were so devastated by their defeat at Lepanto that they never again challenged the nations of western Europe.

It took ten days for news of the victory to reach Venice. When it did, the city erupted in jubilant celebration. The Venetians for the first time in decades were not threatened by a powerful, sinister enemy.

But the jubilation was short-lived. Venice was soon at war with a more ominous and insidious enemy than the Turks. The new enemy struck at the live blood of Venice. The new enemy struck at Venetian shipping. The new adversaries were pirates.

Chapter 14: Pirates on the Mediterranean

As the sixteenth century came to a close, merchants peacefully plying their trade were increasingly victimized by the loss of ships and goods to pirates. These outlaws of the high seas preyed upon any lucrative and unprotected target that came within their grasp.

For the modern individual, living in a fairly orderly world, the notion of pirates brings forth a comical image. Baseball teams are named for them. Halloween costumes of them provide children with playful delight. For the sixteenth century merchant, however, pirates were a major threat to the viability of commerce. For the individual seaman, pirates were a deadly menace. No ship could venture beyond the safety of a protected harbor, free from the fear of attack.

Piracy on the high seas had always been a problem. Along the eastern coast of the Adriatic Sea and at certain points on the northern coast of Africa, the pirates controlled well protected ports from which they could sally forth and raid merchant shipping with impunity.

The pirates in the Adriatic Sea were often exiled criminals from various states, who quite easily took to robbery and plunder. They became excellent seamen and usually were able to out sail the Venetian naval vessels sent to capture them. They would attack a target vessel with many ships of their own, and easily overwhelm the victim. Moreover, their ships were designed for speed, making the task of overtaking a lumbering merchant ship a simple task.

The pirates controlled the towns of their choice, both through fear and benevolence. Sometimes they were coercive. Other times, they shared their plunder with the townspeople, giving everyone a stake in their unlawful activity. In Segna, one of the favorite pirate controlled towns, they even gave one-tenth of their plunder to the Franciscan and Dominican friars, who accepted it gratefully. The Venetian navy was unable to achieve any lasting success against these sea-borne robbers. Aside from the support of the townspeople, and the speed of their vessels, the pirates chose their hangouts carefully. Segna, for instance, was easily defended from attack, and became a stronghold able to defy Venetian military assault.

The Barbary pirates were a separate group of outlaws. They were Muslims, who considered their attacks on Christian shipping to be fully justified as a matter of religious right. Their major strongholds were along the southern shore of the Mediterranean in cities such as Algiers. Like the Adriatic Sea outlaws, the Barbary predators were well prepared to attack and seize any merchant vessel that came within approachable range.

The depredations of the Dalmation pirates raiding from hidden inlets along the Adriatic coast and of the Barbary pirates sailing out of such protected ports as Algiers inflicted a heavy toll on Venetian shipping. But the losses never reached a point where the economic well-being of Venice was seriously crippled. Piracy during the heyday of Venetian expansion was no more than another hazard of commercial life.

Towards the end of the sixteenth century, however, the Venetian merchants faced new enemies on the high seas. The new enemies used all the cunning and lawlessness of the pirates of old, but added resources and fighting power not available to the earlier marauders. The new enemies were the English.

In 1588, the English defeated the Spanish Armada, which had been directed by Philip II to overthrow Queen Elizabeth and to re-establish Roman Catholicism as the state religion of England. As the Spanish ships were pounded to pieces in the English Channel and the North Sea, English confidence in their naval capabilities surged forward.

Having smashed the Spanish Armada, the English in the last decade of the sixteenth century moved aggressively into the Mediterranean. They came as merchants, but did not disdain to act as pirates. Commerce between England and the Mediterranean nations was well established. Wine and currants from Cefalonia and Crete were exported to England. In return, English wool, cloth and tin were shipped to southern countries. For hundreds of years, Venetian merchants handled this trade.

After their defeat of the Spanish Armada, however, the English decided it was time to eliminate the Venetian middleman. To accomplish this objective, the English, in effect, declared war on Venetian shipping. Rather than rely on the ships of Venice, the English sent their own ships to the Mediterranean. But the English did not come as peaceful traders. They came as robbers and thieves, ready to capture and destroy the ships of other nations.

The merchant ships sent by the English to the Mediterranean went armed for battle. They were three masted ships of medium size. They were called *bertoni* by the Italians. The main advantage of these English ships over other vessels was their seaworthiness. They were built solidly with a deep keel, which allowed them to ride smoothly through rough seas. They were frequently armed with twenty or more cannon, as well as with regular firearms. All in all, a *bertone* was a formidable fighting vessel.

The English ships were so over-powering, in large part, because their design had been developed over the centuries in the stormy and unpredictable seas of northern Europe. In contrast to the Mediterranean, the northern seas are subject to violent storms during all seasons of the year. Consequently, the northern mariners had to have ships that would ride out heavy seas and ferocious winds. The ships had to be rugged to survive tempestuous weather, which could drive the seamen far from friendly ports, and durable to get the seamen home again.

The result of the quest for better ships was the development, in the fifteenth century, of the large multi-masted sailing ship. On these new ships, oarsmen were no longer used as a source of power. To withstand bad weather, the ships were stoutly built with their decks high above the water line. Being strongly built, the new ships could also carry heavy cannon, which could not be used on the lightly built Venetian galleys. The recoil of a heavy cannon if fired from a galley would do more damage to the galley than the cannonball would do to the target.

The development of the heavily armed sailing ship by England and other northern European countries fundamentally altered naval warfare. The Venetians never fully understood the impact of this technological change.

The transformation to the new ship design occurred relatively rapidly during the several decades proceeding Columbus's voyages to the new world. By the end of the fifteenth century the ships would have appeared utterly strange to a seaman who lived only a hundred years earlier. Yet, the new design – a design that we associate with large sailing ships – was to endure in its same basic form into the nineteenth century, when sailing ships were rendered obsolete by another technological innovation – the development of the iron-clad steamship.

The hull of the sailing ship resulting from this nautical revolution was longer, relative to its width, than earlier designs. This resulted in a ship that sailed faster. Other changes strengthened the hull and added deck space. But the main difference was in the rigging – the masts and sails of the ship. By experiment, the shipbuilders and sail makers in the fifteenth century found that three masts and a number of square and triangular sails together provided the most effective combination. A century earlier a typical sailing ship would have had one mast and a single square sail.

The new ships brought forth a bewildering array of specialized sails. At the bow were the jibs, followed by the foresails, which in turn were followed by the mainsails. There were also topsails, gallant sails, and staysails. Finally, nearest the stern were the mizzen sails and spanker sails. The advantages of the new design over the old were that the ships were bigger, faster, carried more cargo and supplies, and perhaps most importantly, did not require a proportional increase in the number of crewmen. The new ships were more economical to operate.

But these new fully rigged ships were designed in a haphazard manner. Naval architecture during the period was largely a trial and error process. One of the first mistakes was a ship built by King Henry VIII of England in 1509.

King Henry VIII, a man no more given to humility than to faithfulness to his six wives, named the ship *Henry Grace à Dieu*, Henry Grace to God. His subjects named the ship the *Great Harry*. It was a vessel gargantuan in size. It was rated at 1,000 tons, which was hundreds of tons heavier than any other ship then afloat. It was too heavy. Even under full sail, with a stiff wind, the *Great Harry* hardly moved.

The shipwrights of England in their next endeavor sought to correct the mistake they had made in designing the *Great Harry*. The next ship would not be so heavy. The next ship to be built was named the *Mary Rose*. It was rated at only 600 tons, which was 400 tons lighter than the *Great Harry*.

The *Mary Rose* was also designed to make better use of ship-borne cannon. The technological ability to cast these heavy guns had only recently been developed. The first heavy guns were used on land as artillery to batter down the thin walls of medieval castles. The new guns were muzzle loaded and made of bronze. The old style guns were breech loaded and made of wrought iron. Although the new muzzle loaded guns were more difficult to load, they could be cast in one piece, and were thus much stronger than the old. Being stronger, they could shoot a heavier cannonball farther and more accurately.

The new cannons seemed ideal for use on navy ships. With the development of the new guns, however, seamen had to learn new skills. They had to learn how to hit a target using imperfect cannonballs and gunpowder that varied greatly in quality. In addition, a redesign of the gun carriages was needed. A gun carriage fixed to the deck would transfer the energy of the recoil to the deck itself and in time damage or destroy the ship. The solution was the wheeled carriage tethered by strong ropes.

An additional problem was where to place these new weapons. On the *Great Harry*, the guns were placed on the highest decks. It was soon found, however, that the weight of the guns on the upper decks made the ship top heavy. As a result, the *Great Harry* was cumbersome and difficult to steer.

The solution in the *Mary Rose* was to place the guns on a deck that was just above the water line and to cut gun-ports in the side of the hull. The ship was thus more stable. But unfortunately it was these gun-ports that led the *Mary Rose* to a tragic end.

In the summer of 1545, the *Mary Rose* along with several other ships left Portsmouth harbor to do battle with an approaching French fleet. As King Henry VIII watched anxiously off the Spithead anchorage, the ships drifted aimlessly in a calm. In the smooth water, the Mary Rose sat, with her guns ready, and with her gun-ports open, awaiting a favorable breeze. Suddenly the wind did blow up. But too strongly, and too fast. The great ship heeled over on its side. Normally this would not have been a problem. The ship would have righted itself without harm. With the gun-ports open, however, sea water flooded into the hull. Within minutes, the ship sank.

King Henry, viewing the disaster from shore, watched in horror.

The *Mary Rose* went down so quickly that few, perhaps none, of the men below deck were able to escape. Moreover, few of the men on deck escaped either. To catch falling spars that could be shot down by the enemy cannon, a netting of strong ropes had been fastened over the heads of the men on the deck. As the *Mary Rose* was pulled down by the water rushing in below deck, the rope netting prevented the sailors from swimming free. Of the seven hundred men on the ship, only about thirty survived. On the shore, the families of the crewmen watched in horror as the ship foundered and the sailors drowned.

Immediately after the sinking, efforts were made to raise the ship. At low tide rope cables were attached between the *Mary Rose* and buoyant ships above. As the tide rose, it was hoped the *Mary Rose* would be lifted off the seafloor by the rising tide, at which time the ship could be towed to shallower water. However the effort was unsuccessful, probably because the ropes were not strong enough, and the *Mary Rose* was abandoned. It was a good idea, but what was needed was steel cable, not rope, and steel cable would not be invented for another three hundred years.

The saga of the Mary Rose *does not end with its sinking. In 1836, a marine salvage company responded to complaints from commercial fishermen that their nets were repeatedly getting snagged in a certain area of the Solent, the channel between Portsmouth and the Isle of Wight. The salvage company sent down a diver in an early version of diving bell. He found the* Mary Rose. *Several of the ship's cannons were recovered, but nothing more could be done, the body of the hull being covered with mud and silt.*

Interest in recovering the Mary Rose *revived in the mid-twentieth century.*

In 1971, after years of scanning the seabed with the latest sonar equipment, marine archeologists found — or re-found—the Mary Rose. *More years of careful excavation followed. Finally on October 11, 1982, the* Mary Rose *after 437 years underwater was raised to the surface in a meticulously planned salvage operation, and placed on a specially constructed steel cradle.*

Examination of the wreckage, leads one to conclude that other factors besides the open gun-ports contributed to the rapid sinking of the Mary Rose. *Enough water could not have entered through the gun-ports to sink the ship in minutes. We can surmise that the heavy guns on the upwind side may not have been securely tethered, allowing them to slide downward to the underwater side of the ship as the* Mary Rose *heeled over. And although the* Mary Rose *was less top heavy than earlier ships, it was still top heavy. English ship designers recognized this, and drastically reduced the height of the forecastles and stern castles — the parts of the ship above the main deck — in ships built later.*

The ship is now on display at the Mary Rose Museum in Portsmouth.

Despite the tragedy of the sinking of the *Mary Rose* and the similar fates of other ships, advances in naval architecture continued to be made. The *Mary Rose* sank precisely because it was an innovative design. The Venetians, relying on their centuries old galleys, suffered no losses of the magnitude of the *Mary Rose*. But instead they fell further and further behind in ship design and armament.

In the process, there occurred an event, notable, but unrecognized in its significance. On April 22, 1513, in a battle with the French off the coast of Brest, the British naval ship *Trinity* became the first ship in history to be sunk solely by enemy gunfire.

In time, the English mastered the art of building big fighting ships. In future centuries, these ships would become the mighty ships-of-the-line of the British navy.

Design improvements were also being made in merchant ships. Unlike the navy vessels, the merchant ships were designed to be built and operated in the most economical manner possible. In this regard, the Dutch became the leaders. Dutch merchant ships were cheaper to build, carried more cargo, and required fewer seamen to sail than the ships of any other nation. The merchant ships designed by the Dutch had storage space suited to the intended cargo, and simplified rigging so that a small crew could handle the sails. The frugal Dutch also paid low wages to the seaman, and used every possible scrap of wood in construction.

The Dutch bought their ship timber in Norway, Germany, Russia, and the Baltic. Since the Dutch paid promptly and with hard currency, suppliers offered them the best rates. As a result, the Dutch, at times, were able to buy Norwegian wood at prices that were lower than those charged shipbuilders in Norway, itself.

The Dutch shipbuilding technique also afforded economies over the methods practiced in other countries. In the Netherlands, shipbuilding was practically an assembly-line operation. The Dutch, in addition, used labor saving machinery such as windmill driven sawmills. The advantage of the machinery in making their lives easier was recognized by the Dutch workmen. Once the French, hoping to profit from the Dutch expertise, offered a group of Dutch carpenters much higher wages to work in France. The carpenters turned the offer down, saying that without Dutch shipyard equipment, they would have to work too hard.

One envious Frenchman later described the advantages of the Dutch over the French. Comparing the practices of the two nations, with observations that could also be applied to the Dutch advantage over the Venetians, he wrote:

"The French put 18, 20 or 25 men on a vessel of 250, 300 or 400 tons, the Dutch only 12, 16 or at the very most 18. The French seaman earns 12, 16, 18 or 20 livres a month, while the Dutch sailor is content with 10 or 12 livres and the officers are paid in proportion. French sailors have to be fed bread, wine, biscuit made of pure wheatmeal and it must be white. French sailors also demand fresh and salt meat, cod, herring, eggs, butter, peas, beans and when they eat fish it has to be well-seasoned, and even then they will only accept it on meatless days. The Dutch are satisfied with beer, bread and rye-biscuit, often very black though with an excellent taste, cheese, eggs, butter, a little salt meat, peas, gruel, and they eat a great deal of dried fish without seasoning, every day without distinction, which costs far less than meat."

Continuing his enumeration of the Dutch advantages over other nations, he added:

"The French build their ships of oak timbers, with iron bolts, which cost a great deal; most of the Dutch ships, especially those which sail no further afield than France, are merely made of pine, with wooden pegs, and although they are twice as big, they cost half as much to build as ours."

As a result of all these factors, the Dutch shipowners could make a profit, while giving the merchants the lowest shipping rates in Europe. The Venetians like the French complained much, but did little.

The supremacy of the Dutch in the building of merchant ships is even more remarkable when one realizes that the Netherlands grew no trees fit for ship timber, and has an exit to the sea that is shallow, laden with sand-bars, and often frozen during the winter months of the year. If there was one place on earth with access to the sea where one would not expect a marine community to flourish and to become a world power based upon its naval fleets, it was the Netherlands. Yet this they did.

The Dutch swiftly used their naval superiority to establish an empire reaching from America to Asia. As merchants, the Dutch readily understood that the Portuguese were making huge profits by buying spices in Asia. Seeing no reason why the Portuguese should make all the money, the Dutch in 1594 decided to enter the Asian trade themselves. They organized a "Company of Far Lands" and sent forth two fleets to the eastern lands where the spices grew. Despite heavy losses of ships and men, the fleets returned to yield four fold profits to their investors. "So long as Holland had been Holland," wrote one participant, "such richly laden ships have never been seen."

To better organize the Dutch enterprise, the government of the Netherlands established the East India Company, which easily pushed aside the Portuguese, who after a century of expansion, were over-extended and unable to protect a colonial empire that extended from India to Brazil. In time, the Dutch would suffer the same fate as the Portuguese. However, in the seventeenth century, the "Golden Century" of the Netherlands, the Dutch expanded beyond the Portuguese bases, and established trading factories in Indonesia, China and Japan.

They also incorporated the West India Company to manage the trade in the Americas. The West India Company engaged in many commercial ventures, one of which was the establishment of a colony called New Amsterdam on the island of Manhattan. The settlement ultimately was ceded to the English and renamed New York. The Dutch were more successful in the Caribbean, where the Dutch legacy is still to be found in the islands of Curacao, St. Martin and St. Eustatius.

Thus, the advances of naval architecture allowed the northern powers to establish sea-borne empires that encircled the world. These sea-borne empires substantially undercut the commercial prosperity of Venice. Moreover, for the Venetians the development of the fighting sailing ship in itself would have dire consequences.

An unintended result of the new naval design was a ship with a huge advantage when attacking the much lower and lighter built Mediterranean galley. The high freeboard of the English vessels – the distance between the water line and the deck – gave the English, literally, the upper hand when ramming and boarding a Venetian galley. The galley typically had a very low freeboard so as to maximize the rowing strength of the oarsmen, who were most efficient close to the water.

Since Mediterranean storms are rare, except in winter, the galley also had no need for a high freeboard as protection in heavy seas. During the stormy winter season, the Mediterranean mariner simply did not venture out of port. But the low decks of the Venetian galleys were fatal in an armed encounter with the Northerners. The advantage given by the high freeboard to the English in an attack was, that once the Venetian target ship was grappled, the English had merely to jump down upon the Venetians. The Venetians, in turn, could not easily climb up the side of the English vessel.

The use of cannon shifted the odds even more in favor of the English, for the English cannon could shoot down upon the open and exposed Venetian galley, but the Venetian cannon shooting up at the English would only hit the solid side of the English vessel.

Aside from the piracy, the English by the early seventeenth century were simply more willing to take risks than the Venetians. One English observer noted that an English ship could sail from Venice to Syria and return in half the time it took an Italian ship. One reason given by this observer for the English superiority was that "the Italians pay their Marriners by the day, how long soever the voyage lasteth, which makes them uppon the least storme, putt into harbors, whence only few wyndes can bring them out, whereas the English are payde by the voyage, and so beate out stormes at Sea, and are ready to take the first wynde any thing favourable unto them." A second reason given by this observer was that the Italian mariners were basically "not very expert, nor bold."

Upon entering the Mediterranean as marauders, the English quickly perceived that the ships of Venice made the most lucrative and vulnerable targets. Heavily laden with valuable merchandise and lightly armed, a Venetian ship was a prize worth seeking. The fact that the Republic of Venice was not at war with England was an irrelevant fact to English captains. "They treat every ship they meet as an enemy," wrote an observer at the time, "without distinguishing whether it belongs to friend of foe." To add to the Venetians' problems, the Dutch also joined in the same practices as the English. The Venetian observer noted that "the Dutch attack every ship they meet, no matter whose it is, and, that their misdeeds might not become known, they sew up the crews in sailcloth and let them sink beneath the waves."

The toll taken upon Venetian shipping was horrendous. In 1586, the galleon *Lombardo* with a cargo of wine was captured. The same fate was soon in store for the *Uggiera e Selvagna*, the *Tizzone*, and the *Manicella*. In 1593, the *Costantina* was taken, and its load of grain and lumber sold in Turkey. After that, the *Girarda e Correra* was robbed of its cargo of cotton. Then the *Martinengo*. Then the *San Giovanni Battista* with a load of silken cloth. Then the *Veniera* with goods valued at 100,000 ducats. The list of ships lost to the English pirates appeared to have no end. Some ships were plundered more than once in the same year. One such ship was the *Santa Maria Di Grazia*. She was attacked in one spring off Crete and in the following autumn off Venetico. In the attack off Venetico, her crew was held for four days, while the assailants leisurely plundered the ship. In the end, they stole even the ship's guns.

The merchants, unwilling to jeopardize their ships, stopped sailing on the most dangerous trade routes. Unfortunately, the most dangerous trade routes were also the most profitable. "Due to heavy losses suffered at the hands of the English," reported the merchants in 1605, "trade with the Levant, on which this market chiefly subsists is now reduced to such a wretched state that unless the government takes effective steps it will collapse completely. ... There are ships in this city now ready to sail for the Levant but are unable to leave, because the merchants will not expose their capital and wealth to the certainty of loss." Despite this report, one merchant alone, Francesco Morosini, lost "four good ships and a galleon" in the following year.

The government of Venice, as expected, reacted vigorously to these unlawful attacks. The first response was to send to sea their most powerful fighting ships, the galleasses and the galleons, to do battle with the pirates, indeed to sweep the pirates from the sea-lanes.

The galleasses and the galleons were for Venice the great battleships of the seventeenth century. They were to the Venetian navy what the nuclear aircraft carriers and missile carrying submarines are to the American navy today. So confident were the Venetian naval authorities in the future successes of the galleons, that the President of the Naval Academy of Venice declared that "the mere rumor that the galleon has put to sea will strike such terror into the hearts of the pirates that they will find it in their own best interests to take to other pursuits and leave the sea in peace." Another observer described the ships as the ultimate fighting machines. "Truly," he said, "when you saw them sailing with their castles towering above the sea, they seemed like moving fortresses: and it was said to be the unique achievement of the Republic to build these floating fortresses, for every expert in sea warfare assured us that no ship, no matter how heavily armed, could possibly compare with them."

They were immense ships. Each carried a crew of over 500 men, principally soldiers and rowers. The ships were armed with over thirty cannon. They were indeed floating fortresses. They had to be. The future of Venice depended upon the success of these great warships in driving the pirates from the sea. If they failed, Venice would no longer survive as a maritime power.

The galleasses and galleons, unfortunately, had a major deficiency. They were slow. The ships were so large and heavy, they could not carry enough sail to get moving fast enough to intercept a pirate ship. Even with the added effort of the rowers, the ships were too slow. It was indeed only under unusual circumstances that the warships could capture an enemy ship. In any chance encounter, the pirates had only to maneuver beyond the range of a galley's guns to be virtually assured of escape. A ship's guns in that era were not very accurate anyhow, and the slightest ocean swell was enough to rock the boat sufficiently to require pure luck to hit any target. For the pirate ship able to avoid capture by nightfall, escape was certain. But even chance encounters between pirate and Venetian warship were rare. Because the Venetian ships were so large, they could be seen eight to ten miles farther off than the Venetians could see the pirates. Rather that striking "terror into the hearts of the pirates" as the President of the Naval Academy had hoped, the Venetian warships were easily avoided by the pirates.

The Venetian warships also could not remain at sea long enough to blockade a pirate's harbor. Since the warships carried such a large crew, an extended stay at sea required the ships to carry a large amount of food and fresh water. But because the warships possessed little storage space, they had to return to port every few days to replenish their supplies, thus greatly reducing their pirate fighting opportunities.

Another disadvantage borne by the naval commanders was the quality of their ships crews. The men were for the most part drawn from the lowest elements of society. They were the criminals, the slaves, and the utterly destitute. Nicolo Dona, a high ranking naval official, described the crewmen as "poor, naked wretches."

Venetians, it appears, decided to solve their prison overcrowding problem by sending their prisoners to the navy. As a result, the galleys were crewed by convicts, who were chained to their benches, dressed in rags, and fed nothing more substantial than bread and a watery soup. At times, their daily ration consisted of a few biscuits and a cup of cheap wine. Moreover, the galleys were open ships with no protection against the weather or the waves that washed across the bows in heavy seas. Under these conditions, the convict crewman sat hungry and soaked to the skin at his assigned place with chains about his feet. In winter, he suffered frostbite and illness brought on by unprotected exposure to the elements.

The crewmen were, noted one observer, "drenched by the rain above and the sea below, without even a change of clothing. Often the very bread they have to eat is soaked. They have so little rest, that in a little while they fall down and die." In fact, three out of every five sailors died at sea from sickness brought on from exposure and malnutrition. Aside from the human concern, the problem for Venice created by demoralized and unhealthy crewmen aboard the warships was that the men had neither the will nor the physical strength to do battle with the pirates.

The crews aboard the merchant ships were hardly any better, or any better cared for. In the seventeenth century, merchant ships were expected to defend themselves against the armed attacks of the pirates. But the men hired as crew were not disposed to risk their lives to save the ship's cargo. One merchant noted in anger that "the men who now sail on ships are worthless and unscrupulous creatures, so that when attacked by raiders they not only help them but take to plundering themselves." In 1607, a government commission acknowledged that the crewmen on ships, including those most heavily armed, "were unwilling to fight, either because they hope that being plundered may afford them the opportunity of making large profits, or because they have discovered that they will get excellent treatment from the pirates if they do not fight."

In distinct contrast to the Venetian crewmen who would not fight to protect their ships, the English seamen were highly motivated to plunder. The main reason behind this motivation of the English crewmen was that they were given a financial incentive to capture foreign ships. Generally, when the English seized a ship, the crew received one-third of the booty. With this inducement, a ship's captain had no trouble attracting able-bodied men from the multitude of England's poor and unemployed. Indeed, for a man in England's lower class, striking it rich by being a member of a crew on a ship that had the good fortune to seize a vessel loaded with valuable booty was the only means he had of rising above his miserable condition.

Some captains even named their ships with an eye toward the hoped for windfall. Such names as *Wheel of Fortune*, *Poor Man's Hope*, and *Why Not I?* make their way on to the roster of England's ships. Economic conditions in England in the 1590s' also forced many a man into piracy. Poverty, unemployment, economic depression, and repeated failures of the harvests drove the poor Englishman to privacy as an act of desperation.

The method of seizing a target vessel was simply to ram and board. Immediately upon grappling with the victim, the English crewmen jumped on board with swords, daggers, pikes, hand guns, or any other weapons that happened to be available. Not surprisingly the Venetian prisoner-crewman was not willing to risk his life to protect the cargoes of the merchants.

Piracy by the English was a logical outgrowth of the practice called privateering. Under this practice, English owners of private vessels were authorized by Queen Elizabeth to capture and sell enemy merchant ships and cargoes. Privateering, thereby, added measurably to the naval resources available to the Queen for the defense of the country. Since Queen Elizabeth was also the most frugal of monarchs – she counted every shilling – privateering gave her what she ardently desired, an auxiliary navy at no cost to the crown.

Initially, the use of private ships in privateering ventures was restricted to actions against Spanish shipping, England being at war with Spain. The most famous privateer was Sir Francis Drake, who on one venture captured the Spanish fleet carrying an entire year's treasure from the new world.

Although officially intended to be used only against Spanish shipping, privateering quickly came to be practiced against neutral shipping as well. The English used any pretext to seize a Spanish ship, a Venetian ship, or a ship of any other country. One reason for this practice was that it was highly profitable. Moreover, it was profitable for the Queen, herself, for she received five percent of the take. The Lord Admiral, who was responsible for enforcing the law, also received a cut of the booty, whether it was legally seized, or not.

As a result of these many factors – the development of superior ships by the English and Dutch, the spread of piracy to the Mediterranean, the reliance of Venetian naval authorities on the outmoded galley for defense, the failure of Venice to provide trained and motivated seamen, and the abundance of highly motivated English seamen – the naval superiority of the Republic of Venice, which had stood the tests of a thousand years, was now successfully challenged by the invaders from the north.

Chapter 15: Venice in the Age of Titian, Palladio and Vivaldi

Beginning in the Middle Ages and continuing into the Renaissance, the Republic of Venice was an economic power without a serious rival in Europe. At the end of the fifteenth century, when Christopher Columbus embarked on the voyage that would find a new world, Venice was the supreme naval power in the Mediterranean and the dominant political force on the Italian peninsular.

But in the centuries that followed, Venice faced economic and military challenges from all sides. England, ruled by Henry VIII and Elizabeth I, was striving for international greatness. Spain, fueled by her newly found wealth in the Americas, was seeking to dominate Europe. Holland, propelled by the entrepreneurial skills of her merchants, was gathering within her borders an enviable share of the riches of the world. France, united after years of civil war, was preparing to invade northern Italy. In the sixteenth and seventeenth centuries, Venice entered an era of slow economic decline, in which it was unable to contain the forces that controlled its destiny.

The decrease in stature, however, in no way diminished the vitality of Venetian cultural life. During the early phases of the decline wealth still flowed into the trading accounts of Venice's richest families. Venice's descent from the pinnacle of power was gradual and not particularly troublesome to the patricians of the Republic.

Even as the Venetian economy stagnated, grand and luxurious buildings continued to be built. The fact that these opulent structures were reflective of a wealth that was slowly slipping away simply made the people of Venice savor them more. Many of these buildings were designed by the acclaimed architects, Andrea Palladio and Baldassare Longhena.

The vitality of sixteenth century Venice finds architectural expression in the church of San Giorgio Maggiore on the island of the same name. The island is prominently situated across the Canale di San Marco from the Piazzetta San Marco.

In 1565, the Benedictine monks who maintained the island chose Andrea Palladio to design the church. Palladio was an inspired choice. He is today recognized as Venice's greatest architect. His style is associated with the High Renaissance.

Palladio was born in 1508 in Padua. He began his professional pursuit as a simple stonemason and probably would have remained in this honorable but basically uncreative trade had not an early patron seen in him great ability. The patron provided Palladio with expense money to go to Rome and see for himself the latest architectural developments of the Renaissance.

The Renaissance was greatly influenced by the work of the artisans of Ancient Greece and Rome. Classical forms such as columns and pediments were reintroduced into European architecture in the fifteenth century. A generation before Palladio, Jacopo Sansovino brought the new style to Venice. Palladio however brought the new style to a higher level by adding domes, belltowers and statuary, while retaining Classical harmony and balance.

Palladio's first commissions were from wealthy Venetians for villas in the countryside towns of Veneto. The buildings he designed influenced architecture for centuries to come. In these villas, some of which are simple and some elegant, Palladio applied the Renaissance appreciation of the ideas of Classical Greece and Rome. The Villa Barbaro at Maser for one with its orderly use of Ionic columns, pediments, arches and sculpture is Pompeii reborn.

Palladio's interest in classical architecture provided a guide for later generations of architects. Thomas Jefferson, an amateur architect of extraordinary ability, was one who was greatly influenced by the Venetian's work. Jefferson incorporated Palladio's style into the design for Monticello.

In 1577, even before San Giorgio Maggiore was complete Palladio was given a commission for another highly visible church. This was Il Redentore which was to be sited conspicuously on the island of Giudecca.

Il Redentore was built in thanksgiving for the redemption of the city from a particularly virulent outbreak of the plague. It is a masterpiece of High Renaissance architecture. Like San Giorgio Maggiore, Il Redentore sits majestically across the canal from the Doge's Palace. Viewed from the Piazzetta San Marco, the church looks almost like a heavenly mirage with its white Istrian stone facade of classical pediments, half columns, pilasters, and dentilled cornices. In its interior,

Palladio continued the use of classical orders to give a sense of restrained grandeur.

With the end of the sixteenth century, the economic decline of Venice was finally reflected in fewer commissions for new buildings. Important structures were still being built though. The most impressive was the wonderfully extravagant Santa Maria della Salute, the church that sits prominently at the entrance to the Grand Canal just opposite the Piazza San Marco and the Doge's Palace.

The Santa Maria della Salute was commissioned in 1631 as an expression of gratitude to the Virgin Mary for ending a recurrence of the plague that had killed one-third of Venice's population in two years.

The effect of the plague upon pre-modern Europe is incomprehensible to twenty-first century citizens of developed countries. When it struck, one-quarter to one-third of a city's population could die before the disease ran its course. Other diseases, such as cholera, diphtheria, small pox and influenza, also decimated entire nations before advances in medicine and improved sanitation eliminated the scourge of infectious diseases until recent times in economically advanced countries.

Nevertheless, although the plague took a high toll of human life, it was a stimulating force for the construction of churches such as Il Redentore and Santa Maria della Salute. It also helped the parish fathers shake the money tree. In one case involving the Order of Scuola di San Rocco the plague brought salvation to church administrators if not to members of the congregation. A church being built by the Order proved to be so costly that the friars in charge of the financing despaired of finding the money to complete it. Luckily for the clerics, though, the plague broke out once again, and wealthy Venetians suddenly concerned with the hereafter contributed more than enough to finish the construction.

Jesus may have said, "it is easier for a camel to go through the eye of a needle than for a rich man to enter the kingdom of God." (Matthew 19:24) Nevertheless, many wealthy Venetians were willing to make a valiant effort to convince the Keeper of the Gates that exceptions should be made.

Fortunately money to build the Santa Maria della Salute was not lacking.

The architect chosen to design the Salute was Baldassare Longhena. In the Salute, Longhena incorporated many of the Renaissance elements used by Sansovino and Palladio. These included columns, domes and pediments. But he also went beyond the traditional forms and used elements of the Baroque that was the new European style.

The Baroque architects discarded the Renaissance passion for order, classicism and discipline, and emphasized instead flamboyance, whimsy and drama. Baroque buildings are theatrical, dynamic, and attempted to provide a sense of excitement. Longhena achieved this in the Salute with the twelve giant volutes, each topped with the statue of an apostle.

Like Palladio, Longhena effectively used white Istrian limestone to produce a church exterior that sparkled against the sky. In designing the Salute, Longhena created a structure that complements the Basilica of San Marco. Scholars of architecture have pointed out for example that the dome of the Salute is balanced by the domes of the Basilica, which is within view across the canal.

While the Salute was under construction Longhena also engaged in private commissions. In the 1660's he designed two palaces that rivaled in splendor anything built before. They fully articulated the spirit of the Baroque period with its emphasis on the lively interplay of rich and fanciful architectural elements. These palazzi were the Palazzo Pesaro and the Ca'Rezzonico. Both were designed by Longhena for wealthy patrons who were committed to building palaces that would be more magnificent than any private residence in the rest of Europe. By all accounts, they succeeded.

In art also, Venice experienced its most illustrious period during the sixteenth century. Even as the Venetian economy was battered by European competition, Titian, Venice's greatest artist, rose to become one of the masters of the Renaissance. Titian is considered by many art historians to have been the most important artist in shaping the direction that European painting would take for the two following centuries. Rembrandt, Rubens, Velázquez, Delacroix, Turner and countless other masters of the seventeenth and eighteenth centuries were influenced by Titian's grand, emotional, richly textured style that was at once both evocative and intimate.

Titian was probably born in 1488 though no one knows for sure. Records no longer exist and Titian made himself older or younger as benefited his circumstances.

Although he came to be called Titian, his true given name was Tiziano. To Italians he will always be Tiziano. His family name was Vecellio. The village of his birth was Pieve di Cadore, high in the foothills of the Italian Dolomite Mountains, seventy miles north of Venice.

Pieve di Cadore sits by the Piave River which flows south to find its outlet on the Adriatic Sea a few miles up the coast from Venice. At the center of the town was a piazza with a fresh water fountain. Houses some big some small radiated out from the piazza. Fields, gardens, orchards and pastures lay beyond Pieve di Cadore. On the slopes of the surrounding mountains, which cast their shadows on the town for much of the day, forests of pine, larch and oak rose to the summits.

The Piave River was an important route of commerce between Venice and Germany. Up the river and along the dirt roads that ran beside it, goods from Venice – spices, wine, olive oil, Murano glass, silk and woolen textiles, and every other sort of luxury product – traveled toward Germany and northern Europe. And from the north came in the reverse direction gold, silver, copper, iron, tin, leather, hides and furs. Many of these goods were transported through the Brenner Pass on carts no bigger than a farm wagon drawn by oxen, horses and donkeys.

In addition to being a way-station on this trading route, the Cadore region was a supplier of timber to Venice which had an endless need of wood for fuel, for the building of ships and galleys, and for the wooden piles driven into the sand to provide the sub-structure upon which Venice sits. Nevertheless, Cadore was a somewhat isolated hill town where the soil was thin and the people few.

It is surprising therefore that this provincial town far from the high culture of Venice would be the place where one of the great artists of the Renaissance was born and spent his formative years.

Titian's parents and family were locally prominent. Although Cadore was something of a backwater, the Vecellio for generations had been leading members of the community. Titian's grandfather and other family members held important positions in the government of the town. Titian's father also was highly regarded among the town gentry. He was a member of the town council and a captain in what may be regarded as the local militia. Many years later Titian painted a portrait of his father. The portrait now lost can be seen as an indication of a warm and loving relationship between father and son.

Little is known of Titian's childhood, but he obviously showed great talent as an artist. To further his ambition, his parents knew he had to leave the mountain village of his birth.

Thus when he was no more than twelve years old, Titian gathered together his few belongings, said goodbye to his family and friends, and with an older family member began the journey along the River Piave to Venice. He arrived at almost the same time as the news of the Portuguese discovery of a sea route to Asia reached the city.

Still, Titian was only a young adolescent when he arrived in Venice. He had left the remote town of Pieve di Cadore in the foothills of the Italian Alps where the air was clear and brisk and the people were well known to one another. Now he was in Venice a large, crowded, bustling, pleasure loving city that thrived on commerce in products from lands unseen. It was a city of luxury, poverty, erotic pleasures, strange foods, noise, and people everywhere. It was also a city of art.

Titian was first apprenticed to Sebastiano Zuccato a minor Venetian painter who may have been a friend of the Vecellio family. Shortly thereafter Titian moved to the studio of Gentile Bellini – the most famous if somewhat unimaginative Venetian artist of the time. In these first experiences in professional workshops, Titian learned the basic skills of a painter.

Gentile Bellini and Titian however did not hit it off. It may have been a matter of different temperaments. Gentile's paintings express a personality that is precise and controlled. It is impossible for example to imagine Gentile ever painting *Venus of Urbino*, Titian's great erotic portrayal of female nudity. Titian's personality was always free-wheeling and flamboyant. Many years later after he had become a famous artist, Titian claimed that Gentile had predicted that he would never amount to much. But Titian never missed a chance to tell a good story, and this might have been one of them.

Fortunately, Gentile had a brother Giovanni who was recognized as a much better artist. Today Giovanni

Bellini is regarded as one of Venice's great artists. Titian moved into Giovanni's studio.

Giovanni Bellini is best known for his religious paintings. In these, his Madonna is a young mother — attractive, serene, and full of pride in her newest born. No longer was the Madonna the lifeless icon of the art of the Middle Ages. Bellini also excelled at portraits. One of the paintings Bellini was working on while Titian was apprenticed to his studio was the masterful portrait of the Doge Leonardo Loredano. In this portrait, Bellini captures the personality of the doge — self-confident, self-assured, yet thoughtful and wise.

In Giovanni's studio Titian performed many tasks including the making of paint from a multitude of pigments. Here Titian learned how to make paint with an oil base.

Giovanni Bellini was one of the first in Venice to experiment with the use of oil paint rather than tempera as a painting medium. The earlier painting medium, tempera, had been used for centuries. It consisted of mixing the pigments with egg yolk and water. The egg yolk would bind the pigment to the wood or canvas surface. The water would thin the paint to the proper consistency.

The problem with tempera was that it dried too rapidly to permit an exuberant but slow working artist to express himself creatively. Brush strokes had to be short and quickly applied. This problem was overcome with the use of oil-based paint.

The invention of oil paint as it came to be used by Renaissance painters occurred in Flanders where Jan van Eyck mixed pigments into linseed and nut oils. The results were vibrant colors in a medium that dried slowly enough for the artist to achieve the effect he desired. Oil paint enabled the artist to rework, revise and refine a painting in a manner that tempera never did. Oil paint also allowed for different levels of opacity, from opaque to translucent. The characteristics of oil paint moreover allowed artists to experiment with new techniques and effects. And no artist was more experimental than Titian.

While serving an apprenticeship with Giovanni Bellini, Venice's then most accomplished artist, Titian's ability as a painter became readily apparent. His style, which was vibrant and colorful, abandoned the still and formal style of his predecessors.

It was natural then that Titian would be greatly influenced by Giorgione, the great Venetian painter who transformed art into that of the modern era. He was around ten years older than Titian, and had already upset the established view as to what a painting should be.

Giorgione was born not far from Venice in a town called Castelfranco. His paintings and frescos used drama and color in new and imaginative ways. He quickly found patrons among the Venetian elite, especially amongst young aristocrats who were born rich. These patricians about his own age and with money to burn appreciated Giorgione's flamboyance and disregard of the conventions of the past.

It is in Giorgione's use of drama and narrative – the story a painting is telling – that Giorgione is for many art historians the first painter of the modern era. He represents a break with the static style of the Middle Ages and Early Renaissance.

Yet the narrative of his painting is curious. Typically, the story he tells is ambiguous. It is not clear. Today, this provides art historians with a lot of running room to write windy, vacuous, colleague-impressing academic papers. Maybe this is why they like Giorgione.

His ambiguous narrative style is present in the *Tempest*, a landscape painting in which a naked mother nursing a child sits disconnected from a young man holding a pole while a thunderstorm rages in the distance. What is this all about? Giorgione doesn't say.

A second painting, the *Three Philosophers*, is equally ambiguous. It is a marvelous painting with every element – the three gentlemen, the rocks, the trees, the sky – playing its role in composition. Yet the meaning of the painting is unclear. And perhaps this is how Giorgione meant it to be.

While working on the *Tempest* and the *Three Philosophers*, Giorgione received a commission to paint a fresco on the front exterior wall of the Fondaco dei Tedeschi. The front wall faced the Grand Canal. At the same time, Titian now able to receive commissions on his own was hired to paint a similar fresco on the back wall which faced towards the Merceria. Given Titian's youth – he was not yet twenty – this was a plum assignment and recognition of his rising reputation as an artist.

The Fondaco, which served as a combined apartment-warehouse complex for merchants from Germany, had been recently rebuilt after a disastrous fire in January 1505.

The doge and his counselors had made the decision to commission Giorgione and Titian to paint the frescos to embellish the exterior walls of the new building. We do not know what these leaders of the Venetian government expected. But it certainly was not what they got.

Giorgione's frescos included large random images of nude women, a man from the Levant in a cloak, a young man dressed in the attire of an elite social club, and another man in a striped shirt with red and white sleeves and hose. Titian's frescos followed the same theme.

The present day visitor gliding down the Grand Canal may have difficulty imagining buildings such as the Fondaco dei Tedeschi covered with giant colorful frescos of men and women some without any clothes on. The frescos must have looked like those three story high Victoria's Secret's billboards on Manhattan office buildings. Only with less clothing for some. This part of the Grand Canal in the sixteenth century could have looked like an early version of Times Square or the Las Vegas strip except for the lack of flashing lights.

Giorgio Vasari didn't like the Giorgione-Titian frescos. Vasari was an artist and writer who lived in Florence and other Italian cities while Titian created masterpieces in Venice. To the everlasting gratitude of art historians, Vasari wrote a multivolume series of books titled *Lives of the Most Excellent Painters, Sculptors and Architects*. In it he recounted the biographies of major Italian Renaissance artists including Michelangelo and Leonardo da Vinci.

Without Vasari we would know little about the artists of the sixteenth century. Vasari however did not include Titian in the first edition of this book, an omission that Titian never forgot.

But Vasari had definite opinions about the frescos on the Fondaco dei Tedeschi. "Giorgione," Vasari wrote, "merely painted figures according to his fancy. ... I for one was never able to fathom his meaning. ... I never was able to interpret what the painter intended to represent."

The frescos unfortunately did not last. The moist climate from the sea and the northerly winter winds from the mountains caused the frescos to disappear within decades.

And a few years after painting the frescos Giorgione died during an epidemic of the plague.

Fortune though favored Titian. A few years after completing the Fondaco frescos, he was commissioned by the Franciscan order to paint the central altarpiece of the Santa Maria Gloriosa dei Frari. The altarpiece is called the *Assumption of the Virgin* and is popularly known as the *Assunta*. The *Assumption of the Virgin* is one of the great paintings of the Renaissance. It is as important as Michelangelo's painting of the ceiling of the Sistine Chapel. Given the painting's prominent position in one of Venice's foremost churches, the *Assunta* commission affirmed the recognition of Titian who was still in his twenties as one of the Renaissance's leading artists.

The *Assunta* is the focal point of the high altar at the center of the Santa Maria Gloriosa dei Frari. It is a very large painting – over 22 feet tall and nearly 12 feet wide. Standing before the large Gothic windows of the apse, the *Assunta's* visual impact is immediate. Its dramatic effect is heightened by Titian's bold use of color – a characteristic that Titian would develop in future work. Bright reds, yellows, blues and greens at once draw the viewer's attention.

The *Assumption of the Virgin* dramatizes the religious experience to a degree that no previous artist had ever attempted. The observers eye is drawn upward from the tormented Apostles in the foreground to the Virgin, and finally to a peaceful God above it all. The *Assunta* was completed in 1518 when Titian was only thirty years old. Despite the initial concerns of the church leaders that the figures were too large the *Assunta* immediately was recognized as a masterpiece of the Renaissance.

In the *Assunta* the Virgin rises to be embraced by God. By Titian's rendering of her wind-blown gown and cloak one sees her upward movement as dynamic and energetic. The Virgin with anxious expression and raised arms as she is about to enter heaven also adds to the painting's dramatic impact.

Below the Virgin the disciples look up with awe and wonder. Above, God waits to accept her. Yet for all its visual excitement, the composition of the painting is orderly, even traditional. The disciples provide a solid base as the eye is drawn upward by the Virgin's sweeping garments until God looking down from heaven provides visual closure. Titian also heightened the dramatic effect with strong diagonals – one may note how the red garments of two of the disciples lead upward to the red gown of the Virgin.

With the *Assunta*, Titian broke away from the traditional means of composing an altarpiece. The *Assunta* is about movement, energy, excitement and exuberance. The traditional altarpiece was static, restrained and formal.

Like every painting that breaks new ground, the *Assunta* met with opposition. The most out-spoken critics were the Franciscan monks who had commissioned the painting in the first place. They wanted something more traditional. Only when a wealthy patron of the arts offered to buy it if they were willing to sell, did the Franciscan brothers realize that what they had was extraordinary.

Also in the Frari is a second altarpiece by Titian. This altarpiece in one of the side altars on the left aisle presented Titian with interesting problems for which he found innovative solutions. The main problem was that the patron, Jacopo Pesaro, wanted to be included in the painting along with members of his family. The traditional means of dealing with such requests was to place the Virgin in the center with the patron and his family grouped devoutly at her feet. But for Titian who did not think in traditional terms the standard presentation was static and unimaginative.

Titian's approach was to place the Virgin at the right side with St. Peter below her in the center and Jacopo Pesaro kneeling at the left side. Pesaro family members are grouped below the Virgin but in the main look at St. Peter rather than at the Virgin. This was a most original composition. Titian added drama to the scene by careful use of color. The Virgin's gown is red, St. Peter's robe is golden yellow, and an orange-red flag balances the other elements. Strong diagonal features in the composition add to the dramatic effect.

Another aspect of placing the Virgin at the right side of the altarpiece is that observers as they walk down the nave first see the Virgin and then one by one the other figures in the unfolding of the painting's narrative.

One more delightful element in the altarpiece is having a boy – his name is Giovanni Pesaro – turn his head and gaze at the viewer. With this simple gesture Giovanni, who like most boys is obviously not particularly interested in prayers, engages the viewer who becomes almost an extension of the altarpiece.

In addition to these paintings for the altars of the Santa Maria Gloriosa dei Frari, Titian was at the same time becoming known by knowledgeable patrons as an outstanding painter of portraits. In his portraits, like in his altarpieces, Titian brought freshness and innovation to painting. He sought to capture his subject's personality as well as his likeness. In the sixteenth century, this was a new idea. Through his subject's position, gesture and facial expression, Titian conveyed such human attributes as arrogance, humility, defiance and satisfaction with life's pleasures.

His first commissions for portraits came from wealthy Venetians. But soon aristocrats throughout northern Italy were asking for their own portraits.

The Duke of Ferrara, Alfonso d'Este, gave Titian a commission as did the Marquis of Mantua, Federico Gonzaga. The Duke of Urbino, Francesco Maria della Rovere also wanted portraits of himself and members of his family. These in turn led to commissions from

Emperor Charles V and his son and successor Philip II. Many of these portraits can be seen at the Uffizi and Pitti Museums in Florence and at the Prado in Madrid.

Another important patron was the Farnese family whose wealth and influence were pervasive in sixteenth century Italy. The pontiff, Pope Paul III, was of the Farnese family. The first portrait for the family was of Ranuccio Farnese, the pope's twelve-year old grandson. It was painted in 1542 and can now be seen at the National Gallery of Art in Washington. The portrait is simple and direct. Ranuccio stands clear eyed and pensive, looking to his right. His highlighted face and rich, embroidered uniform stand out against the dark background.

When Ranuccio was fifteen his grandfather, Pope Paul III, named him a cardinal.

The Farnese were much impressed with the portrait of Ranuccio and upon its completion Titian was asked to paint the pontiff himself.

The portrait of Pope Paul III, now at the Capodimonte National Gallery in Naples, portrays an aged, but determined pontiff. Like the painting of Ranuccio Farnese, the background is understated. The focus is on an over burdened pope who is dressed in luxurious garments but weighed down by the cares of his office.

Although most of Titian's commissions for portraits came from patrons outside of Venice, he did paint a magnificent portrait of Doge Andrea Gritti. This portrait which now hangs in the National Gallery of Art in Washington presents the Doge as the powerful, strong willed, tough minded leader that he was.

It was Doge Gritti who directed Jacopo Sansovino to build in the Piazza San Marco the Libreria and the Zecca. As the doge responsible for making the Piazza San Marco one of the most beautiful public places in the world, Doge Gritti receives his due in the Titian portrait.

The aristocrats who commissioned portraits of themselves and members of their families also requested paintings with mythological themes. Many of these paintings had strong erotic overtones.

One of the first of these paintings which idealized the nude female figure was the *Venus of Urbino*. This painting which Titian completed in 1538 now hangs in the Uffizi in Florence.

Titian continued the sensual theme of *Venus of Urbino* in two additional paintings based on the Greek legend of the seduction of *Danaë*, the daughter of Acrisius, king of Argos, by Jupiter. Like Venus, *Danaë* in both paintings lies naked in a suggestive manner upon a couch. The expression on her face is dreamy, wistful, open to hedonistic activity.

The first *Danaë* painted seven or eight years after *Venus of Urbino* created a sensation. The papal nuncio in Venice declared that it would sexually arouse the most puritanical cardinal. Another aristocrat who saw it wrote that "her breasts …would make martyrs unfrock themselves." The painting had been commissioned by Cardinal Alessandro Farnese, a Church leader with obvious libertine and not always pious views towards matters of sexuality. But then, this was the Renaissance.

And Cardinal Farnese was Italian. He was also another grandson of Pope Paul III.

The second *Danaë*, similar to the first, was painted for Philip II, who it appears wanted to have whatever goodie Cardinal Farnese had.

The first *Danaë* hangs in the Museo Nazionale di Capodimonte in Naples. The second at the Prado in Madrid.

The impact of *Venus of Urbino* and the *Danaë* must be understood in the context of the times. In the sixteenth century, paintings were the only visual media that could convey a sensual ideal. Photographs, videos, movies, DVDs, iPads and smartphones were centuries into the future.

Moreover, the erotic nature of the *Danaë* and the *Venus of Urbino* paintings was in itself a major innovation in Western art that previously had been almost entirely religious in theme. The overt sensuality of these paintings, in addition, could probably only have been tolerated in Venice, where the Republic's government had a more liberal attitude towards self-expression than any other European state. Even Michelangelo, Leonardo and Raphael in Rome and Florence would not have been allowed such latitude.

Throughout his long life Titian continued to explore the robust use of color and the potential of oil paint. He and the other Venetian artists experimenting with oil and with color were fortunately placed because Venice had greater access to pigments than any other city in Europe. Many of these pigments originated in remote places in the world. Yet the world transportation routes to Europe still led through Venice.

The semi-precious mineral lapis lazuli, which was used to make the rich purple-blue color ultramarine, for example, was only mined in what is today the Badakshan region of Afghanistan. It reached Venice by much the same routes as did the spices and silk textiles from the Far East. The blue-green pigment azurite, a form of copper carbonate, was mined in Hungary. As were other pigments, it was sent to Venice because Venice was the pre-eminent center of trade where buyers and sellers knew they would find a market. Some of these minerals, such as orpiment and realgar, which produced vivid yellows and oranges, were arsenic based, but much favored by the artists looking for ways to use oil paint.

With oil paint Titian was able to achieve a sense of naturalism and depth that eluded earlier artists.

As Titian grew older, his style evolved. Unlike most artists who become more conservative as they grow older, Titian became more experimental and unconventional. The hallmark of his late style is a looser, freer brushwork that imparted vigor and vitality to his paintings. Like the Impressionists of the nineteenth century, Titian even as an old man was seeking to expand the range of painting, to push it where it had never gone before.

Not everyone was pleased with the artistic direction Titian was taking. Michelangelo for one never fully understood the path Titian was pursuing. He considered

Titian's work to appear to be unfinished and to lack design qualities.

Yet Michelangelo in Rome was constrained in ways he did not even realize by the demands of the Vatican. Titian breathed the freer air of Venice, whose citizens were the most tolerant of unconventional thought of all the peoples of Europe. In this manner Venice became the crucible for later developments in Western art.

Titian died on August 27, 1576. Twenty-four years later Peter Paul Rubens a young Flemish artist visited Rome, Florence and Venice. Here, the impact of Titian's paintings upon Rubens affected him forever. As the center of art shifted northward, Rubens, Van Dyke and Rembrandt studied the works of Titian as students of a great master. Despite Michelangelo's greatness the next generation of artists would look to Titian for inspiration and instruction.

Titian painted altarpieces for the great churches of Venice; he painted the portraits of the aristocrats; and he painted, for the palaces of the wealthy, works that unabashedly celebrated erotic, hedonistic and sensual behavior. He painted with equal grace the altarpiece for the Church of Santa Maria dei Frari titled *Assumption of the Virgin*, a portrait of *Eleonora della Rovere*, the aging wife of a Venetian nobleman, and the intoxicated scene of *Bacchanal of the Andrians*, where the wine flows without limit.

Above all, Titian loved color. He used it to achieve rich, dramatic effects. The skin of his subject is always natural and sensual. His subject's silk and satin clothing is sumptuous and richly textured. The women in his allegorical scenes are voluptuous goddesses. The works of Titian project human emotion and physical action. His paintings perfectly reflected the spirit of Venice in the sixteenth century. Even though the economic well-being of the republic was in irreversible decline, life was still to be experienced and enjoyed. Excess in the pursuit of pleasure was the norm.

Titian's work greatly influenced later European artists, most notably Rembrandt, who was born in the Netherlands, thirty years after Titian's death. Rembrandt studied Titian assiduously. We know that Rembrandt owned a book containing copies of nearly all of Titian's paintings. We also know that a noted Amsterdam art collector had in his home an original Titian titled *Portrait of Man with a Blue Sleeve*. In this portrait, the subject is facing sideways, with his head turned to the left to look directly at the viewer. The subject is dressed in a resplendent, blue silk shirt. His arm rests arrogantly on a stone railing. In 1639, Rembrandt painted himself, in one of his many self-portraits, in almost the exact pose as Titian's *Man with a Blue Sleeve*. The painting titled *Rembrandt Leaning on a Stone Sill* is considered one of his best.

Nor was Titian Venice's only great artist. Following Titian, Paolo Veronese succeeded as the favorite artist of the rich and powerful. He continued what had become the Venetian High Renaissance style: grandiose, exuberant paintings with a fresh, dynamic use of bright color. His sumptuous paintings celebrating the triumphs of the republic were chosen to adorn the Sala delle Udienze del Consiglio dei Dieci—the Council of Ten, the government's most powerful body, in the Doge's Palace.

Nevertheless, one painting got Veronese into deep trouble with the ecclesiastical authorities. He was commissioned to paint the Last Supper for the dining hall of the Santi Giovanni e Paolo. Unfortunately, the completed work was too worldly for the Church fathers. It contained, along with Christ and the apostles, drunks, buffoons and German soldiers. The Church fathers were outraged. Veronese was commanded to appear before the Inquisition.

The Inquisition convened on Saturday, July 18, 1573. The court got straight to the point:

Inquisitor: Do you know for what reason you were summoned here?

Veronese: No, sirs.

Q: Can you imagine the reason?

A: Indeed I can.

Veronese thereupon brought up the subject of the painting of the Last Supper. After a description of the painting, he was asked

Q: Who are those at the Lord's table?

A: The Twelve Apostles.

Q: What is St. Peter doing, that is the first of them?

A: He is dividing the lamb, to pass it to the other end of the table.

Q: And the other man, beside him?

A: He holds a dish ready to receive what St. Peter will give him.

Q: Tell us what is being done by the man who comes next.

A: He is picking his teeth with a fork.

The Inquisitor proceeded to question the accuracy of Veronese's painting, suggesting a lack of reverence— namely, an Apostle should not be shown picking his teeth with a fork. Veronese responded that Michelangelo in the Sistine Chapel had used similar artistic license. The Inquisitor noted that to the contrary Michelangelo's paintings did not contain jesters, dogs, weapons or any such buffooneries.

Veronese was ordered to remove the offending figures from the painting.

A less adventurous man would have bowed to the demands of the Inquisition, then at the height of its power. Not Veronese. He simply changed the name of the painting to the *Feast in the House of Levi*, thereby removing its association with the Last Supper. The painting now hangs in the Gallerie dell'Accademia.

Other great artists of the sixteenth century in Venice are Giorgione and Jacopo Tintoretto. In the seventeenth century, Giovanni Tiepolo continued the traditions of Venetian art.

As in its art and architecture, Venice's colorful and exuberant spirit influenced its music. Despite the downturn in the Republic's economic fortunes, the music of the Baroque flourished in Venice. Here, Antonio Vivaldi, one of Europe's most important composers, turned out his prodigious production of concertos, oratorios and operas.

Vivaldi was born in 1678. He trained for the priesthood, but found his true vocation at the Conservatory of the Pieta as the conductor, composer and teacher of music. The Conservatory was founded as a home for orphans and illegitimate children. Music was an important part of the education provided the children. One observer wrote, after attending a concert at the Conservatory: "Each concert is given by about forty girls. I assure you there is nothing so charming as to see a young and pretty nun in her white robe, with a bouquet of pomegranate flowers in her hair, leading the orchestra and beating time with all the precision imaginable. ... They are reared at public expense and trained solely to excel in music. And so they sing like angles, and play the violin, the flute, the organ, the violoncello, the bassoon."

Compositions flowed from Vivaldi's pen. He claimed that he could compose a concerto faster than a clerk could copy it. He is known to have written 49 operas, 75 sonatas, and no fewer than 454 concertos. The most famous of his works are the violin concertos titled *The Four Seasons* which are over-played pieces that do not reflect Vivaldi's versatility.

One reason for the great number of his compositions was that Venetian music lovers constantly demanded new productions. They were not satisfied to merely hear the old stand-bys. They expected a new piece for each concert. Baroque music was to the eighteenth century Venetian, what the latest music fad is to an American teenager. Vivaldi's style was fresh, clear, vigorous and spontaneous. His music later greatly influenced Johann Sebastian Bach, who used at least nine of Vivaldi's concertos as the basis for his own works.

Nor was Vivaldi the only great musician to find favor in Venice. Years earlier, Claudio Monteverdi and Giovanni Gabrieli had been warmly received by Venetians who recognized immediately the outstanding qualities of the compositions being played. Many of the works were performed in the Basilica of San Marco, where the vast and lofty nave reverberated with the trumpets, violins, organs, bassoons, and accompanying choirs used so effectively by the composers. Today, over three centuries later, the compositions of these great men still excite music listeners everywhere.

But the music of a Vivaldi, the art of a Titian, the architecture of a Sansovino could only thrive as a creative process in a state where wealth was available to finance cultural endeavors. By the eighteenth century, Venice was no longer a wealthy city. International trade was now dominated by other nations.

Chapter 16: The Last Doge

Venice was not to remain the independent republic that it had been for a thousand years. In 1797, Napoleon and the armies of France rolled across Europe. As the winter of that year gave way to spring, the French forces stood before Venice. Napoleon ordered the leaders of the Republic to surrender. The Doge and Great Council had no other option.

On May 12, 1797, as the French troops were about to enter the city, the government of the Republic of Venice voted itself out of existence. On that day, the last doge, Ludovico Manin, in his final act as head of the government, called the members of the Great Council to order in the Great Council Hall, their customary meeting room in the Doge's Palace. He then presented to the patricians of that ruling body the French demand that they vote to abolish the old form of government.

The ornate ceiling of the Great Council Hall was decorated with Paolo Veronese's painting titled the *Apotheosis of Venice*, completed two centuries earlier. Since the word apotheosis means glorification to the rank of a god, the title and the painting itself must have seemed entirely out of place on this occasion. At the end of the great chamber, Tintoretto's magnificent *Paradiso* covered almost the entire back wall. Other paintings depicting the glorious military and cultural history of Venice decorated the remaining walls.

As the pale and trembling Doge spoke to the silent and fearful members of the Council, a volley of musket fire was heard in the distance. The members, thereupon, in great haste capitulated to the French demands. The vote taken, nearly all the Council members fled for their lives. Many feared that a guillotine would be erected on the Piazza San Marco in short order, and that the patricians of Venice would be treated in the same manner as had been the aristocrats of France.

The Doge announced to the virtually empty chamber that the resolution had passed. Then he calmly gathered up his papers and walked without purpose to his private quarters. There, he removed the clothes that signified his now defunct office. To his valet, he handed the ducal cap, and said sadly: *"Tolè, questa no la doperò più"*— "Take it, I will not be needing it any more."

The city, which had stood proudly as an independent republic since early medieval times, which had contributed so much to the civilization of the West, and which had never been occupied by a foreign invader, ceased to be a sovereign state.

The French quickly confiscated many of Venice's outstanding art treasures, some of which can be seen today at the Louvre in Paris.

So ended the sovereignty of the Republic of Venice, the state that had played a dominant role in European economic and cultural development since the Fourth Crusade nearly six centuries earlier.

We can now look back and ask questions as to the outcome of the Venetian experience. Was it Venice's inevitable fate to decline from the preeminent economic power in Europe to a role of minor importance? Could the Venetians have done anything beyond what they did do to prevent what became an unending slide in power, influence, and vitality? Could not Venice with all its resources have met the challenge? We must look at the record.

When the Portuguese broke the Venetian monopoly on the spice trade by discovering the sea route to Asia, the quantity of spices reaching Venice from Asia dropped drastically. Profits and employment dropped just as precipitously. After recovering from the shock that a shattering blow had struck their prosperous, centuries old trade with the east, the Venetian merchants responded as best they could.

The first option was to destroy the Portuguese merchant and naval fleets that were sailing between Europe and Asia. The Venetians wisely left this task to their Muslim counterparts who were also suffering significant economic losses due to the Portuguese establishment of trading routes that did not require the desert caravans. The main source of Muslim revenue was derived from these caravans. Their profits came from the resale of the Asian spices to the Venetians and through taxes on the caravans traversing Arabian territory. But the Muslim effort to destroy the Portuguese fleet failed. The Muslims were simply technologically too far behind the Portuguese in ship design and weapons development to mount effective opposition.

Having failed to destroy the Portuguese fleet, the Muslims next tried to destroy the Portuguese bases at Goa, Calicut and Malacca. The Portuguese, however, had chosen the locations for their bases well. All the strategic strongholds used natural terrain for maximum defensibility against numerically superior forces. Thus, due to the advantageous location of the Portuguese bases, the incompetence of the Muslim military leadership, and the Portuguese control of the sea, the Muslim effort to defeat the Portuguese on land also failed.

Consequently the Portuguese, victorious at sea and undefeated on the Asian continent, were able to land the precious spices at Lisbon and Antwerp without opposition from Venetian or Muslim competitors. The Portuguese were restricted only by the forces of nature from creating a total monopoly of the spice trade. The perils of the 14,000 mile sea voyage between Portugal and India, however, severely limited the quantity of spices which could be brought back to Europe. The coast of Africa was littered with the shipwrecks of vessels that failed in the effort.

Overall, the Portuguese challenge to Venice for control of the spice trade was not a long term problem for the Venetian economy. The traditional land routes still provided Venice with sufficient supplies. The Portuguese, choosing to maximize their own profits, also helped the Venetian merchants by refusing to engage in extensive price cutting. It was not in the Portuguese self-interest to allow prices to drop. Moreover, the European appetite for spices was growing, allowing Venice to profit from a smaller share of a larger market.

A much greater challenge to the power and dominance of Venice came from the unlawful sinking of its ships by English and Dutch pirates. This undeclared warfare by England and Holland, whose shipbuilders had designed ships of superior strength and seaworthiness, caused more devastation to the Venetian economy than did the Portuguese capture of a portion of the spice trade.

The geographical location of England and Holland, facing into the stormy North Sea and the tempestuous Atlantic Ocean, forced the people of those two countries to design stronger ships simply to survive the rigors of their environment. When these ships were sailed into the placid Mediterranean, they quickly overwhelmed the lightly built Venetian galleys. The advances in naval gunnery added to the imbalance, the northern ships being better able to absorb a hit than the Venetian galleys, which could be sunk by a single well placed cannonball.

To meet the challenge from the North, the Venetians would have had to build warships of sufficient strength to drive the English and Dutch from the Mediterranean. To a degree, the Venetian Signoria did respond in this manner. Certainly, the round ships of the Republic were similar in design to the ships of the northern invaders. The main hope of the doges and Venetian naval commanders, however, remained in the galley, the ship with which they had for centuries successfully driven all competitors from the sea. The Venetian faith in the fighting qualities of the galley was reinforced by their decisive victory over the Turks in the Battle of Lepanto.

The leaders of the Republic thought that if a new direction in naval policy had to be made, the change should be to build galleys that were bigger and carried more men. The result was the great galley, a huge ship which they confidently expected would overwhelm all sea-borne opposition. Unfortunately, as a fighting vessel the great galley was too big to be fast, and too light to effectively engage in combat the frigates of the English and Dutch.

The naval leaders of Venice could not understand that the basic design of the galley was inadequate to the task of defeating the intruders from the north. With its reliance on oarsmen, the galley did not make effective use of the power of sail. Moreover, being low in the water and being lightly built so as to allow the oarsmen to be able to row, the galley was of a design that was at an extreme disadvantage when confronted by the high decked, strongly built sailing ships of the English and Dutch. The Venetians did arm their merchant ships so as to better defend themselves against attack. But this alone was not sufficient to prevent the slow destruction of the merchant fleet.

Looking back, we can ask why the Venetians did not adopt the superior ship designs of the English and Dutch. The only answer appears to be resistance to change. The galley had served the Venetians so well for so long that the naval commanders refused to believe it was an out-moded design. Only in the mid-seventeenth century did the Venetians build their first fully rigged sailing fighting ship. Even then, they needed an English ship to use as a model.

But even when the need to modernize the fleet was recognized, the supply of timber, particularly oak, limited the number of new ships that could be built. The oak forests of the Adriatic region had been cut over and depleted. The oak forests of Scandinavia were too far away, and were under the control of the northern powers anyway.

As we have seen, though, the destruction of much of the Venetian merchant and naval fleets by the English and Dutch, and the loss of a good part of the spice trade to the Portuguese were not the only problems facing the Venetian republic.

The Venetian textile industry, which provided employment to a large segment of the Venetian workforce, was also being devastated by competition from low cost producers in the north.

During the seventeenth century, the textile industry in Venice declined steadily. At the end of the century it was one-tenth the size it had been a hundred years earlier. English and Dutch competition overwhelmed the Venetian manufacturers with lower cost products.

However, the main reasons for Venice's failure to meet the competition were internal. The Venetian manufacturers did not produce the types of cloth that were most popular in the marketplace. It is ironic that this most capitalistic state ignored the demands of the consumers. A major problem was the regulations of the Signoria. Venetian regulations prohibited the production of goods that did not conform to rigid

specifications. But the regulations did not reflect the needs and demands of the consumers, who wanted cheaper, lighter, and more colorful fabrics. The English and Dutch unhindered by such regulations adapted their products to the market.

The Venetian manufacturers were also hampered by guild restrictions that had the effect of raising the labor costs of every item. A final burden upon the Venetian textile manufacturer was a tax system that heavily taxed the woven cloth. The tax, first put in place when Venice faced little competition, remained in force even when producers in other countries were not taxed at all, or worse, were subsidized by their governments.

Overall, many factors contributed to the economic decline of Venice. Some of the factors were clearly beyond the control of the Venetians. The Portuguese discovery of the sea route to Asia, and the resulting loss of a large share of the spice trade, was the inevitable result of the Portuguese building better ships and of their desire to explore the unknown seas. Also beyond the Venetians control was the depletion of the Mediterranean forests of oak that provided the wood for their ships. The deforestation could have been slowed, but not prevented.

In many other areas, however, the Venetians were simply too resistant to change. They were too rigid, too unyielding, too wedded to the past. In the design of fighting ships, they refused to recognize the deficiencies of the galleys in confrontations with fully rigged sailing ships. In the manufacture of cloth, they refused to respond to the competitive demands of the marketplace.

We can debate endlessly the question of whether Venice's economic decline was inevitable. The only conclusion we can reach is that all nations live in a competitive and ever changing environment. The nations that continue to prosper are those that adapt to the new conditions.

Yet, even a government more responsive to changing economic conditions would not have been able to maintain Venice's independence in the emerging age of nation-states. With its limited population and resources, Venice could not remain as the most prosperous entity in Europe.

But for a thousand years the Republic of Venice had graced the world with magnificent architecture, art and music. It had been a preeminent center of learning and scientific achievement. When the rest of Europe was convulsed in various forms of barbarity, Venice was always a haven of law and a sanctuary of comparative tolerance.

The vitality of the *Serenissima Repubblica* lives forever.

Bibliography

Aczel, Amir D. *The Riddle of the Compass*, New York: Harcourt , 2001.

Albion, R., *Forests and Sea Power,* 1926.

Andrews, Kenneth R. *Trade, Plunder and Settlement, Maritime Enterprise and the Genesis of the British Empire, 1480-1630*, Cambridge, England: Cambridge University Press, 1985.

Ball, J. N. *Merchants and Merchandise, the Expansion of Trade In Europe 1500-1630*, New York: St. Martin's Press, 1977.

Bell, Christopher *Portugal and the Quest for the Indies*, New York, 1975.

Bowden, Peter J. *The Wool Trade in Tudor and Stuart England*, London: Macmillan, 1962.

Boxer, Charles R. *The Dutch Seaborne Empire: 1600-1800*, New York: 1965.

_____, *The Portuguese Seaborne Empire, 1415-1825*, New York: 1969.

Bradford, Ernle *The Sundered Cross, the Story of the Fourth Crusade*, Englewood Cliffs, NJ: 1967.

Braudel, Fernand *The Mediterranean, and the Mediterranean World in the Age of Philip II*, volumes 1 and 2, translated by Sian Reynolds, New York: Harper & Row, 1976.

_____, *The Structures of Everyday Life: The Limits of the Possible, 15th-18th Century*, New York: Harper & Row, 1982.

_____, *The Wheels of Commerce: 15th-18th Century*, New York: Harper & Row, 1984.

_____, *The Perspective of the World: 15th-18th Century*, New York: Harper & Row, 1984.

Chambers, David and Brian Pullan, edited by, *Venice, A Documentary History, 1450-1630*, Toronto: University of Toronto Press, 2001.

Cipolla, Carlo M. *Before the Industrial Revolution, European Society and Economy, 1000-1700*, New York: W. W. Norton, 1980.

_____, *Guns, Sails and Empires*, Minerva Press, 1965.

_____, "The Economic Decline of Italy" in *Crisis and Change in the Venetian Economy in the Sixteenth and Seventeenth Centuries*, edited by Brian Pullan, London: Methuen & Co., 1968.

Coryate, Thomas *Coryate's Crudities*.

Crowe, Joseph A. and Giovanni Cavalcaselle *The Life and Times of Titian*, London: 1881.

Davis, John *Venice*, 1973.

Davis, Ralph *The Rise of the English Shipping Industry*, London: Macmillan & Co., 1962.

Dubnov, Simon *History of the Jews*, New York: 1971.

Duffy, James *Shipwreck & Empire, Being an Account of Portuguese Maritime Disasters in a Century of Decline*, Cambridge: Harvard University Press, 1955.

Evelyn, John *The Diary of John Evelyn*, Oxford: 1955.

Freeman, Charles *The Horses of St. Marks*, London: 2004.

Bibliography

Gough, J. W. *The Rise of the Entrepreneur*, New York: Schocken Books, 1969.

Goy, Richard J. *Building Renaissance Venice*, New Haven: Yale University Press, 2006.

Graetz, Heinrich *History of the Jews*, Philadelphia: 1894.

Granzotto, Gianni *Christopher Columbus*, New York: Doubleday, 1985.

Greenlee, William B. *The Voyage of Pedro Álvares Cabral to Brazil and India*, London: 1937.

Grout, Donald J. *A History of Western Music*, New York: 1960.

Guilmartin, John F. *Gunpowder and Galleys, Changing Technology and Mediterranean Warfare at Sea in the Sixteenth Century*, Cambridge, England: 1974.

Hale, Sheila *Titian, His Life*, New York: 2012.

Haskell, Francis *Patrons and Painters*, New Haven: 1980.

Hilton, R. H. *The English Peasantry in the Later Middle Ages*, Oxford: Clarendon Press, 1975.

Hope, Charles *Titian*, London: National Gallery Company, 2003.

Hopkins, Andrew *Baldassare Longhena and Venetian Baroque Architecture*, New Haven: Yale University Press, 2012.

Howard, Deborah *The Architectural History of Venice*, New Haven: Yale University Press, 2002.

_____, "Civic and Religious Architecture in Gothic Venice" in *Venice, Art & Architecture*, edited by Giandomenico Romanelli, Cologne: 1997.

_____, "Jacopo Sansovino and the Romanization of Venetian Architecture" in *Venice, Art & Architecture*, edited by Giandomenico Romanelli, Cologne, 1997

_____, *Jacopo Sansovino, Architecture and Patronage in Renaissance Venice*, New Haven: Yale University Press, 1975.

Jayne, Kingsley G. *Vasco da Gama and his Successors, 1460-1580*, New York: 1910.

Kurlansky, Mark *Cod*, New York: Walker, 1997.

Labalme, Patricia H. and Laura Sanguineti White (editors) *Cita Excelentissima, Selections from the Renaissance Diaries of Marin Sanudo*, translated by Linda L. Carroll, Baltimore: The Johns Hopkins University Press, 2008.

Lane, Frederic C. *Venice, A Maritime Republic*, Baltimore: Johns Hopkins University Press, 1973.

_____, *Venetian Ships and Shipbuilders of the Renaissance*, Baltimore: Johns Hopkins University Press, 1934.

Lauritzen, Peter and Alexander Zielcke *Palaces of Venice*, London: Calmann & King, Ltd., 1978.

Levathes, Louise *When China Ruled the Seas*, New York: Simon & Schuster, 1994.

Ley, Charles David (ed.) "A Journal of the First Voyage of Vasco da Gama in 1497-1499" in *Portuguese Voyages 1498-1666*.

Lithgow, William *The Totall Discourse*, Glasgow.

Lipson, E. *The Economic History of England*, London: 1931.

Bibliography

Longworth, Philip *The Rise and Fall of Venice*, London: Constable, 1974.

Madden, Thomas F. *Enrico Dandolo & the Rise of Venice*, Baltimore: The Johns Hopkins University Press, 2003.

Mann, F. O., (ed.) *The Works of Thomas Deloney*, Oxford.

Martin, John and Romano, Dennis, (eds.) *Venice Reconsidered*, Baltimore: The Johns Hopkins University Press, 2000.

Martines, Lauro *Power and Imagination, City States in Renaissance Italy*, New York: Knopf, 1979.

Martinez-Hidalgo, Jose Maria *Columbus' Ships*, Barre, MA: 1966.

McNeill, William H. *The Pursuit of Power*, Chicago: The University of Chicago Press, 1982.

McKee, Alexander *How We Found the Mary Rose*, 1982.

Morison, Samuel Eliot *Admiral of the Ocean Sea, A Life of Christopher Columbus*, Boston: 1942.

Moryson, Fynes *Itinerary (Shakespeare's Europe)*, Benjamin Bloom, New York.

Murray, Peter J. *The Architecture of the Italian Renaissance*, New York: 1963.

Norwich, John Julius *A History of Venice*, 1982.

Parker, Geoffrey *The Military Revolution*, Cambridge, England: Cambridge University Press, 1996.

Pears, Edwin *The Fall of Constantinople*, London: 1885.

Phillips, Jonathan *The Fourth Crusade and the Sack of Constantinople*, New York: Penguin Books, 2004.

Prestage, Edgar *The Portuguese Pioneers*, New York: 1933.

Price, William Hyde, *The English Patents of Monopoly*, Cambridge: Harvard University Press, 1913.

Prottengeier, Alvin E., (trans.), *From Lisbon to Calicut*, University of Minnesota Press, 1956.

Pullan, Brian *Rich and Poor in Renaissance Venice*, Oxford: 1971.

Queller, Donald E. *The Fourth Crusade, the Conquest of Constantinople 1201-1204*, Philadelphia: University of Pennsylvania Press, 1977.

Rapp, Richard Tilden *Industry and Economic Decline in Seventeenth-Century Venice*, Cambridge: Harvard University Press, 1976.

Robert of Clari *The Conquest of Constantinople*, translated by E. H. McNeal, New York: 1936.

Romano, Dennis *The Likeness of Venice, A Life of Doge Francesco Foscari 1373-1457*, New Haven: Yale University Press, 2007.

Roth, Cecil *History of the Jews in Venice*, New York: Schocken Books, 1975.

Ruskin, John *The Stones of Venice*, 1853.

Russell, Peter *Prince Henry the Navigator, A Life*, New Haven: Yale University Press, 2007.

Sella, Domenico "The Rise and Fall of the Venetian Woollen Industry" in *Crisis and Change in the Venetian Economy in the Sixteenth and Seventeenth Centuries*, edited by Brian Pullan, London: Methuen & Co., 1968.

Bibliography

Tapie, Victor *France in the Age of Louis XIII and Richelieu*, 1974.

Tawney, R. H. *The Agrarian Problem in the Sixteenth Century*, 1967.

Tenenti, Alberto *Piracy and the Decline of Venice, 1580-1615*, Berkeley: University of California Press, 1967.

Thacher, John Boyd *Christopher Columbus*, New York: 1967

Unger, Richard W. *The Ship in the Medieval Economy, 600-1600*, London: Croom Helm, 1980.

Villehardouin, Geoffroi de *Memoirs of the Crusades*.

Watkins, Ronald *Unknown Seas, How Vasco da Gama Opened the East*, London: John Murray, 2003.

Journals and Articles

Barbour, Violet, "Dutch and English Merchant Shipping in the Seventeenth Century" in *The Economic History Review*, January, 1930.

Coleman, D. C., "An Innovation and its Diffusion: the New Draperies" in *The Economic History Review*, December, 1969.

Fisher, F. J., "Commercial Trends and Policy in Sixteenth-Century England" in *The Economic History Review*, November, 1940.

Lane, Frederic C., "Venetian Shipping During the Commercial Revolution" in *American Historical Review*, January, 1933.

————, "The Economic Meaning of the Invention of the Compass" in *American Historical Review*, April, 1963.

Rapp, Richard T., "The Unmaking of the Mediterranean Trade Hegemony: International Trade Rivalry and the Commercial Revolution" in *The Journal of Economic History*, September, 1975.

Wagner, Donald O. "Coke and the Rise of Economic Liberalism" in *The Economic History Review*, October, 1935.

Bibliography

The author and publisher gratefully acknowledge permission to reprint material from the following works:

Boxer, C.R., The Portuguese Seaborne Empire, Reprinted with permission from Random House, Inc.

Braudel, Fernand, The Mediterranean, translated by Sian Reynold, Reprinted with permission from HarperCollins Publishers, Inc.

Braudel, Fernand, The Perspective of the World, translated by Sian Reynold, Reprinted with permission from HarperCollins Publishers, Inc.

Duffy, James, Shipwreck and Empire, Reprinted with permission of Harvard University Press, Cambridge, Mass., copyright©1955 by the President and Fellows of Harvard College.

Prottengeier, Alvin E., From Lisbon to Calicut, Reprinted with the permission of the University of Minnesota Press.

Rapp, Richard T., Journal of Economic History, Reprinted with the permission of Cambridge University Press.

Tenenti, Alberto, Piracy and the Decline of Venice, 1580-1615, Reprinted with permission from the University of California Press.

Clipper Ship Publishing

Made in the USA
San Bernardino, CA
16 October 2018